Liberal Terror

For Christine

—— Liberal Terror ——

—— Brad Evans ——

polity

First published in 2013 by Polity Press

Polity Press
65 Bridge Street
Cambridge CB2 1UR, UK

Polity Press
350 Main Street
Malden, MA 02148, USA

ISBN-13: 978-0-7456-6531-3
ISBN-13: 978-0-7456-6532-0(pb)

A catalogue record for this book is available from the British Library.
Typeset in 11 on 13 pt Sabon
by Toppan Best-set Premedia Limited
Printed and bound in Great Britain by the MPG Books Group

For further information on Polity, visit our website: www.politybooks.com

Contents

Preface

One of the more challenging tasks during the final stages of a manuscript's production is deciding upon a suitable and appropriate cover. No image could ever of course truly capture the narrative's essence. Such truthful representations simply don't exist. Just as every manuscript is open to multiple interpretations, so every image conveys many different feelings, emotions, and political sentiments depending on the person viewing the composition. Despite, however, the well-rehearsed claim about not judging a book by its cover, it is perhaps inevitable (especially in our 'image-conscious' societies) that some assumptions will be made before a single page is turned. The author must therefore be mindful that the cover is an aesthetic complement to the text, even though it is anticipated that any preconceptions will eventually be disrupted. The decision to use the image of the fallen man for this book was made after considerable deliberation. Inspired by the advertising campaign for the launch of *Mad Men* season 5 in the United States, the image seemed to capture the contextual logic of terror normality so central to the book's narrative. While the *Mad Men* campaign drew criticism as it invoked memories of the fallen victims of 9/11, that the image was emblazoned across Manhattan at all was testament to the fact that we are in a different political moment. The image of a falling person, it seemed, was no longer sacrosanct; it was, as the show's producers insisted, simply advertising.

Beneath the superficial level of what many believed was a shameless exploitation of the image for commercial reasons (revealing in itself given the focus of the television series), the Mad Men campaign has subsequently proved to be remarkably political. More than reclaiming the meaning of a symbolic act such that it cannot be reducible to one specific moment in history, however deeply troubling, the campaign allows us to *move beyond* and yet *think before* the atrocities of the 9/11 attacks. Indeed, despite the fact that the horrifying scenes of that day have left a lasting imprint on the memory, the campaign proved significant by reminding us that representations of falling victims (actual or metaphorical) are not entirely novel. As Matt Weiner, the creative director for the series, pointed out, 'I hate to say it, but a businessman falling out of a window is a symbol that far precedes that event.' Such representations cannot, however, avoid the charges of insensitivity, or, worse, trivialization of the tragic events of 9/11. This is not simply a danger from which we must retreat. It is a *political responsibility* that requires careful consideration and ethical debate. We may deal with claims of insensitivity here by posing the following two supplementary questions: Why were the images of the falling victims deemed so intolerable? And what is there to be gained politically by drawing reference to wider discourses on the falling subject?

Many people were undoubtedly touched by the raw reality of Richard Drew's infamous photographs. While a number of media outlets felt obliged to publish these troubling images, critics argued that their publication somehow disrespected the victims as final moments were recorded in horrifying detail. But what was so different about these images as opposed to those of the initial explosion or the cascading towers, which have been continually reprinted ever since? It could be argued that the images of the falling were personally difficult to come to terms with since they forced each of us to confront the pure contingency of the situation. Had any of us happened to visit Manhattan that day for the first time, it is likely that a trip to the World Trade Center's viewing gallery would have been on the itinerary. How would any of us have reacted should we have found ourselves by the brutal chance of fate alone in such a terrifying predicament? While there is no answer to be given in advance to what can only be termed a 'non-decision decision' (i.e. a decision that cannot be made within any bounds of reason), we should remain categorical that the term 'suicide' is not in any way appropriate for describing what followed. As Primo Levi once intimated in respect to Auschwitz, even in the most horrifying moments, when death seems almost certain, it is nevertheless possible to still find some degree of freedom, however terrible the inevitable outcome. Maybe, if there is anything positive whatsoever to be salvaged from these tragic moments, we should think about the fallen in those terms.

There was, however, something more at stake here which points to the political intolerability of the photographs. By effectively removing the individual from the dominant frames of perception, so the attack upon the symbolic ordering became the more truthful representation. Personal testimonies as such would be subsumed within a broader narrative in which the quantifiable numbers of the dead affirmed, as the symbolic violence unequivocally illustrated, that something truly exceptional was happening. War was very much taking place. Images of modern warfare are replete with examples of urban destruction. This is not incidental. If utopia remains an urban dream, so dystopia finds sure representation in architectural catastrophe as structural power proves to be illusionary. The images of falling victims, in marked contrast, required a more sombre and humane reflection. Their more serene composition demanded that we refocused our attention instead upon the personal, the intimate, the qualitative, the micro-specific, and the complexity of the stories. Such images defied the absolutist and highly reductionist narrative of the event, which proved so central to the subsequent drums of war. In short, then, the images of the falling didn't function in a manner that was compatible with the political ambitions to bring about justice, violent retribution, and foreign invasion. How, may we ask, would the world look today if the images of the falling victims had become the defining emblem of the 9/11 attacks? And what would the contemporary state of relations be amongst the world of people had we dared to consider all the human stakes?

Beyond the sacralizing narratives of the 9/11 attacks, the idea of the fall is a recurring motif within Western culture and its metaphysical heritage. Homer's *The Iliad*, for instance, narrates the fall of Troy by explaining how the besieged consciously jumped from the tops of burning buildings to avoid the raging fires. Not only has the biblical story of human treachery in the Garden of Eden remained central to Christian eschatology, its prevailing message that we have a predisposition to act without consideration for the greater moral good (what many deem to be a more worldly conception of evil) has also proven wholly compatible with secular reasoning and its allied forms of security governance. Secularism hasn't, then, fully abandoned the idea of original sin but has reworked it into the modern productive schematic. In this regard, as Gilles Deleuze once insisted, we all remain within the spectre of the Kantian revolution in thought. Not that we are heirs to some inalienable framework for universal right or that we are driven to become perfectly reasonable subjects. Burdened by the weight of an imperfect past while haunted by a future that is insecure by design, liberal societies require some form of divine intervention to help mitigate the 'imperfections of man'. The idea of the fallen subject thus appears absolutely integral to understanding the liberal account of terror which, emanating out of an endangered sense of belonging in the world, demands the most sophisticated forms of human interventionism on account of the fact that life is the author of its very own (un)making.

Brad Evans (May 2012)

Acknowledgements

This book owes a considerable intellectual debt to a number of remarkable colleagues who still recognize that the essential function of the university is to continue to hold power to account and challenge the troubling moves in academia towards necessary policy entrepreneurship. As always, however, the limits and intellectual deficiencies forever remain my responsibility. I would like to express my continual thanks to Professor Raymond Bush (University of Leeds), Professor Michael Dillon (Emeritus Professor University of Lancaster), Professor Mark Duffield (University of Bristol), and Professor Julian Reid (University of Lapland), whose friendship, collegiality, inspiration, along with their intellectual courage in the face of conformist pressures, are testament to the value of critical pedagogy. I have also been fortunate to have had the intellectual counsel of a number of remarkable scholars whose pioneering work highlights with political surety the less than objective dogmatism of the positivist political sciences. Particular friendship is extended to Philip Armstrong (Ohio State University), Ian Buchanan (Wollogong University), Terrell Carver (University of Bristol), Simon Critchley (The New School, NY),

Henry Giroux (McMaster University), Michael Hardt (Duke University), Gregg Lambert (Syracuse University), Todd May (Clemson University), John Protevi (Louisiana State University), Saskia Sassen (Columbia University), Michael Shapiro (University of Hawaii), Cynthia Weber (University of Sussex), and Samuel Weber (North-Western University), along with my close friends Paul Amourdedieu and Tim Hedger, whose conversations are forever cherished. I would also like to extend my sincerest thanks and gratitude to Louise Knight and the team at Polity Press, whose professionalism and commitment to new ways about thinking about the political ensure that the academic world retains its intellectual dignity. Last but not least, I do not forget students past and present who continue to decry the 'esoteric' label so easily applied by those who feel intellectually challenged by Continental thought. None of this, however, would have been possible if it wasn't for the support of my wonderful wife Christine, my loving parents and family, along with my beautiful daughter Amelie, who continually reminds me that there are moments in life that words simply cannot capture.

Segments of this book have been previously published in: Brad Evans, 'Foucault's Legacy: Security, War and Violence in the 21st Century', *Security Dialogue*, vol. 41 no. 4 (2010), pp. 413–33; and Mark Duffield and Brad Evans, 'Biospheric Security: The Development-Security-Environment-Nexus [DESNEX], Containment and Retrenching Fortress Europe', in J. Peter Burgess and Serge Gutwirth (eds), *A Threat against Europe? Security, Migration and Integration* (Brussels: VUB Press, 2011), pp. 93–110. I would like to express my thanks to the publishers for granting permission for republication. All rights reserved.

– 1 –

Imaginaries of Threat

States of Normality

Walter Benjamin once warned that while exceptional moments of crises were politically dangerous, it was the effective normalization of rule that could be altogether more sinister.[1] With order finally restored, what previously shattered the boundaries of acceptability now begins to reside in the undetected fabric of the everyday. Such is our warning. What marks the contemporary period is *terrifyingly normal*. Haunted by the spectre of another attack for over a decade, we have learned to live with terror. It has become part of the everyday political lexicon. Some may even argue that the term has lost all political appeal, displaced by a plethora of new challenges which are more important in defining the twenty-first-century security terrain. That is not to suggest a return to some pre-9/11 normality. The world has been spatially and temporally transformed to the lasting death of the Westphalian Order. This evidences the real triumph of liberal reason, attained not through some universal ascription to liberal values, ideals, or principles. Demanding an inclusive imaginary on account of the way life is radically endangered by its own planetary ambitions, the age of liberal reason is made real as 'the outside' no longer appears as a credible political referent – geo-politically or intellectually.

What we may term 'liberal terror' refers to this global imaginary of threat which, casting aside once familiar referents that previously defined the organization of socie-ties, now forces us to confront each and every potential disaster threatening to engulf advanced liberal life. Binding terror to the everyday does not simply tie the phenomena to political forms, though it does require the trauma of the past to impress the logic. Neither does the problem register exclusively as a militaristic affair, though the encounter with some form of violence remains its principal form of conditioning. What terrifies is of the order of the cata-strophic. It is the future scenario so often played out in our ways of thinking about the world to come. It is the seemingly predictable yet unpreventable that reminds us of the insecure sediment of our very existence. It is the chance encounter with a violent force that doesn't dis-criminate one's political subjectivity. And it is infinitely possible, which, threatening to appear at any given moment, dangerously affirms with each passing occur-rence the precariousness of the human condition. The Terror – our terror – is therefore the contingent possibility of a future-coming catastrophic event which increasingly shapes the normality of the times.

The state of normality defining liberal terror runs counter to those 'States of Exception' discourses which became popular in the post-9/11 moment.[2] This paradigm, for some, was seemingly self-evident. The initial attacks upon New York City and Washington were deemed excep-tional by any conceivable measure. Enemies to be fought, it was said, appeared like none ever encountered. In response, the United States and its allies coupled this exceptionality with their own exceptional abuse of sover-eign power as they sought to hunt down terror in all its forms. For many, therefore, the subsequent retreat from Iraq and Afghanistan represented far more than a change in the strategic direction of the war effort. It symbolized a return to the civic normality lost, the hope that our civilization credentials would slowly be resuscitated as we began mapping out those comforting demarcations which formerly held between the lawful & unlawful, the citizen & the soldier, the abiding & the recalcitrant, the inside & outside, along with times of peace & times of war. Here Carl Schmitt appeared to be an unlikely ally for those who wanted to distance themselves from excessive militaristic behaviour. Invoking Schmitt's famous *Concept of the Political*, which defines sovereignty as the ability to decide upon the exception,[3] cosmopolitan theorists resurrected his (dis)comforting fixed order of things in order to challenge the abuse of state power. As Martti Koskenniemi has noted:

> Whatever Schmitt's political choices, readers have been struck by the expressive force of his critiques when applied to contemporary events: the war on terrorism as a morally-inspired and unlimited 'total war', in which the adversary is not treated as a 'just enemy'; the obsoleteness of traditional rules of warfare and recourse to novel technologies – especially air power – so as to conduct discriminatory wars against adversaries viewed as outlaws and enemies of humanity; Camp Delta in the Guantánamo naval base with its still over 500 prisoners from the Afghanistan war as a normless exception that reveals the nature of the new international political order of which the United States is the guardian – the source of the normative order, itself unbound by it.[4]

These types of analysis, however, failed on a number of levels. Firstly, since they remained tied to the telluric world of nations, the state remained the only credible referent for political assessment. Not only was this trope therefore dominated by theories of state power, it offered a very outdated analytic in which the state still appears to be the natural ontological and epistemological foundation for political belonging and contestation.[5] What is more, since these types of analysis proposed a new planetary idealism premised upon the structural remnants of the Westphalian order, so the constituted sovereign power remains primary. Nobody is saying here that states don't exist, or that sovereignty is some abstract or redundant concept. It is, however, to accept, as Boutros Boutros-Ghali once insisted, that '[t]he time of absolute and exclusive sovereignty . . . has passed; its theory was never matched by reality.'[6] Many academics who remain committed to the idea of a Westphalian order will no doubt have been troubled by Boutros-Ghali's honesty. Tony Blair, however, was a learned disciple: 'Before Sept. 11, I was already reaching for a different philosophy in international relations from a traditional one that has held sway since the Treaty of Westphalia in 1648 – namely, that a country's internal affairs are for it and you don't interfere unless it threatens you, or breaches a treaty, or triggers an obligation of alliance.'[7]

Secondly, since these approaches have taken distinct sites of abandonment, e.g. Guantánamo Bay, to be paradigmatic, Schmitt's ideas have been deployed in order to condemn the 'international' nature of liberal interventionism, while in the process rescuing its more humane 'cosmopolitan' variant.[8] The politics of exceptionalism thus became the principal rallying cry for those who, lamenting a still fractured terrain, highlighted the inherent dangers of spatial division in order to summon its lasting foreclosure. This position was invariably compromised – theoretically and ontologically. 'Truer liberals' would actually start their theoretical position by taking the worst aspects of Schmitt's thought (i.e. ontologically prior enmity) in order to use it against its resulting tensions. This proved convenient (not to say self-fulfilling) as neatly identifiable forms of geo-strategic separation (the dangerous reality) could be taken to fully vindicate the eventual closure of political space (the cosmopolitan promise). Questions of legitimate power as such would be firmly tied to competing grand visions of political formation. With Schmitt's nightmare vision of the fall of *jus publicum Europaeum* therefore recast as the liberal condition of possibility for the twenty-first century,[9] selective appropriation of his ideas put Schmitt in a peculiar bind as the diagnostician in chief along with the chief adversary to be vanquished at all political costs. What happened to Schmittean ontology, however, remained a complete mystery.

The third reason for the failure of a Schmittean approach was that, since universality was taken here to be the natural foundation for all analysis – even though the empirical reality of the world continuously eschews any factual basis for universal ascription – the political subject was always assumed to be a universal subject in waiting. Questions of ontology and epistemology would therefore be colonized by what we may term a 'universal image of thought', which, proposing a linear way of thinking, offered a profoundly faith-based ontological positioning. Humanity thus appeared as always naturally there in waiting, yet to reveal itself. It would logically follow that whatever challenged this universal orientation would not only be disqualified as a less than authentic political subject; it could also be presented to be a direct challenge to a world of lasting security, peace, and prosperity. Ontologically speaking, however, not only has this arcane aspiration appeared in direct conflict with the contemporary bio-philosophy of life which, counter-intuitively, argues that the more interconnected life becomes, the more its form actually proliferates and differentiates (see below), but it is precisely the adoption of such universal imaginaries which has effectively allowed systems of power to mask the contingent use of power, while retaining political difference as the start-point for the liberal understanding of war, injustice, and political contestation.

David Chandler was correct to point out that the selective use of Schmitt provided the 'last refuge of critical theorists' working in the International Relations discipline. By using Schmitt's framework devoid of any ontological consideration – hence as a heuristic device in order to affirm existing normative frameworks and pre-existing visions of the world – he was juxtaposed with his apparent resulting tensions, highlighted the 'weakness and defensiveness of critical theoretical positions themselves'. Previous structural musings are excavated, and Schmitt is simplified without ever questioning his contemporaneousness. As Chandler explains: 'The clarity and cause of the critical position is becoming increasingly uncertain as the clear frameworks of state-based international relations are undermined, not by progressive movements constituting new collectivities beyond the state, but by leading western states and international institutions which claim to be operating beyond the sphere of national interests and in the interests of the emancipatory subject.' This 'lack of clarity', Chandler argues, enables Schmitt to be used 'symbolically or rhetorically to reassert clear lines of political division, demarcating the "purity" of the critical theorist from those alleged to be serving the interests of power'.[10] These marks of separation weren't incidental. Despite the failures in liberal policies, it was possible, by means of tactical separation, to retain a lasting faith in the project as a shared *telos* of the world of peoples.

This brings us directly to the problem of temporality. Time is one of the most important political concepts. It is inextricably bound to the entire truth-telling process upon which regimes of power depend. Time, however, is not simply value-neutral. Neither does it only appear *diachronically*, i.e. seconds, minutes, hours, days, years. While this concept of time has undoubtedly dominated the modernist industrial period, it increasingly appears arbitrary and redundant. As John Hall writes, '[D]espite how nearly ubiquitous measurement of time has become, people in different social settings organize and experience even objective temporality in highly divergent ways.'[11] Time in fact has always been a *construct* which reveals many different rhythms, meanings, interpretations, quantitative forms, and qualitative expressions. Once the concept of time is broached politically, we discover that history 'remains fundamentally an account, and what is called explanation is nothing but the way in which the account is arranged in a comprehensible plot'.[12] This bracketing of time is not simply about the historical record. In the process of narrating the past, what needs to be done in the present begins to find its most purposeful expression: '[B]ecause diachronic time makes possible the projection of alternative future events, it puts into play the planning of the future, such that any given present is no longer simply a "here and now," but also the realization of a (past) projected future and the anticipation of events to come, already plugged into diachronic schedules.'[13]

Take the events of 9/11. It was common to date the history of the violence to that fateful morning. This played into the narrative of the unprovoked attack: 'They simply hated us for who we were.' It also fostered a collective belief that everything had changed. So what had previously been taken for granted would now become the source of uncertainty, anxiety, and despair. '*The kaleidoscope* has been shaken,' Blair famously explained. 'The pieces are in *flux*.' Armed with this truth, what followed proved to be reminiscent of what Merleau-Ponty referred to as being a 'historical epoch': 'one of those moments where the traditional ground of a nation or society crumbles and where, for better or worse, man must reconstruct human relations'.[14] It was the perceived lack of provocation in particular which constituted the truth of the event, as well as ascribing a certain validity or righteousness to the retributive violence which followed. In this way, as Paul Ricoeur once noted, 'the very notion of the history of a long time-span derives from the dramatic event . . . in the sense of the emplotted event.'[15] Making 'sense of the event' was essential to the conditioning of what then became possible. Of course, if we decided here to broaden the time-frame ever so slightly and delve further into the history of the violence, alternative and less politically expedient histories of the events of 9/11 begin to surface that are altogether less comfortable. Or as Merleau-Ponty would no doubt have more critically put it, 'We do not have a choice between purity and violence but between different kinds of violence.'

Times of exceptionality have followed the lines of a diachronic temporality. They have been neatly bracketed in time by the threshold that binds lawfulness/unlawfulness so that the course of events could be subjected to the legitimate routines of calculated power. Time in this sense has revealed a particular *disjuncture* since it would be fully bound to the normalized laws of what we may term the *Sovereign Chronos*, while nevertheless suspended by the sovereign moment on account of its juridical abandonment. Times of exceptionality therefore corresponded to the time witness of particular regimes whose temporal imperfection was to categorically refute the *timelessness* of universal law. While the time of the exception appeared diachronically certain inasmuch as there was an absolutely pin-pointable start-point for the unfolding of the exceptional moment, i.e. the point where it all went wrong, it also appeared 'out of time' in the pure teleological sense of its lasting completion, i.e. universal peace. This highlighted a familiar time/space continuum with which to castigate political entities which (a) temporally abandoned a commitment to international norms on account of some desire to reassert sovereign authority or (b) permanently operated outside of the rule of international law, i.e. the Geneva Conventions. There was, however, a ready-made easily digestible fix. Since a clear break in time could be detected, so the time of the exception could be put to an end once the legitimate exercise of sovereign power was finally restored.

This linear understanding of time has proved to be completely problematic and woefully inadequate. It neatly synchronized political activity to ideological persuasion, while time itself was fully colonized by the juridical imperative. History thus became tied to a narrative of greater/lesser perfectibility on the road to either (a) the natural unfolding of the world into its promise of a universal state of lasting peace and (b) the unnatural continuation of war, misery, and suffering. Just as the problem of sovereignty would therefore be bracketed in order to allow for highly reductionist structural narratives which were easily digestible, the time of the exception equally provided epistemic comfort by resurrecting the untroubling familiarity of rehearsed spatial orthodoxy. It necessarily followed that any political statement which threatened to disrupt this time-sequence of events was seen to be, at best, self-serving, or, at worst, an example of outright deception. So while these types of approaches took issue with Schmitt's own lack of faith in human nature (especially its completion), they, too, rested upon a conspiratorial approach to power in which the political classes could not be taken at their word. Statements which ordinarily evidenced allegiance to liberalism's foundational principles were simply read as a deceptive mask to geo-political ambition: 'We have no desire to dominate, no ambitions of empire. Our aim is a democratic peace.'[16] Mitchell Dean has been less deceived by the convenience of partial historical memory:

This [perceived] contest between European cosmopolitanism and American conservatism misses the point of the intrinsic connection between the contemporary liberal critique of sovereignty and the authorization of the use of deadly force. Even the most Kantian and philosophical among contemporary commentators on International Affairs, Jürgen Habermas, recommended a police action in the name of human rights and justified the NATO bombing of Yugoslavia in 1999 as possible anticipation of the leap from the classical conception of international law for sovereign states toward the cosmopolitan law of a world society. At the very least such a stance would seem to suggest that even cosmopolitans are willing to suspend current international law in an emergency in order to advocate the use of military violence if their morality dictates it.[17]

Cosmopolitan approaches to universal law are idealistic at best. There is no law without enforcement or relations

of power. As Jacques Derrida explained by drawing specific reference to Immanuel Kant's *Theory of Right*,

> There is no law that does not imply in itself, *a priori*, in
> the analytical structure of its concept, the possibility of
> being 'enforced' applied by force. . . . There are, to be
> sure, laws that are not enforced, but there is no law without
> enforceability, and no applicability or enforceability of the
> law without force, whether this force be direct or indirect,
> physical or symbolic, exterior or interior, brutal or subtly
> discursive – even hermeneutic – coercive or regulative, and
> so forth.[18]

Implicit in Derrida's 'Force of Law' is that no enforceability exists without some intimate relation to crises. This
contingency of law's enforceability is crucial. Every law,
every decision, responds to an exceptional moment.[19] It
brings force to bear upon that which breaks from the norm
in order to rework the basis of normality anew. There is
therefore no pure theory of the exception, no absolute
break from law. An exception simply infers the 'order-
word' proper to the continuous recovery of sovereign
power out of the unending cinder of its own disorder. Law,
in other words, reserves the right to transgress its own
foundations after the experience of 'crises-events', which
profoundly alters our sense of meaning and action in the
world. It is no surprise, then, to find that states of exception are all too frequent once the broad sweep of history
is considered. Temporal crisis simply permits the reworking of the 'legitimate' normative boundaries out of the
ashes of a disrupted existence. In doing so, law continues
to illustrate a fluctuating shift from (dis)ordered sovereign
recovery to further emerging disruptions that continue to
define the modern condition.

Our task is to move beyond the simple linearity which
colonizes our political understanding of space and time.
This requires us to question the political and philosophical
stakes of late liberalism, in which familiar modernist

concepts of space and time have effectively entered into lasting crises. What happens, for instance, when space is no longer an obstacle to power? And what happens when past/future frames of reference blur into a unifying strategic framework that shapes the present? It is important to point out here that these spatial and temporal crises are not incidental. As we shall discover, they are fully integral to the bio-philosophy of late liberalism, which, proposing an entirely new social morphology of life that promotes complex, adaptive, and emergent qualities, demands new spatial and temporal awareness that moves beyond fixed frames of reference. With this in mind, our task is not to show allegiance to the messianic nature of the liberal promise, whatever the perceived nature of its perpetual glory. Our task is to understand how this faith-based narrative conditions the present so that serious questions can be raised about the profoundly onto-theological dimensions to the liberal will to rule planetary life. Only then can we begin to set aside the universalizing moral entrapments of liberal humanism, which reduces political ethics to a question of relations amongst already compliant political subjects.

The Terror Diagnostic

Terror – or at least terror(ism) – is not a new problem. Ever since Maximilian Robespierre orchestrated his *régime de la terreur* (1793–5), it has become a permanent feature of the modern political vernacular. While Robespierre's 'reign of terror' is credited with coining the term, for the most part the phenomenon has been directly associated with *internal* challenges to sovereign authority. A supplementary function, then, to 'legitimate' juridical power, terror has been condemned for occupying an *excessive* or extra-juridical position in relation to the legitimate order of things. Importantly, given that no sovereign power has ever perceived itself to be illegitimate – that is to say, from the moment of its inception it always believes in the *timelessness* of its rule – terror has effectively been openly recruited into a profound metaphysical game in which notions of truth, order, righteousness, and justice have continued to depend upon each other. Metaphysics (without oversimplifying) refers to a mode or style of thinking which seeks to be able to grasp and recover the very *truth* of being out of some *transcendent* exteriority. Metaphysics, as such, places specific demands upon thought. It makes it incumbent upon the thinker to believe that since the political 'subject' has been thrown back upon some insecure ground, the true 'object' for thought is to authenticate life by establishing firm and secure foundations. As Michael Dillon explains:

> Metaphysics, then, is the masque of mastery; securing some foundation upon which to establish the sum total of what is knowable with certainty, and conforming one's everyday conduct – public and private – to the foundation so secured. Such foundations may go by different names but that of the project itself does not. Hence, the responsibility, traditionally incumbent upon the philosopher – his 'true' mission – consisted in securing ultimate referents or principles. Philosophy was, as Nietzsche put it, a matter of valuation, 'that is, establishment of the uppermost value in terms of which and according to which all beings are to be'.[20]

Plato is partly credited with beginning this tradition. His allegory of the cave not only gave the metaphysical world real tangible purchase by proposing the authentic subject; insisting that this subject necessarily produces its own *mimetic rival* allowed him to couple authenticity with an intimately bound copy or imitation. This was necessary for the authentic to have any true meaning. For Plato, this mimetic rival, like a shadow on the wall of a cave, is a product of a world of *re-presentation*. Originality has its own unique presentation – a truly unique form which accompanies the reality of its presence – whereas the imposter merely resembles or falsifies that presence. Platonic reason thus gave to us the necessity of the image (*eidolon*), which enables one to differentiate between the true/false, original/fake, authentic/imposter, secure/dangerous, and so forth. Importantly, while the Platonic world of representation proved compatible with the iconography of Christianity, modernity has taken this aesthetic compulsion and made it his own.[21] Confronting the dangers of its own making, the modern condition has required what Martin Heidegger once termed the 'certainty of representation', in which truth can find its optical expression.[22] Indeed, as Gilles Deleuze and Félix Guattari once indicated, 'the form of subjectivity, whether consciousness or passion, would remain absolutely empty if faces did not form loci of resonance that select the sensed or mental reality and make it conform in advance to a dominant reality.'[23] Such mimetic rivals have been thoroughly recast throughout the representational schema of the modern political sensibility. Imitating and aspiring, they continue to appear like some virus, feeding off the system, copying its behaviours, while directing its productive energies back upon itself for destructive ends.

This mimetic approach to terror is conceptually beneficial. It certainly goes some way to explaining why a concise definition is difficult to obtain. Since systems are constantly evolving – politically, socially, culturally, and technologically – so too must the nature of threat. Philip Bobbit is a principal advocate of a mimetic approach to terror. In his volume *Terror and Consent* he adopts such an approach to present an entire history of the phenomenon's evolving nature.[24] Central to Bobbit's thesis is the assumption that every human order produces its own novel brand of terror whose defining features show a remarkable resemblance to the system it wishes to destroy: 'In each era, terrorism derives its ideology in reaction to the *raison d'être* of the dominant constitutional order, at the same time negating and rejecting that form's unique ideology by mimicking the form's structural characteristics.'[25] So just as the colonial seafaring powers had to contend with the terror of piracy, while modern industrial capitalist societies had to deal with the terror of the industrial-minded communist vanguard, contemporary market states must deal with their own parasitical entrepreneurs which show hostile self-destructive intent. Terror is thus like a distorted mirror image of the vision of peace it continually haunts. It turns strengths into weaknesses, freedoms into vulnerabilities, optimisms into despair, hopes into fears, and the means of production into the means for destruction. This proves to be conceptually significant. While adopting a mimetic approach to terror allows us to account for its omnipresent nature, it also permits us to appreciate (without any contradiction) why the phenomenon is a highly contingent product of its own productive time:

> Just as earlier forms of terrorism reacted against the values while mimicking the techniques of the prevailing constitutional order, this new mode of terrorism reflects the new constitutional order coming into being, the informational market state. . . . [T]he market state finds it has generated a terrorism that negates the very individual choice that the state exalts, and puts in service of that negation the networked, decentralized, outsourcing global methods characteristic of the market state itself. . . . Market state terrorism will be just as global, networked, decentralized, and devolved and rely just as much on outsourcing and incentivizing as the market state.[26]

Bobbit effectively consolidates here a number of strands of thought that have been in currency for well over a decade. Network theorists have for some considerable time been proposing a mimetic approach for understanding the changing nature of social organization, none more so than the military and strategic analysts who at the forefront of this strategic rethink inaugurated an entire revolution in global military affairs. The RAND Corporation in particular has been a notable advocate of network theory, promoting its now well-established doctrine of *Networked Centric Warfare*: 'The term we coined was *Netwar*, largely because it resonated with the surety that the information revolution

favoured the rise of network forms of organization, doctrine, and strategy.'[27] Crucially, for RAND, the advent of
network-centric thinking is not confined to any particular
sector.[28] It points to a much wider revolution in thought in
which the 'age-old ideas about life as a "great chain of
being" or as a progression of nested hierarchies are giving
way to new ideas that networks are the key to understanding *all of life*.'[29] Militarism alone is not therefore shaping
the world. It is responding in equal measure to the new
science of life which is fundamentally transforming, for
better and worse, all life-world systems beyond any previous comprehension. Militarism may not be the principal
driver behind this revolution, but it does stress the theory's
imperative since organization literally becomes a matter of
life and death. As the two main architects of the US transformation in military affairs once so forcefully explained,
'Across the 1990s global rule sets became seriously mis-
aligned, with economics racing ahead of politics . . . and
technology racing ahead of security (e.g., the rise of transnational terrorists exploiting globalization's growing
network connectivity). Now it is time to play catch-up.'[30]

Borrowing heavily from post-structural thinking,[31] this
brought to the fore a number of key principles which have
left a lasting imprint on the twenty-first-century security
terrain:

1 Nothing and nowhere is strategically marginal. With
   the capacity for terror to happen 'anywhere, any-
   place, anytime', geo-strategic concerns have become
   displaced by planetary problems which must be
   matched in ambition, scope, and mission.
2 It is the radically singular which has the capacity to
   inflict most damage. Unlike conventional warfare,
   in which the enemy's capability was dependent upon
   material massification (soldiers, bombs, etc.), in
   these open conditions where the ability to remain
   undetected is more of a tactical advantage, less is
   actually more.

3   Success requires pre-emptive action. Since human capabilities (including the catastrophic attack) have increased exponentially, waiting is simply not an option.

4   Since total security is impossible, one has to appreciate that further attacks are inevitable. As lasting insecurity becomes the default setting, so unending emergency becomes the norm.

5   All conventional referents blur into a zone of indistinction. So the major distinctions that once marked out conventional modern thought – i.e. war/peace, enemies/friends, soldiers/citizens, outside/inside, law/strategy, politics/economy – have been firmly undermined by the complex account of life, whose adaptive ontology actually takes pride in the abandonment of compartmentalized mentalities and the effacement of neat lines of identification.

When the source of potentiality becomes the source of the problem, improved capability effectively heightens the stakes. There are a number of reasons for this. Firstly, whereas hierarchical forms of organization have provided clear epistemic guidance, network forms are more problematic since their outcomes are ambivalent: 'The same technology that aids social activists and those desiring the good of all is also available to those with the darkest intentions, bent on destruction and driven by a rage reminiscent of the Middle Ages.'[32] Secondly, since the network form affords greater organizational efficiencies, they are exponentially more powerful: 'This distinctive, often ad-hoc design has unusual strengths, for both offense and defense. On the offense, networks tend to be adaptable, flexible, and versatile vis-è-vis opportunities and challenges. . . . In terms of their defensive potential, networks tend to be redundant and diverse, making them robust and resilient in the face of attack.'[33] And thirdly, whereas hierarchical models presuppose fixed (hence epistemologically certain) properties, networks pose entirely new problems by radically altering the strategic terrain, collapsing once familiar dialectical terms of engagement: 'The blurring of offense and defense reflects another feature of net-war (albeit one that is exhibited in many other policy and issue areas): It tends to defy and cut across standard boundaries, jurisdictions, and distinctions between state and society, public and private, war and peace, war and crime, civilian and military, police and military, and legal and illegal.'[34]

Networks promote radical forms of interconnectivity which dissipate all meaningful demarcations. Their principal message is *systemic complexity*:

> Seemingly out of nowhere, in the span of a few years, network theory has become one of the most visible pieces of the body of knowledge that can be applied to the description, analysis, and understanding of complex systems. New applications are developed at an ever increasing rate and the promise for future growth is high. Network theory is now an essential ingredient in the study of complex systems.[35]

This has undoubtedly radicalized the strategic terrain. With everything potentially (re)connectable, all that was once solid truly melts into air. As Luis Amaral and Julio Ottino explain, 'A complex system is a system with a large number of elements, building blocks or agents, capable of interacting with each other and with their environment.' While 'interaction between elements may occur only with immediate neighbours', they may also 'move in space or occupy fixed positions, and can be in one of two states or of multiple states'. 'The whole', as such, is 'much more than the sum of its parts'.[36] Importantly, since there are no elements (human/non-human, animate/inanimate, actual/virtual) which are to be considered *outside* of the strategic play, everything matters, for every element in this complex arrangement has the potential to be truly disastrous. As Duncan Watts argues:

> When it comes to epidemics of disease, financial crises, political revolutions, social movements, and dangerous

ideas, we are all connected by short chains of influence. It doesn't matter if you know about them, and it doesn't matter if you care, they will have their effect anyway. To misunderstand this is to misunderstand the first great lesson of the connected age: we may all have our own burdens, but like it or not, we must bear each other's burdens as well.[37]

Such burdens have redefined our understanding of social responsibility. As Zygmunt Bauman acutely observed, today 'there is no "outside", no escape route or place to shelter, no alternative space to isolate and hide in. . . . On this planet, we are all dependent on each other and nothing that we do or refrain from doing is indifferent to the fate of everyone else.'[38] This has a number of telling implications. With the world effectively *foreclosed*, every frame of reference is deemed *in*clusive. Catastrophe therefore finds a new location – integral to the living conditions which sustain advanced life. It logically follows that since the potential for catastrophe is the product of our radically interconnected times, dealing with its unknowability is to accept the *possibility* that the worst can happen. Only then does it become possible to bring that which is beyond comprehension within our calculable models for assessment, damage limitation, and future amelioration. So not only have we become ever more dependent on complex, adaptive, dynamic, and distributed systems for the sustenance of life, it is assumed with equal measure that within this systemic trope even the smallest of disruptions can end up having enormous and sometimes catastrophic consequences:

> The novelty of the global risk society lies in the fact that our civilizational decisions involve global consequences and dangers, and these radically contradict the institutionalized language of control – indeed the promise of control – that is radiated to the global public in the event of catastrophe (as in Chernobyl, and now also in the terror attacks on New York and Washington). Precisely this constitutes the *political* explosiveness of the global

risk society. This explosiveness has its centre in the mass-mediated public sphere, in politics, in the bureaucracy, in the economy, though it is not necessarily contiguous with a particular event to which it is connected.[39]

Terror terrifies precisely because of its *radical interconnectivity*. This is not new thinking. It was fully understood by Paul Wolfowitz, who in a testimony to the US Congress in October 2001 was already of the opinion: 'Along with the globalization that is creating interdependence among the world's free economies, there is a *parallel globalization of terror*, in which rogue states and terrorist organizations share information, intelligence, technology, weapons materials and know-how.' For Wolfowitz, what made this new form of terror particularly dangerous was its 'parasitical' nature. It operated within the very system that ordinarily gives form to life, appearing like some *intelligent virus* intent upon destroying its host. Terror in this regard is seen to be altogether more terrifying precisely because it displays intelligent co-evolving capabilities. It is constantly on the move, traversing fixed boundaries, mutating to avoid meaningful detection, while continually infecting the vital global networks of advanced liberal societies. As Bobbit further explains:

> The problem of terrorism is similar in some ways to that of an epidemic. Like new antibiotic-resistant strains of tuberculosis, market state terrorism is a function of what we have done to eradicate old threats. That is, its principal causes are the liberalization of the global economy, the internationalization of the electronic media, and the military-technological revolution. . . . New, mutated strains of tuberculosis are resistant to antibiotics for similar reasons, that is, they are the direct result of the successful attack on earlier forms of the virus, remnants of which have mutated in order to survive.[40]

These viral/vital analogies are routinely deployed in a metaphorical way to offer a meaningful understanding of highly complex phenomena. They also serve a very useful political function. Drawing together the biological with the digital, these narratives personalize the terror by relating the virtual nature of the threat to the vital world inhabited. Indeed, providing a recombinant language which is dangerously fitting to a world in which virtuality connects all things vital, the broadest strategic focus is demanded on account of the post-vital stakes. So living freely today becomes a thoroughly dangerous business. For to live in an age in which complexity provides the clearest epistemic guidance, risk-taking is encouraged, emergence is liberated, and the speed of flows has increased exponentially necessarily entails living in an age in which life, cast onto the uncertain shores of the contingent encounter, finds itself open to many more catastrophic possibilities that this art of free living now entails. Understood this way, it is no longer possible to discuss terror in terms which cast it outside the political realm. Integral to our ways of living, terror *conditions what is liberally possible*. Our intellectual choice is therefore straightforward. We can either approach the problem of terror (including all its subsequent affects) as a *de facto* given – thereby accepting the political and philosophical stakes – or we can properly deconstruct the term in a meaningful way so that the dominating systemic rationalities from which it emerges can be better understood.

The Global Real

Manuel Castells conjured upon brilliantly the contemporary phase of globalization by mapping out what he termed the 'global space of flows'.[41] For Castells, what defines this space is the shift from the industrial to the information age. Historical change as such is brought about by the advent of new information technologies – especially those in the fields of communication and biology. Since this profoundly alters our sense of space and time, networks are not simply a new form of social organization. The network form has become a key feature of an entirely new 'social morphology' in which everything changes. Network theory, in other words, provides us with a new science of life that radically undermines spaces of fixed residency. In some respects, this hypothesis extends Paul Virilio's earlier claims that speed was finally conquering political space.[42] Speed in this context wasn't simply about questioning the intensities of means of passage. It was a milieu through which life itself is radically transformed. One evident effect of this has been to expose the fragility of limit conditions. Whatever the boundary, speed-space displaces time-space, so that once impenetrable divisions become increasingly porous. As Hall explains:

> Increased speeds of communication and transportation have led to a compression of objective time and space. The consequence of these shifts is time has become 'liquid': events of the past slip away, soon to be forgotten; new events and things arrive ever more quickly. People come to exist in a blur of vivid present ever more jam-packed with activities that displace the here-and-now, or construct it from the outside. . . . The times of modern life, predicated on history and the clock, are malleable and emergent.[43]

There is an important caveat to address here. Globalization does not necessarily refer to the uninhibited free movement of peoples. For the term to have any meaning, that which is global must be felt locally. In this sense, globalization is the ability to connect different localities so that local experiences undergo some form of transformation in their political, social, economic, or cultural fabric. This has long since been appreciated by the famous theorist of nomadism, Deleuze, who noted that it is not a condition of nomadism to actually move around physically. Like nomadism, globalization can be felt as the world passes through different localities. Our world invariably comes to us in many different guises. We are the consumers of many different global products, none perhaps more powerful or immediately recognizable than our instantaneous daily consumption of global media services, which, following the latest technological advancements in handheld devices, at their very moment of arising, places worldly occurrences quite literally into our hands. As Virilio explains, in the age of the 'hyper-modernity of real time', 'the problem is no longer so much with the standardization of the products and behaviours of a bygone industrial age, as the synchronization of sensations that are likely to suddenly influence our decisions.' Synchronicity is 'the combined effect of the acceleration of History and of a shrinking of geographical space, triggering an individualization of each and every one of us, as well as the various destinations of actions'.[44]

Contemporary news media are all about *global events*. Such events do not need to constitute any linear sequence. Neither does their immediacy need to reaffirm any lasting structural impression. The global media event conveys the evident contingency of the world. It continuously reaffirms with increasing frequency that the world is constantly on the move. Its 'grid of intelligibility' tells how the dynamism of the times eschews any notion of permanence. And its complex mapping seamlessly moves from one event to the next, permitting ever wider (spatial and temporal) connectivity on account of the events it traces. Despite the monopolistic ownership of news media, it would be wrong to suggest that the viewing public represents some docile mass. In his highly influential study on *Cinematic Geopolitics*,[45] Michael Shapiro coins the term 'cinematic heterotopias' to explain how one's encounter with visual media can actually effectuate real socio-political change in spite of the setting of political agendas. This becomes apparent when visual media are broached less in terms of the polemical representations of progressive political issues, than in terms of their ability to formally challenge the perceptual limits of spectator subjects who possess political agency. In these terms, it is possible to identify within any event-narrative multiple interpretations which evidence what Jacques Rancière called 'the re-partitioning of the political' so as to invite a more contested terrain of interpretations:

> Aesthetics is not a discipline dealing with art and artworks, but a kind of, what I call, distribution of the sensible. I mean a way of mapping the visible, a cartography of the visible, the intelligible and also of the possible. Aesthetics was a kind of redistribution of experience, the idea that there was a sphere of experience that didn't feed the traditional distribution, because the traditional distribution adds that people have different senses according to their position in society. Those who were destined to rule and those who were destined to be ruled didn't have the same sensory equipment, not the same eyes and ears, not the same intelligence. Aesthetics means precisely the break with that traditional way of embodying inequality in the very constitution of the sensible world.[46]

Two particular global media events stand out in recent memory. The first was to happen on 9 November 1989. The fall of the Berlin Wall was in many ways unprecedented. It was perhaps the first live global media moment. The images that were being projected seemed to indicate that globalization had truly come of age. We shared the collective outpouring of emotion as the visibly linear construction behind which an oppressed people had been shadowed was demolished by a popular tide. At the time, it felt that this was more than the collapse of some dividing partition. What had also been erased in the process were the political, social, and ideological lines that had kept the world for too long resting upon their destructive razor-edge. As the intellectual virtues of orthodox Marxism structurally imploded, it was assumed that the world would no longer be divided into 'camps'. Instead it was to be defined by ever greater co-operation and integration. Francis Fukuyama captured the optimism of the times by famously declaring, 'What we may be witnessing is not just the end of the Cold War, or the passing of a particular period of post-war history, but the end of history as such: that is, the end point of mankind's ideological evolution and the universalization of Western Liberal Democracy as the final form of human government.'[47]

Some eleven years and 307 days later another global event would be transmitted into our collective consciousness. On this occasion the message was entirely different. No doubt there were similar epoch-shifting parallels to be drawn. It would, however, be the symbolic differences that would traumatize Western audiences. Structurally, it was not the imprisoning walls that would crash into vertical decent but one of modernity's proudest landmarks. Ideologically, it was not the system of oppression that would collapse but a physical formation that was meticulously built with liberated hands. And symbolically, it would not be the hammer that would be put to an unintended use but all which symbolized our ability to roam and soar to great heights. The climate had clearly taken a turn for the worse. With these changing winds, the air of optimism was now replaced by a suffocating cloud of despair. We went from being spectators in a collective salvation of an entire continent to being broadcast voyeurs in the slaughter of thousands. Through the endless re-runs, every angle was covered, so that we could all watch in 'real-time' reality television in its most abhorrent and compelling form. Death broadcast LIVE. Contrary, therefore, to misguided beliefs, the 'Global' would not be made 'real' through the triumphant advance of liberal reason. We experienced the global through the raw reality of a catastrophe:

> Our preliminary reaction is that the shattering impact of the September 11 attacks can be accounted for only against the background of the borderline which today separates the digitalized First World from the Third World 'desert of the Real'. It is the awareness that we live in an insulated artificial universe which generates the notion that some ominous agent is threatening us all the time with total destruction.[48]

The events of 9/11 were undoubtedly spectacular. 'Everywhere', Alain Badiou commented, there was 'the evidence of a certain affect'.[49] We all became mutually assured of our own vulnerabilities.[50] But why did the events have such an impact? It certainly cannot be explained in terms of scale alone. While the events were tragic, the numbers pale when compared to the annul of human suffering. The spectacle itself proved more compelling. Never before has the world been democratic witness to the horror of mass casualty violence upon liberal subjects. This was part of the intention. Manhattan epitomizes the 'Global City'.[51] It is the central node of the global media network. It concentrates global attention more than anywhere on the planet. So as the most famous of towers fell, the world was always going to be watching. In this regard, despite our revulsion, it could be argued that the attack was perfectly logical in terms of its execution. As Virilio explained, '[H]yper-terrorism no longer requires the mass armoured divisions because its weapon system is mainly constituted by the array of mass communication tools turned back on the enemy.'[52] It works by 'synchronizing emotion' through 'mass individualization': 'the emotional synchronization of the hordes, a process in which terror must be instantaneously felt by all, everywhere at once, here and there, on the scale of a global totalitarianism'.[53] Since what strategic analysts used to once term 'the frontline' has therefore been 'ousted by the surface of the screen', the new media environment has assisted in making us all active participants in 'a kind of instantaneous aleatory war of which Clausewitz could have no inkling'.[54]

9/11 forced us to confront the dangerous uncertainty of an unequal world that was increasingly closing in upon itself without a political framework for dealing with the problems such shrinkage necessarily created. The violence showed 'how *global* events can truly be. It gave flesh to the heretofore abstract idea of global interdependence and the wholeness of the globe.'[55] Highlighting the frailty of all boundaries, it fitted 'the role of the symbolic end to the

era of space better than any event in recent history'.
Importantly, for Bauman, once the violence of 9/11 is
contextualized within the global space of flows, it is possible to write of planetary frontier-land conditions in which
movement becomes defining: 'The adversaries are known
to be constantly on the move – their might and nuisance-
making power lie in the speed, inconspicuousness and
secrecy of their moves. For all practical intents and purposes, the adversaries are *extra-territorial*. Capturing the
territory they occupied yesterday does not mean today's
victory, let alone "termination of hostilities".'[56] Despite
some of the evident geo-strategic misadventures that have
dominated political discussions in the post-9/11 moment,
planetary movement remains central to understanding
every type of threat encountered in the present.

The symbolic end to time-space was fully written into
the narrative of 9/11. Spatially it was made certain as the
war effort seamlessly shifted from 'terrorism' to 'terror'.
By shortening the signifier, so the signification was extended
to deal with all 'radical uncertainty'.[57] This has left a
lasting imprint. As Jean Baudrillard observed, 'Terrorism,
like viruses, is everywhere. There is a global perfusion of
terrorism, which accompanies any system of domination
as though it were its shadow, ready to activate itself anywhere, like a double agent. We can no longer draw a
demarcation line around it. It is at the very heart of this
culture which combats it.'[58] What is at stake here is the
nature of the problem: 'It is not a question . . . of a "clash
of civilizations", but of an – almost anthropological – confrontation between an undifferentiated universal culture
and everything which, in any field whatever, retains something of an irreducible alterity.'[59] This concern with the
alterior was clear from the outset. As President George W.
Bush quickly reminded Congress on 20 September 2001:
'Our war on terror begins with al-Qaeda, but it does not
end there.' Indeed, as Bush later added with even more
significance to the contemporary security agenda, 'The war
on terror is a war *into the future*.' As the task of securing

tomorrow becomes an integral part of the strategic remit, so the inevitable unfolding of time is infected with a terrifying potency.

The temporal collapse was highlighted in the subtle media-packaged move from September 11 to 9/11. September 11, 2001 is a simple date in the Gregorian calendar. It repeats itself every year in familiar diachronic rotation. 9/11, however, allows both definition (i.e. fixed memory) and sequencing (fractional alteration). It is a designated moment in history from which all our futures can project. Moving out of the realms of yet another day in the history of human suffering, it becomes *the* point of reference. As Susan Neiman observed, 'The perception was so wide and swift that for the first time in history not space but time became shorthand. If naming a city – Lisbon or Auschwitz – was enough for earlier ages to record deepest shock and horror, the twenty-first century began by naming a date.'[60] 9/11 forced a quantum shift in significance. Each and every subsequent catastrophe may draw upon and connect to the imagery of that day. A potent strategic merger is therefore permitted between the powers of the image and the power of the network. The spectacle becomes networked as the visualization of non-visualized forms and the potential for further catastrophe are manifest through the power of the images of their combined affects. Ground Zero as such symbolizes more than the epicentre for global remembrance. While a particular memorializing form of time is permanently set at the point of Zero so as to reinforce the claims that 9/11 was the original sin of globalization, the suffix still remains open to infinite possible connections.

Two Regimes of Fear

Terror poses a *danger*. Danger is the hidden potential or the unknowable in that which is knowable. It cannot be known, otherwise it would be a calculable problem that could be overcome – hence no danger. To say 'we have a problem' is not the same as saying 'we are in danger'. For while danger is a problem, it does not follow that a problem with a solution is necessarily dangerous. Dangers, however, do require certain exposure to the possibility. Life must be made aware of the potential for endangerment in order to thwart its eventual realization. The nature of this exposure largely depends upon the political strategies recruiting inasmuch as the nature of threat is always rationality specific. So how does possible danger manifest itself in a meaningful way politically? This is where fear comes into play. 'Fear', Brian Massumi writes, 'is a staple of popular culture and politics. There is nothing new in that. In fact, a history of modern nation-states could be written following the regular ebb and flow of fear rippling their surface, punctured by outbreaks of outright hysteria.' Indeed, for Massumi, fear has become central to contemporary regimes of power: 'What aspect of life, from the most momentous to the most trivial, has *not* become a workstation in the mass production line of fear?'[61]

Fear is a complex phenomenon. It defies neat description. Some fears, for instance, may appear completely rational, some paranoiac. If there is a singularity to fear it is *uncertainty*. It is brought about by a sense that the course of events is beyond the subject's control. It also provides security with a distinct affective purchase. As Frank Furedi pointed out, 'The rise of catchphrases such as the "politics of fear", "fear of crime" and "fear of the future" is testimony to the cultural significance of fear today. Many of us seem to make sense of our experiences through the narrative of fear.' For Furedi, there is an important conceptual problem to overcome here: 'Though sometimes used as a synonym for risk, fear is treated as an afterthought in today's risk literature; the focus tends to remain on risk theory rather than on an interrogation of fear itself.' This can be rectified by understanding that 'Fear Rules'. Fear, in other words, operates politically through the construction of threats to express certain emotions upon particular forms of existence. In this regard, it doesn't matter whether fear matches the empirical reality of the world. Fear is more like an *apparition* – a partially recognizable yet disrupted form whose realm of signification draws upon some spectral violence of the past in order to affect the future-present: '[T]he fact that more and more areas of life are seen as targets for terrorists – buildings, power stations, the economy and so on – has little to do with the increased capabilities of terrorists; rather it reflects the growth in competitive claims-making around fear and terror.'[62]

Deriving from the Latin *terrere*, fear implies some heightened state of anxiety brought about by a certain defencelessness. While this emotional state of affairs may not always be political in a familiar sovereign sense i.e. a fear of the identifiable Other, in the most general way it 'denotes extreme fear, usually stemming from a vaguely defined, relatively unknown and largely unforeseeable threat'.[63] Fears are not, however, always self-evident. Many are constructed. Indeed, so that fears have any political function they must resonate with prevailing rationalities. Fear in this regard is not about rendering subjects immobile; it is about conditioning what is possible. Liberal regimes deal with society's fears in a particularly novel way. Unlike totalitarian systems, which are defined by closure, liberalism brings everything into the open. It continually exposes that which threatens the fabric of the everyday. Since the sources of our anxieties do not therefore arise from a fear of the unknown, i.e. the advent of *disappearance*, what causes anxiety belongs to the realm of all *appearances*. What is more, since visual representations of threat so integral to our contemporary imaginaries have become globally networked – hence effectively rendering any localized drama greater affective power than ordinarily afforded – the radically interconnected nature of liberal terror is quite literally the sum of all fears. When everything is connectable, our fears are included.

We are reminded here of Virilio's two regimes of fear.[64] Mapping out the distinctions between totalitarian and

liberal regimes, Virilio reveals some disturbing connections. While the former invokes paranoia by working in
the shadows, the latter strikes at the same senses through
overexposure. The former, in other words, stifles reality
through repression and censorship, while the latter over-
loads the imaginary in a frenzied assault so that we are
anxiously synchronized yet blinded to the attempted
mastery of social space. The relationship to violence is
particularly telling. While the embodiment of totalitarian
regimes is pre-figured in the 'disappeared' – those unac-
countable bodies who offer no empirical verification –
liberal violence is virtuously declared. It takes place as an
'open event'. Importantly, for Virilio, since these affective
relations are never simply articulated in a linear top-down
fashion, like a networked system they endlessly feed-back:
'the synchronization of sensations that are likely to affect
our decisions'.[65] Since what matters here is less about particular fears than creating the conditions for a more generalizable logic, liberalism replaces the neat tensions of
sovereign (dis)order with the paradox of human potentiality in which the emotional experience of life is always
greater than any singular living entity. This profoundly
impacts upon the logic of fear as it feeds off the many
potential horrors which continue to register affectively by
circulating throughout living systems. As Massumi explains:

> Threat is as ubiquitous as the wind, and its source as
> imperceptible. It just shows up. It breaks out. It irrupts
> without warning, coming from any direction following any
> path through the increasingly complex and interconnected
> world. The longer it has been that a threat has not
> materialized, the greater the prospects must be that it will:
> it is difficult to overstate an indiscriminate threat. It is
> impossible to stop. Absence makes the threat loom larger.
> Its form is a priori neither human nor natural. Its form is
> in the looming: as-yet undetermined potential to just sud-
> denly show up and spread. Threat is self-organizing, self-
> amplifying, indiscriminate and indiscriminable, tirelessly
> agitating as a background condition, potentially ready to

irrupt. The potential of threat is already, in the waiting, an incipient systemic disruption.[66]

This brings us directly to the problem of emergence. The concept of emergence is at the forefront of complexity thinking.[67] It allows us to make sense of the dynamic and circulatory nature of complex systems. It also helps explain the nature of terror in the contemporary world. Complexity science is not simply content with understanding forms of self-organization; it is all about explaining processes of adaptation and change, i.e. why some entities evolve and remain resilient while others die away. Its concern is with the politics of the unpredictable, along with the infinitely possible. As Stuart Kauffman maintains, we cannot 'prestate the configuration space of a biosphere'.[68] The term 'emergence' reveals an interesting genealogy. As Melinda Cooper explains, 'The microbiologist René Dubos was the first to coin the term "emergence" as a way of describing the temporality of biological evolution. By "emergence", he understood not the gradual accumulation of local mutations, but the relentless, sometimes catastrophic upheaval of entire co-evolving ecologies; sudden field transitions that could never be predicted in linear terms from a single mutation.' Dubos' findings certainly seem to resonate. As Cooper further explains, 'If we are at war, Dubos contends, it is against an enemy that cannot be sequestered; a threat that is not containable within the boundaries of species life; is both inside and out; necessary for our survival yet prone to turn against us; and capable of reinventing itself in response to our "cures".'[69]

Emergence defines contemporary liberal societies 'governed by terror [and] in the process of trying to bring terror within the orbit of their political rationalities and governmental technologies'.[70] It is the emergent, i.e. 'what is to come', which creates anxiety/fear in the present. Since, however, paradoxically, emergent life is also promoted – indeed being hermetically sealed in some suspended incubus is the surest way to bring about one's demise[71] – 'the more effort is put into governing terror, the more terror come to govern the governors'. Here we begin to encounter a distinct aporia of our times. What is emergent cannot be known in advance. We can only second-guess its likely form and its probable occurrence. This places us in a double bind. We cannot simply fear a memory of the past, since this is never going to be repeated. Nor can we be content to fear some imagined future, since our scenarios never perfectly go to plan. Two steps removed, what we fear is fear itself:

> [W]hen we speak in terms of a bio-political productivity of fear today, what we are really describing is the produc-tion of a *fear of fear* itself, or a *fear of being fearful* . . . [so that] the main way for emergent living things of dealing with the impending source of doom is simply to fear more and more or to proliferate self-monitoring and self-carcer-alizing techniques that can only confirm that they have good enough reasons to remain fearful.[72]

Our economies have adapted. As Bauman explains, 'The consumer economy depends upon the production of con-sumers, and the consumers that need to be produced for fear-fighting products are fearful and frightened consum-ers, hopeful that the dangers they fear can be forced to retreat.'[73] This feeds into the sense of normality. As Didier Bigo observes, since all manner of threats have been inserted into a wider continuum of generic unease,

> many different actors, as in a stock market, exchange their different fears and determine their hierarchy and the prior-ity of the struggles against these dangers, through a process of competition based on their supposed authority coming from their knowledge reputation, the scale of the informa-tion they gather and exchange, their technical know-how and their capacity to claim secrecy when questioned. This process of assemblage escapes the will of a dominant actor or coalition of actors and is the result of their overall rela-tions of competition, alliance and strategies of distinction,

and as such its list of priorities appears as 'natural' to all of them, as a 'reflection' of reality justifying their common beliefs in the rise of a dangerous globalized world.[74]

Terror *emerges* from within our afflicted communities. It is integral to the modalities which sustain our advanced living systems. As Stephen Graham points out, this creates a 'fear of dislocation' which is now 'endemic in the population of all great cities'.[75] This paranoiac systemic awakening, he argues, is having 'huge implications for the very conceptual distinctions used in the analysis and definition of organized political violence'.[76] Disrupting the sense of civic normality, terrors appear like a sudden break or rupture that, maturing for some considerable time, terrifies precisely because it has gone unnoticed within our daily routines. It is therefore no coincidence to find that contemporary accounts of terror demand *environmental* frames of reference.[77] What we fear is what we actually *produce*. Since what endangers arises from within our living systems, what threatens is part of that very existence.[78] Not only does this imply that terror is necessarily indiscriminate; as Massumi noted, it is *in*discriminable and *in*distinguishable from the general environment.[79] It precludes any prior elimination of the fact on the basis that its sheer possibility inaugurates its simulated occurrence. No longer, then, a conventionally singular problem, i.e. nuclear attack, contemporary fears register in the multiple. Anything can become the material source of our physical undoing. With sequential notions of catastrophe therefore firmly displaced by an unending continuum of endemic crises, selective immunity is replaced by the demands for an auto-responsive logic that strategically connects all things liveable. The political as such is effectively over-written by a catastrophic aversion complex as the normalization of threat takes aim at those dangers which are not quite locatable but remain forever lurking. A recent contribution to the RAND Corporation's tenth anniversary reflections on 9/11 retains this emphasis:

Nation-states are geographic; they have addresses. As important, they come with lengthy 'stories' attached, and intelligence is ultimately about helping people adjust the stories in their heads to guide their actions. . . . We know what states are like, even states as different from the United States as North Korea. They are hierarchical and bureaucratic. They are a bounded threat. Many of the items of interest about states are big and concrete: tanks, missiles, massed armies. Terrorists are different in every respect. They are small targets, like bin Laden, yet a single suicide bomber can do major mayhem. They are amorphous, fluid, and hidden, presenting intelligence with major challenges simply in describing their structures and boundaries. Not only do terrorists not have addresses, they aren't only 'over there.' They are 'here' as well, an unpleasant fact that impels nations to collect more information on their citizens and residents and to try to do so with minimal damage to civil liberties. Terrorists come with little story attached.[80]

Being witness to the events during the build-up to the tenth anniversary of the 9/11 attacks provides some telling insight into this state of terror normality. Some three days before the official commemoration, new media channels reported the possibility of another devastating attack. The event itself already heightened the stakes. The Department of Homeland Security warned of 'specific, credible but unconfirmed threat information'. The United States, it seemed, was preparing itself for an attack of epidemic proportions. To be expected, many specialists provided expert opinion on the likely nature of the attack. While the intelligence seemed to point to car bombs (thereby placing severe restrictions on the movement of traffic to strategically important areas of New York City), nothing was to be ruled out. Once again, the airwaves were full of professional doomsayers speculating about an attack on the transport system or within a prominent public space. Others also discussed the relative merits of some airborne biological agent or contamination of water systems. The threat was seemingly ubiquitous. It could not be divorced from the lived environment. What was therefore ordinarily taken for granted once again became the source of anxiety as the threat appeared everywhere yet remained elusive. Meanwhile, for defensive agencies, the frontier between warfare, public life, transportation, and the life-world systems that sustained the ordinary functioning of this dynamic environment once again became strategically indifferent. *The Daily Herald* poster which adorned newspaper stands throughout New York on the morning of 9 September encapsulated the tragic irony to this anxious predicament: '9/11 Terror Threat'.

Catastrophic Topographies

While all modern political communities have been constituted by a security imperative, the catastrophic imaginaries of liberal regimes of security governance advance a new topography for political action that is planetary in vision. Geo-politics is therefore seconded by a catastrophic risk landscape of which the modern nation-state is merely a part of a global network of interconnected endangerment. It is most revealing to find that economic agencies are at the forefront of this security policy. During the 1990s, organizations such as the World Bank increasingly became interested in security concerns as the focus of their work (along with economics more generally) went from the managed recoveries of national crises to the active promotion of better lives.[81] Transforming their remit from economic management to security governance, such organizations became moral agents in their own right advocating economic solutions to the ravages of civil wars, criminality, shadow economies, poverty, endemic cultural violence, and political corruption. This was matched by a particular revival in the ideas of liberal political economists such as Friedrich von Hayek who long since equated the free market with political orientations. While we will deal with Hayek's legacy later, it is important to stress that he wrote specifically about the concept of emergence in order to dismiss the conscious creation of rational agents invested in some grand universalizing metaphysical structure.[82] For Hayek, since the most important structures (including laws) are emergent, so the *Nomos* assumes altogether contingent qualities. In doing so, Hayek more than paved the way for liberal political economies to assume a moral status as they were tasked with alleviating worldly injustices and unnecessary suffering. Providing the intellectual foundations and self-appointed moral justifications for intervention, he set in place the logic that poor economic management is central to understanding local problems which potentially have global consequences.

More recently, the World Economic Forum (WEF) has taken up this challenge in a comprehensive way, allowing us to truly visualize the catastrophic topographies of twenty-first-century liberal rule. In 2005, the WEF published its first annual *Global Risk Report*, whose 'top ten risks' included: 'Instability in Iraq', 'Terrorism', 'Emerging Fiscal Crises', 'Disruption in Oil Supplies', 'Radical Islam', 'Sudden Decline in China's Growth', 'Pandemics – Infectious Diseases', 'Climate Change', 'WMD's' and 'Unrestrained Migration and Related Tensions'. Every year since, the reports have become more rigorous in their analysis, more expansive in the numbers of potential threats (the current figure now includes the main fifty with geo-politics merely a nodal element), and accompanied by sophisticated digitalized mappings which highlight the interconnectedness of this global security terrain. With each report providing fully interactive 'Global Risks Interconnection Maps', analysts can be alert to the latest information on continually evolving radically connected situations which have the potential to become truly catastrophic. According to the 2012 report:

As the world grows increasingly complex and interdependent, the capacity to manage the systems that underpin our prosperity and safety is diminishing. The constellation of

risks arising from emerging technologies, financial interdependence, resource depletion and climate change exposes
the weak and brittle nature of existing safeguards – the
policies, norms, regulations or institutions which serve as
a protective system. Our safeguards may no longer be fit
to manage vital resources and ensure orderly markets and
public safety. The interdependence and complexity inherent in globalization require engaging a wider group of
stakeholders to establish more adaptable safeguards which
could improve effective and timely responses to emerging
risks.[83]

Global risks are presented here as a complex and contingent narrative for contemporary society. Working on the
'objective' basis of scientific evaluation, they enable us to
work out through sophisticated algorithms the best and
worst case scenarios. Presupposing the accidental (hence
collapsing the future into the present), they offer considered value and attribute assayable costs to that which is
otherwise incalculable. There is, however, a distinct
politics at work here. The catastrophic imaginary is not
premised on value-neutral science. As Dean has acutely
observed, risk is a set of different ways for 'ordering
reality, of rendering it into a calculable form. It is a way
of representing events in a certain form so they might be
made governable in particular ways, with particular
techniques and for particular goals.'[84] So while the WEF
presents risks like some uncontroversial truth, Dean
encourages us to focus on the 'intelligibility' of certain
'representations that render reality in such a form as to
make it amenable to types of action and intervention'.[85]
Dean's critique here is notably indebted to the work of
François Ewald, who once explained: 'Nothing is a risk in
itself; there is no risk in reality. But on the other hand,
anything *can* be a risk; it all depends on how one analyses
the danger, considers the event.'[86]

Proposing new methods for acting upon subjects'
behaviour, risk-based analysis displaces any ideologically
principled notion of equitable social insurance with highly

technocratic 'rule by experts'. As Peter Miller and Nikolas Rose have observed, 'The ethics of lifestyle maximization, coupled with a logic in which someone must be held to blame for any event that threatens an individual's "quality of life", generates a relentless imperative of risk management.'[87] Risk thus becomes axiomatic since any effort at risk awareness cannot help but establish a new horizon of risks. As Furedi notes, '[T]erms like "risk" or "at risk" are used in association with just about any routine event reflecting our unprecedented preoccupation with risk.'[88] That is to say, the more we are able to control/reduce known risks, the more risks proliferate and appear to warrant further attention. For this reason, Dillon argues, '[r]isk is one of the single most important devices' for security strategies 'currently pursued'.[89] On the one hand, it proposes a remedial solution to the problem of finitude, for 'it may appear that, in taming chance, you may tame time. Moreover, tame time and you may tame the future. Tame the future and you may, finally, secure a being – human being – whose very existence is temporal.'[90] On the other hand, it cannot provide a solution since 'contingency is itself constitutive of what it means to be a living thing.'[91] Risk as such is not something to be simply averted at all costs. Securing life through the embrace of risk-based technologies becomes the preferred method for regulating the conduct of lives:

> Whatever else might be said of the ontology of a contingent universe . . . , 'risk' does not exist 'out there', independent, as it were, of the computational and discursive practices that constitute specific risks as the risks that they are. Risk is a carefully crafted artefact. Risks are thus created, circulated, proliferated and capitalized upon in a whole variety of burgeoning ways. Underwriting secures self-governance through contingency by employing technologies of risk. This, then, is not exactly the risk society explored by Ulrich Beck, whose account of risk is almost wholly preoccupied with cataloguing the growth of man-made dangers. This is the truth-telling of a governmental

technology that enacts a world of self-regulating subjects bound in continuous calculation and commodification of their variable exposure to contingency.[92]

Catastrophic topographies are overwhelmingly future-orientated. Raising awareness of the interconnections between all potential dangers, security agencies begin to govern through the constellation of catastrophic emergencies liberal societies face. While interconnected mapping doesn't offer any hierarchy of endangerment in terms of some universal political aspiration, what does appear central to all deliberations is 'the Event'.[93] Crucial here are issues of *preparedness* and *resilience* in the face of the catastrophic occurrences. Resilience is now the lingua franca of contemporary security discourse. It provides us with a technical term for all manner of threats to existence.[94] It is no coincidence, however, to discover that its contemporary meaning can be traced back to the ideas of Crawford Stanley Holling, who defined the resilience of an ecosystem as the measure of its ability to absorb changes (particularly sudden catastrophic events) and still exist.[95] Resilience is something more than survivability. It encourages actors to learn from catastrophes so that societies can become more responsive to further catastrophes on the horizon. It promotes adaptability so that life may go on living despite the fact that elements of our living systems may be destroyed. And it creates shared knowledge and information that will continually reshape the forms of communities and affirm their core values, thereby determining what is absolutely 'vital' to our ways of living.

Resilience is premised upon the ability of the endangered subject to continually re-emerge from the conditions of its ongoing emergency. Life *becomes* a series of events. Its bio-graphical make-up therefore has no intrinsic value other than a non-linear set of (post-)vital problems which at the point of their arising continue to defy the dream of perfect calculation long since abandoned by technologies of systemic rule. So as the resilient subject continually navigates throughout the complex landscape which defines the *topos* of contemporary politics – the catastrophic topography of the times – what becomes a condition of possibility is the contingency or eventfulness of life itself. Unlike Continental approaches to the event, however, which propose a concept of freedom on account of life's facticity which precedes any compulsion to make secure, the resilient subject – while not secure in any fixed sense – embodies the subject which is no longer tasked with imagining a different concept of the political. It is, from the perspective of difference, a *post-political* subjectivity which, accepting the eventual fatefulness of existence, proposes an emergent ontology that is exclusively bound to mastering the control of life-shaping events by pre-emptively governing those catastrophes (actual or potential) which shape the normality of the times. Resilient life as such offers no political concern with a future that may be politically different. What concerns the resiliently minded is whether or not the future is at all liveable.

Late liberalism has reached its point of political finitude where existence is being increasingly governed by an immanent ordering of life that witnesses the triumph of economy over the political, and the catastrophic imaginary is most revealing of its particular onto-theological expressions. This brings into sharp relief the differences between the apocalyptic imaginaries of monotheistic regimes of religious power and the catastrophic imaginaries of liberal regimes of security governance. While both fixate on the event-to-come, the apocalyptic is founded upon the eventual revelation of the One (true God, true religion, Supreme Being). The catastrophic, in contrast, proposes a future-orientated discourse that is fuelled by the infinitely possible. Whereas apocalyptic narratives therefore put forward a Sovereign eschatology that impresses upon the subject's imaginary the plagues of judgement such that onto-theological rule can shape actions of believers in the present, catastrophic narratives construct the basis for their onto-theologically driven rule by promoting life as an emergent, adaptable, pre-epistemic eschatological complex. So whereas apocalyptic imaginaries propose an altogether teleological religiosity whose eventual revelation is a prophesied truth, the catastrophic imaginary offers a non-linear eschatology of the living that moralizes the government of life on a planetary scale *in lieu* of the fact that nothing can be known with absolute certainty.

– 2 –

Liberal Security

The Security Debates

Giorgio Agamben showed considerable foresight when he mused that 'security' was fast becoming 'the sole criterium of political legitimation'.[1] In the post-9/11 moment, security would be presented like some verifiable truth which calls for unquestionable allegiance. It was something we *must* all believe in. While this imperative remains a constant, the concept remains highly contested and open to dispute, not least in terms of its definition. Which referents' objects should be brought within its remit? And what forces does it bring to bear upon the political? Ulrich Beck, for instance, argues that in order for security to be effective and have any legitimate meaning, it must be applied without condition to planetary life. For Beck, it is no longer 'a nation-based "faith in the community" that creates legitimacy, it is a *belief that the risks facing humanity can be averted* by political action taken on *behalf* of endangered humanity'.[2] Against this tendency, authors like Agamben warn of the political dangers faced in a security-obsessed world. The politics of security, Agamben argues, contains an 'inherent risk' which can actually lead to a 'gradual neutralization of politics'.[3] How, then, are we to explain security in today's global age? What have been the political implications of a broadened and deepened focus in the security agenda? What happens when security discourses and practices take planetary life to be their object? Is security primordial? Or is there something more imperial at stake here which should demand a new analytical focus?

For many, the critical turn in security studies provided welcome relief from the dogmatism of regime theories which dominated International Relations thinking. In recognizing that conventional approaches were defined more by what they actually left out, i.e. their humanitarian 'omissions', those who advocated a broadening of the security agenda effectively challenged political realism.[4] In doing so, *critical security studies* extended 'our moral horizons beyond national-based conceptions of citizenship'.[5] Serving up a mixture of normative and empirical arguments, this approach included issues such as human rights, development, illicit economies, epidemics, and trans-border criminality in our frameworks for understanding, while emphasizing various methods for prioritization in relation to the nature and magnitude of these types of threat. This represented a new departure inasmuch as it offered a shift away from the narrow and reified notions of state security towards 'life-centric' paradigms that encompassed the 'whole of humanity'.[6] Replacing the traditional ontology of soldiers and diplomats, critical security studies therefore placed 'the victims at the centre of its enquiries'.[7] The intended outcome, as Richard Falk imagined, was a 'community for the whole of humanity which overcomes the most problematic aspects of the present world scene . . . [and where] difference and uniformities across space and time are subsumed beneath an overall commitment to world order values in the provisional shape of peace, economic well-being, social and political justice, and environmental sustainability'.[8]

While Kant presented the case for a global security agenda in the latter part of the eighteenth century, it wasn't until the 1990s that a global imaginary of threat allowed for the possibility to govern all illiberal life on the basis that the species as a whole would be less endangered. This ability to collapse the local into the global resulted in an unrivalled moment of liberal expansionism.[9] Importantly, however, despite the normative basis for intervention, it is far from clear that the liberal advance happened because of some universal subscription to its value and belief systems. Localized forms of suffering in zones of political instability and crises permitted new opportunities for political engagement. Liberalism as such proceeded on the basis of catastrophic emergencies. Since liberal interventionism bypassed traditional sovereign integrities, a number of key assumptions were consolidated to provide justification:

1   The 'New Wars' offered a new set of problems which could no longer simply be scripted in terms of Cold War rivalry.
2   Conditions of underdevelopment replaced notions of outright barbarity or ideological contest to become the principal diagnostic for understanding the causes of conflict and violence.
3   Because indiscriminate violence became the hallmark of these crises, more sustained obligations were demanded.
4   Interventionism could be justified on humanitarianism grounds providing that the ends justified the means.
5   With maladjusted populations open to remedy and demanding engagement, the wholesale transformation of societies could be sanctioned in the name of creating lasting conditions/capacities for peace.

Ultimately, then, since underdeveloped life was seen to be capable of its own (un)making, new analytical tools were demanded in order to overcome the problems life posed to itself:

In (re)defining the threats to human life as its most basic operation, the discourse of human security must begin by defining and enacting the human in bio-political terms. The target of human security, whether broad or narrow, is to make live the life of the individual through a complex of strategies initiated at the level of populations. In defining and responding to threats to human life, these strategies have as their aim the avoidance of risk and the management of contingency in the overall goal of improving the life lived by the subjects invoked in their own operation. In this sense, as with Foucault's understanding of the bio-political, the health and welfare of populations is human security's frame of reference.[10]

It was tempting to suggest that the War on Terror set aside these positive advances in our understanding of security. What we witnessed, it could be argued, represented a return to the 'Old War' mindset, so that constructed enemies could be neatly defined and easily defeated using conventional methods. Mary Kaldor, for instance, lamented that 'Bush's response has been an attempt to re-impose international relations, that is to say, to put the threat of terrorism within a state framework.' In doing so, '[T]he wars in Iraq and Afghanistan have not reduced terror; on the contrary, the bombing in Madrid, London, the Middle East and Asia seem to suggest that terror and the war on terror feed on each other.'[11] For Kaldor, the way out of this cycle is a return to the emancipatory idea enshrined in the discourse of Human Security which took hold in the 1990s: 'I do not see any other way out of the current dangerous impasse than trying to establish a set of global rules based on consent. We have to try and find ways to minimize violence at a global level, in the same way that early modern thinkers envisaged civil society as a way of minimizing violence at domestic levels.'[12] Steve Smith shared a similar platform:

The events of September 11, 2001, give us good reason to reassess the meaning of the concept of security. While at

first glance the events seem to strengthen the traditional
view of security as primarily a military domain, closer
examination reveals that to explain the events requires a
much wider and deeper notion of security. Both the moti-
vations of those who undertook the attacks on September
11, and the way in which the ensuing conflict unfolded,
simply do not fit within the traditional realist view of
security. Indeed, they strongly support the claims of those
who wish to conceive of security more broadly.[13]

President Barack Obama's election victory promised a
return to this type of thinking. Before assuming office, he
was already of the opinion that the 'misrepresentation of
enemies' had led to the wrong type of war being fought in
Iraq. In an address on global terrorism delivered at the
Wilson Center in August 2007, he called this a 'failure of
strategic thinking' which held firm to outdated realist
paradigms: 'A rigid twentieth-century ideology that insisted
that twenty-first-century stateless terrorism could be
defeated through the invasion and occupation of a state.'
Once in office, Obama seemingly instigated this revival of
human security thinking by giving strategic priority to the
doctrine of *counter-insurgency*. This witnessed the move
away from high-impact war to a concern with the underlying causes of violence.[14] Obama announced this overriding
commitment on 27 March 2009 symbolically flanked by
both civilian and military members of his administration.
Central to his agenda was the need to offer a more comprehensive approach that afforded greater emphasis on
investment, development, and education.[15] Recourse to
violence, should it be required, was not, of course, to be
excluded, but the local population was no longer to be
simply exorcized of its radical elements by use of military
force alone. The population was now seen to be an asset,
the object for new positive relations which could prove to
be an active part and integral to the global war effort that
promises 'our security' through 'their social betterment'.
    It could be argued that this strategic turn stemmed from
the tactical failures of conventional military practice. These

sentiments have been echoed by Rupert Smith, who argued that a new paradigm of conflict had now taken hold which he called *war amongst the people*.[16] Within this paradigm, enemies are displaced by insurgencies against which military force has little utility; in fact, it fuels and internationalizes the resistance encountered. To counter this, strategic priority is given to the winning of 'hearts and minds'. Such approaches are, however, deceiving. While it has been common to suggest that hard/military versus soft/developmental approaches to conflict represent entirely different 'world-views',[17] the claim that they are incompatible or ideologically opposed is misguided. They have in fact both proven to be complementary strategic facets of a *liberal way of war* that has been slowly maturing for some considerable time.[18] Michael Ignatieff has been candid in this regard. For Ignatieff, while humanitarian agencies may continually exist in an uneasy tension with the forces of militarism, it is nevertheless necessary for 'imperial armies' to have 'cleared the ground and made it safe for humanitarians to act'.[19] What Ignatieff terms *Empire Lite* refers to a 'humanitarian empire' in which 'humanitarian relief cannot be kept distinct from the imperial project', since tackling the underlying causes of conflict requires fighting the 'forces of evil'. This understanding was clearly spelt out in the US *Quadrennial Defense Review Report* (2010), which explains with a renewed sense of moral surety:

> The wars we are fighting today and assessments of the future security environment together demand that the United States retain and enhance a whole-of-government capability to succeed in large-scale counterinsurgency (COIN), stability, and counterterrorism (CT) operations in environments ranging from densely populated urban areas and mega-cities, to remote mountains, deserts, jungles, and littoral regions. . . . Accordingly, the US Armed Forces will continue to require capabilities to create a secure environment in fragile states in support of local authorities and, if necessary, to support civil authorities in providing essential

government services, restoring emergency infrastructure, and supplying humanitarian relief.[20]

Counter-insurgency was actually reintroduced within the War on Terror framework before Obama came to power in 2009. It also drew upon a wealth of experience within the NGO world that had been developing in zones of instability and crises since the early 1990s. Contrary to expectations, this period did not witness the promises of global peace, prosperity, and political harmony. Instead, from the Occupied Territories in Palestine, to the jungles of Mexico, the streets of Somalia, the coastal towns of Sierra Leone, the shanty towns of Haiti, the fields of Rwanda, and even onto the doorstep of Europe, so-called 'New Wars' were breaking out that posed a fundamental challenge for those seduced by Francis Fukuyama's 'End of History' thesis. As the United Nations related in its *Human Development Report* for 1994, 'Global conflicts seem to be changing – from wars between states to wars within them. Of the 82 conflicts between 1989 and 1992, only three were between states.' Martin van Creveld, the prominent military historian, supported these changing conditions by adding, 'In today's world, the main threat to many states . . . no longer comes from other states. Instead, it comes from small groups and other organizations which are not states.'[21] Invariably, facing these post-Clausewitzean conditions, not only were the traditional rules which once governed the conduct of war being firmly set aside; in the process, these conflicts brought an entirely new set of problems which were far more devastating in their human consequences. Amongst the most prominent of these were the following:

1 The violence had no obvious central command (networked).
2 For those actors engaged in these confrontations there appeared to be no attempts to 'capture' state power (post-vanguard).

3 The violent actors were notably 'ethnic' in orientation (identity-based).

4 The violence was of a non-discriminatory nature (especially against women and children).

5 The violence was especially acute in zones of economic failure (underdevelopment) and political failure (product of state failure).

6 Perhaps most worrying, the conflicts were seemingly being exacerbated by the forces of globalization, in which certain populations were far removed from the rich financial benefits that trade permits, while at the same time intimately exposed to the worst unregulated aspects of global market mechanisms (dislocation).

Boutros Boutros-Ghali led the search for new meaning. His influential 'An Agenda for Peace' noted how the post-Cold War environment of opportunity had failed to deliver upon its promises.[22] Kaldor was of the same opinion: 'The point is . . . that the processes known as globalization are breaking up the cultural and socio-economic divisions that defined the relations of politics which characterized the modern period. The new type of warfare has to be understood in terms of global dislocation.'[23] This required moving our analysis beyond familiar geo-strategic co-ordinates. As Castells observed,

A new world, the Fourth World, has emerged, made up of multiple black holes of social exclusion throughout the planet. The Fourth World comprises large areas of the globe, such as much of sub-Saharan Africa, and impoverished rural areas of Latin America and Asia. But it is also present literally in every country, and every city, in this new geography of social exclusion.[24]

Kaldor agreed. New Wars 'involve a myriad of transnational connections so that the distinction between internal and external . . . or even between local and global are difficult to sustain'.[25] This notion of the Fourth World certainly resonated. In a highly original thesis, Subcomandante Marcos of the indigenous Zapatistas, for instance, wrote of a 'Fourth World War' which, inverting Tony Blair's framework of the universal versus the particular, pitted the forces of liberal markets against those who are politically *different*: 'The Fourth World War is destroying humanity as globalization is universalizing the market, and everything human which opposes the logic of the market is an enemy and must be destroyed. In this sense, we are all the enemy to be vanquished: indigenous, non-indigenous, human rights observers, teachers, intellectuals, artists. Anyone who believes themselves to be free and is not.'[26]

William Shawcross was not in any doubt that international agencies had abandoned any pretence of political neutrality. He observed that while the humanitarian interventions of the 1990s underwent their gradual politicization, by the end of the millennium they had reached their 'logical conclusion', becoming overtly militaristic.[27] On 24 March 1999, NATO began its bombing campaign against Serbian positions, in defence of the ethnic Albanian population in Kosovo. While this campaign proceeded without specific UN authorization, the principal architects were assured in the purpose of their mission. Blair, for instance, insisted that unlike previous conflicts, which were conducted for national interests, this war would be the very first military operation to be carried out for 'humanity's progress'. It was the clearest embodiment of 'just war', which was based 'not on any territorial ambitions but on values'. Kosovo was thus both the litmus test and wake-up call for liberal internationalism. It not only showed that liberals were willing to defend their ideals, in the process it forced liberal idealists to confront the realization that peace comes at a price. Reflecting upon this abandonment of neutrality, Ignatieff argued that the Kosovo war was without question a defining moment in the history of humanitarian interventionism. Not only did it show that liberal societies were willing to use force; this particular mission made it perfectly clear that in the short run successful humanitarian interventions cannot avoid imperial ascriptions. Hence, for Ignatieff, while Kosovo was a test case for liberal war, these relationships have since governed nearly every humanitarian mission which has followed.[28]

Instead of marking a radical change in political direction, what the shift towards counter-insurgency represents is the onset of a more 'enduring political relationship: a post-interventionary terrain of international occupation'.[29] In this regard, as General David Petraeus more recently explained, counter-insurgency and human security have become co-extensive in that they are the 'two key principles' capable of separating 'the reconcilables from the irreconcilables'.[30] This kind of warfare figures as 'a condition of possibility' for the production of power relations in which human life is 'variably recruited, set free, manipulated, and put to work in the development of social arrangements'.[31] With development as such 'rediscovered' as a tool to combat both insurgency and terrorism on a planetary scale, the idea of 'the Long War' comes more into focus, to the lasting effacement of exceptional narratives:

> From the beginning the War on Terror has been both a battle of arms and a battle of ideas – a fight against terrorists and against their murderous ideology. In the short run, the fight involves using military force and other instruments of national power to kill or capture the terrorists, deny them safe haven or control of any nation; prevent them from gaining access to [weapons of mass destruction]; and to cut off their sources of support. In the long run winning the War on Terror means winning a battle of ideas, for it is ideas that can turn the disenchanted into murderers willing to kill innocent civilians.[32]

Foucault's Intervention

Michel Foucault's recent renaissance has undoubtedly added renewed political force to his remarkable intellectual oeuvre. Much of this owes to the influential works of Michael Hardt and Antonio Negri,[33] along with Agamben,[34] whose application of Foucauldian thought to the areas of security, global war, and violence has highlighted his relevance to some of our most pressing political concerns. This has been matched by the translated publications of the lecture series Foucault gave at the Collège de France from the mid- to late 1970s.[35] In the wake of these lectures, which bring to the fore his thinking on 'biopower' and 'biopolitics', alternative critiques of governmental practices become possible. What has been taking place here is a necessary rewriting of Foucault's legacy. Not only do these endeavours move us beyond the normative 'Question of Truth' (which, to be frank, served the dialectical entrapments of Frankfurt theorists such as Jürgen Habermas more than it ever did Foucault),[36] they also force us to pose new questions concerning the nature of power in our modern societies. Foucault's resurrected spectre does, however, come with its challenges. As Foucault himself would explain, when one begins to pose the problem of power biopolitically, an entirely different grid of intelligibility is adopted which no longer provides us with the comfort of a rehearsed orthodoxy:

> Instead of deducing concrete phenomena from universals, or instead of starting with universals as an obligatory grid of intelligibility for certain concrete practices, I would like to start with these concrete practices and, as it were, pass these universals through the grid of these practices. . . . Historicism starts from the universal and, as it were, puts it through the grinder of history. My problem is exactly the opposite. I start from the theoretical and methodological decision that consists in saying: Let's suppose universals do not exist. And then I put the question to history and

historians: How can you write history if you do not accept a priori the existence of things like the state, society, the sovereign, and subjects? . . . [N]ot, then, questioning universals by using history as a critical method, but starting from the decision that universals do not exist, asking what kind of history we can do.[37]

Enthusiasm for Foucault's revival has been expectedly muted in certain quarters. Some Foucauldian scholars – albeit of a distinct liberal persuasion – have even expressed their concern with the applicability of his lecture series to contemporary political analysis.[38] Leaving aside the claim that this body of work somehow represents Foucault's 'wasted years' – or, for that matter, the concepts explored during this period were not really Foucauldian at heart (especially biopolitics), the most serious charge concerns the lack of sufficient academic rigour which the lecture series offers. Beatrice Hanssen, for instance, has correctly pointed out that despite the attention given to race war, the history of colonization is scantly considered.[39] This is certainly true. It is also the case that when Foucault did apply his biopolitical method to colonialism, he attended only to the colonial heartland, not to the overseas dominions/borderlands. It is fair, therefore, to say that Foucault's efforts are somewhat incomplete. They leave us wanting more empirical depth. That is not, however, to deny their usefulness. As John Marks argues,

[T]he lectures are an expression of Foucault's attempt to analyse power in terms of its operation, functions, and effects, rather than in terms of sovereignty and juridical models. They are a continuation of his project to look at power from the perspective of its functions and strategies, as it operates 'under the radar', as it were, of the juridical system of sovereignty.[40]

So while these lectures may lack rigorous empirical depth, they nevertheless introduce concepts which can be put to use today *politically*.

For Foucault, biopolitics referred to the political strate-gization/technologization of life for its own productive betterment. Effectuating the active triangulation between 'security, territory, and population', biopolitics forges a new normative alliance with human development/progress in a manner which complements traditional security para-digms. Importantly, for Foucault, since the biopolitical operates by openly recruiting life into political strategies for the internal defence of societies as a whole – what we may term 'doing what is necessary out of life necessity' – so our question becomes: What happens to security discourses and practices when life itself becomes the principal object for political strategies? That security is now written in human terms is well established. The concept in fact only now makes theoretical and practical sense once *humani*-tarian qualities are assumed. While this shift in our under-standing is not in doubt, the political implications have tended to avoid rigorous scrutiny. That is to say, while the critical turn in security studies has been visibly re-energized in the post-Bush era, we are yet to fully come to grips with the manners in which life-centric discourses on security continue to mask a more contested terrain of political occupation which remains fraught with imperial tendencies.

This brings us to our earlier suspicions of critical secu-rity studies. While its moves to broaden the narrow con-ceptions of security represented an important theoretical shift within the mainstream academies, what was being offered in terms of a critical alternative proved upon further reflection to be highly problematic. Indeed it seems that what passed for 'critical security' was a fantastic appropriation of the term, in that the idea of security not only remained ontologically entrenched, but was actually afforded more reverence. Security was taken to be the unequivocal basis for all assessment that must extend to all aspects which affect human existence. As such, there was no attempt to question whether the politics of security could in any way be imperial, let alone question our incessant ontological commitment to securing the political subject. In other words, the critical was determined by consciously intensifying and expanding security's reach, without ever entertaining the notion that it is the ontological priority afforded to the politics of security which should itself be open to critical question. What is more, since the broadening of the security agenda was presented to be a radically new benevolent departure, there was a failure to understand the real historically consistent singularity to liberal rule, which, although appearing in many different guises, has always sought to secure life for its own productive betterment. Once we move beyond the faith-based affinities of the universal liberal aspiration, it is precisely this biopolitical imperative that appears above all else to set liberalism apart from other political rationalities.

The Security *Dispositif*

Foucault suggested that security implied the modification of 'something in the destiny of the species'.[41] Taking life to be the principal referent object for security discourses and practices, biopolitics attends to those general strategies for power which, in the process of making life live, entail the *regulation of populations* for society's overall betterment. Bio-security, for Foucault, thus involves 'not so much establishing limits and frontiers, or fixing locations, as, above all and essentially, making possible, guaranteeing, and ensuring circulations'.[42] Promoting species life, it is all about *letting things happen*: 'a question of constituting something like a milieu of life, existence'.[43] There is nothing negative about this. As Michael Dillon and Andrew Neal suggest, 'Making live cannot be secured by locking up life processes. Securing life poses quite a different game.'[44] With this in mind, entirely different analytical methods are invariably sought. As Didier Bigo explains, 'Security pre-supposes that one analyses mobilities, networks and margins instead of the frontier and isolation that goes with demarcation. Security is thus a dispositif [i.e. apparatus] of circulation within a life environment and not a dispositif of disciplining bodies. A security dispositif does not isolate, it is built as a network.'[45] Biopolitics as such 'not only functions through mechanisms that elevate contingency into a dominant field of formation for western societies as a whole, it similarly also opens up an entirely different spatial configuration of security. If distribution is the spatial figuration that characterizes traditional geopolitical rationalities and technologies of security, *circulation* is the spatial configuration that characterizes the bio-politics of security.'[46]

Foucault illustrated more than one way to rationalize/conceptualize security, war, and political violence. Specifically attending to *internal* conceptions of threat, he wanted us to consider how notions of threat actually provide societies with their *generative principles of formation*:

> [W]e see the emergence of a completely different problem that is no longer of fixing and demarcating the territory, but of allowing circulations to take place, of controlling them, sifting the good and the bad, ensuring that things are always in movement, constantly moving around, continually going from one point to another, but in such a way that the inherent dangers of this circulation are cancelled out.[47]

That security has a *performative* function has been understood for some time. David Campbell's *Writing Security*, for instance, provided us with a wonderful insight into how the domains of inside/outside, self/other, and domestic/foreign are constituted directly in relation to the writing of threat.[48] Importantly, for Campbell, the process of signifying threat is not simply bound to some negative process of exclusion; it is also a productive condition of possibility. Nevertheless, while Campbell's work displays evident allegiance to Foucault, his method still remains committed to sovereign tensions. The question of subjectivity is therefore constituted here in relation to some epiphenomenal decision which provides the endangered political community with its shared sense of belonging. Where Foucault's biopolitical analytics, however, mark their most important departure is to turn our attentions away from these conventional markers. In his method, which exposes instead the nature of those ordering/securing mechanisms which operating in the name of species progress/development are more immanent to the conduct of life, sovereignty is seconded by a more positive account of securitization that is synonymous with the production of freedom realized:

> If I employ the word 'liberal', it is first of all because this governmental practice in the process of establishing itself is not satisfied with respecting this or that freedom, with guaranteeing this or that freedom. More profoundly, it is a consumer of freedom. . . . It consumes freedom, which means it must produce it. It must produce it, it must organize it. The new art of government therefore appears as the management of freedom, not in the sense of the imperative: 'be free', with the immediate contradiction that this imperative may contain. The formula of liberalism is not 'be free'. Liberalism formulates simply the following: I am going to produce what you need to be free. And so, if this liberalism is not so much the imperative of freedom as the management and organization of the conditions in which one can be free, it is clear that at the heart of this liberal practice is an always different and mobile problematic relationship between the production of freedom and that which in the production of freedom risks limiting and destroying it.[49]

We should not underestimate this shift of analytical focus away from the primacy of sovereign power towards the problems posed by a productive account of freedom which is always haunted by its own capacity for self-destruction. Demanding a more positive approach to power, this perspective exposes one of liberalism's key foundational myths: 'If natural law could not cover all the juridical exigencies and contingencies which confronted the operationalization of the social contract legislatively, neither was law, alone, sufficient to discharge the task of rule which Liberalism posed. Although positive law was, therefore, required to supplement natural law, governance was required to supplement the law as such.'[50] From this perspective it can be argued that the problem of security is not simply a problem of law or legal transgression. The problem of security is always a problem of *security governance*. If we are therefore to conduct any thorough investigation of contemporary securitization processes, it is necessary to account for all the sets of practices and mechanisms (whether they are juridical, technical, or military) involved in securing the political subject – this is what Foucault termed the *dispositif de securité*:

> By the term apparatus (*dispositif*) I mean a kind of formation, so to speak, that a given historical moment has as its major function the response to urgency. The apparatus therefore has a dominant strategic function. . . . I said that the nature of an apparatus is essentially strategic, which means that we are speaking about a certain manipulation of relations of forces, of a rational and concrete intervention in the relation of forces, either so as to develop them in a particular direction, or to block them, to stabilize them, and to utilize them. The apparatus is thus always inscribed into a play of power. . . . The apparatus is precisely this: a set of strategies of the relations of forces supporting, and supported by, certain types of knowledge.[51]

Mark Duffield's critique of the development/security nexus has provided a rich account of the liberal security *dispositif* as it operates in zones of political crises.[52] Importantly, for Duffield, it was through mapping out these connections that we begin to discover a global cartography of power relations which is being effectively shaped by the liberal encounter. 'Initially,' he argued,

[I had thought that development involved a universalizing of the technologies that Foucault had outlined in relation to Europe, a sort of scaled-up biopolitics that acts on a 'global' population. The answer, however, now seems as obvious as it is simple; rather than a universalizing biopolitics, development is the opposite. It is a means of dividing humankind against itself in the generic form of developed and underdeveloped species-life.[53]

Such divisions proved crucial. Not only did they provide a considered genealogy of the formative figures of political modernity (the civilized, the savage, and the barbarian), they also directly challenged liberal claims of political emancipation:

[U]nderstanding conflict has also moved its locus from wars between states to conflicts within and across them. Like sustainable development, households, communities and populations furnish the terrain on which such conflicts are fought. Within this continuation of total war by non-industrial means, both development and war take communities, livelihood systems and social networks as their point of reference. For the former they are sites of entry, protection and betterment; for the latter they are objects of attack and destruction. . . . In other words, both sustainable development and internal war – albeit for opposing purposes – take life or population and not the state as their reference point.[54]

In the post-9/11 moment, underdeveloped populations became a global concern. Afghanistan, for instance, was no longer a 'failed state' but a 'terrorist haven' which allowed the forces of global destruction to develop. The implications have been telling. As Rosa Ehrenreich Brookes explained,

Shifts in the nature of security threats have broken down once clear distinctions between armed conflict and 'internal disturbances' that do not rise to the level of armed conflict between states and non-state actors, between combatants and non-combatants, between spatial zones in which conflict is occurring and zones in which conflict is not occurring, between temporal moments in which there is no conflict and between matters that clearly affect the security of the nation and matters that clearly do not.[55]

With the lines that once allowed for the sovereign principle of non-interference therefore entering into lasting crises, 'saving strangers', as one author once put it, no longer registers as a benevolent moral duty or humanitarian obligation alone.[56] It is completely self-interested inasmuch as a lack of security elsewhere can have disastrous consequences for stability in the metropolitan homelands. Since what is therefore 'outside' the liberal pale quite simply cannot be left to chance, what previously registered as an idealistic intellectual political ambition to realize lasting planetary peace now becomes *the* moral imperative for political action.

The Life-World System

Over two hundred years ago, Kant imagined the perfect unification of the human species through common citizenship. What he envisaged as being 'Nature's Supreme Design' has in some sense arrived inasmuch as political problems have taken on a distinct global outlook. In this sense, for better or worse, Kant is the political philosopher whose time has come. While many contemporaries debate the significance of these developments, Kant was fully aware of the ontological stakes were space and time to enter into lasting crises. Not only did he present a vision of a *Perpetual Peace* that was internally fraught with continual political strife, as he completed his project, the question of ontology becomes profoundly onto-theological as the problem of *evil in the world* appears. This was not incidental. While Kant turned his attention to questions of ontology, something of the order of the Divine equally appeared to belong to the world. As we shall later discover, the divine providence Kantianism forces us to inherit cannot be explained by drawing reference to some timeless juridical structure. It is not sovereignty. Neither is it located in the final completion or unity of the people as invested in some all-embracing concept of humanity. What we may term 'the Kantian Divine' reconciles in a highly emergent and problematic way what is the infinitely possible (hence infinitely problematic) with the finitude of existence (hence infinitely endangering). Such is Kant's ontological relevance to the catastrophic imaginaries of our times.

Ever since Kant imagined the autonomous individual at peace with its wider political surroundings, the liberal subject has always been inserted into a wider terrain of productive cohabitation that is potentially harmonious and free from conflict. While this logic has been manifest locally since the dawn of liberal reasoning, during the 1990s a global imaginary of threat appeared which directly correlated liberal forms of governance with less planetary endangerment. This ability to collapse the local into the global resulted in an unrivalled moment of liberal expansionism.[57] Such expansion did not, however, result from some commitment to embrace liberal ideals. Even the most fundamental terms of engagement, i.e. security, freedom, right, and justice, are of course more than liberal in interpretation. Liberal interventionism proceeded instead on the basis that local emergencies in zones of crises demanded a response on account of the fact that they threatened to spill over into zones of influence. Modes of incorporation were therefore justified on the grounds that while these were populations which still existed beyond the liberal pale, for their own betterment they *should be included* – albeit in a fashion that was wholly conditional! This is fully acknowledged by the sympathetic Kantian scholar Andrew Linklater:

> Inside-Out analysis works in liberal political theory by arguing the way in which states treat national citizens is

not simply a domestic matter that can be ignored in accounts of external affairs. If strategic action prevails in domestic politics, then the commitment to communicative action is unlikely to shape that state's foreign policy, other than for pragmatic and self-interested reasons. But if communicative action is central to the domestic political order, then the prospects for transcending purely strategic concerns in foreign policy will be significantly enlarged. These are the considerations that underpin Kantian and more contemporary liberal analysis of the relationship between transformation of political community and the advancement of human security.[58]

None of this was lost on Foucault. Biopolitics concerns 'control over relations between the human race, or human beings insofar as they are species, insofar as they are living beings, and their environment, the milieu in which they live'.[59] It is therefore a 'problem of environment' to the extent that our sense of space 'has been created by the population and therefore has its effects on population'. The concept of the milieu is crucial here: '[S]ecurity will try to plan a milieu in terms of events or series of events or possible elements.'[60] Since the space of security in other words refers to 'a series of possible events', biopolitics is concerned with 'the temporal and the uncertain, which have to be inserted within a given space. The space in which a series of uncertain elements unfold is, I think, roughly what one can call the milieu.' In this sense, space is never politically neutral. It is overlaid with modes of signification which bind life to its world through a series of articulated problems. This entails thinking about life in a new spatial context so that space itself is effectively activated with life-like qualities. Space as such loses it natural objectivity, framing instead the entirely possible. As Hardt and Negri have therefore observed, once power takes planetary life itself to be its object, the 'notion of security' inevitably becomes a 'form of bio-power' in that 'it is charged with the task of producing and *transforming* social life at its most general and global level'.[61] This in turn, as Eyal Weizman explains, necessarily engenders an all-inclusive 'environmental' frame of reference:

> The logic of 'security' . . . presupposes that the danger is already inside, presented by a population in which subversive elements exist. The relation that 'security' implies between 'inside' and 'outside', as well as between military and police action, is ambiguous. . . . 'Security' conceives new spatial practices and arrangements. It erects barriers and channels and rechannels the flow of people and resources through space. According to the logic of security, only a constantly configured and reconfigured environment is a safe environment.[62]

Peter Sloterdijk has made a compelling case for understanding the relationship between terror and the environment in which it operates. Putting forward his 'atmo-terrorism' thesis, he suggests that terror makes sense only once we factor in the conscious attempt to attack the very conditions which sustain life: 'Terror operates on a level beyond the naïve exchange of armed blows between regular troops; it involves replacing these classical forms of battle with assaults on the environmental conditions of the enemy's life.'[63] Importantly, for Sloterdijk, since terror 'presupposes an explicit concept of the environment', it relies upon the 'malign exploitation of the victim's life sustaining habits . . . integrating the most fundamental strata of the biological conditions for life into the attack'.[64] This move away from epiphenomenal explanation is telling. Such terror actually 'voids the distinction between violence and people and violence against things: it comprises a form of violence against the very human-ambient "things" without which people cannot remain people. By using violence against the very air that groups breathe, the human being's immediate atmospheric envelope is transformed into something whose intactness or non-intactness is henceforth a question.'[65] Since terror therefore awakens inhabitants out of the 'silent condition' of existence, it 'breeds a prolonged climate of fear, placing the defendants in a permanent state of readiness against attacks they are helpless to counter'.[66] This creates a fateful paradox. Given that what is threatened is the 'otherwise imperceptible milieu of everyday life', terror effectively forces the victim to become the 'unwilling accomplice in his own annihilation'.[67]

Kathleen Stewart's idea of 'trauma time' brings this directly back to the problem of temporality.[68] Trauma time, Stewart explains, is a condition '[w]here the here and now drifts between the future-making of awakened expectations and the dragging dread of lurking threats and half-remembered horrors'.[69] Caught, then, in a dynamic state of temporal purgatory, '[t]hings seem to be simultaneously leaping forward and falling back.' Since this temporality is continually haunted by a 'peripheral vision that demands hyper-vigilance', it marks out the 'nightmarish vulnerabilities of a subject who is subject to forces beyond her control or understanding and yet given total responsibility for everything that happens to her and to others'.[70] Not only does this propose a rethinking of vulnerability as a problem of political responsibility, it foregrounds a new notion of subjectivity which is based less on fixed allegiances than on one's experience to endure the catastrophic normality that defines the contemporary order of things – an 'experience of life on the level of surging affects, forces unfolding, events erupting, and impacts suffered or barely avoidable'.[71] Despite, therefore, the dream of lasting security, risk societies actually continue in practice to undermine this ambition by serving up 'the worst-case scenario in the very effort to insure against it'.[72]

Biopoliticized Desire

Foucault famously reorientated our understanding of power in order to excavate what could be termed the 'history of the present'. This moved us away from the limited understanding of power as form, i.e. the state form, to focus our attentions upon relations of force, i.e. power relations. No longer would we see power as a material property that was capable of being 'captured' or to which some exclusive political class was granted 'privileged access'. Neither would we look for an identifiable core essence. Power produces reality in a highly contingent way by fashioning out ever-wider circuits of influence. This proved reminiscent of what Gilles Deleuze (borrowing from Spinoza) called 'affect': 'an ability to affect and be affected. It is a pre-personal intensity corresponding to the passage from one experiential state of the body to another and implying an augmentation or diminution in that body's capacity to act.'[73] Foucault's intervention has had a direct bearing upon our understanding of what we think we know about what we know of the formation of political problems – the framing of the problem itself: '[W]hat I am attempting to bring to light is the epistemological field, the *episteme* in which knowledge, envisaged apart from all criteria having reference to its rational value or its objective forms, grounds its positivity and thereby manifests a history which is not that of its growing perfection, but rather its conditions of possibility.'[74] In doing so, it becomes possible to restore to 'our silent and apparently immobile soils its rifts, its instability, and its flaws . . . the same ground that is once more stirring under our feet'.[75]

Key to Foucault's method is the need to move beyond the question of sovereignty: 'That model pre-supposes the individual as a subject of natural rights or original powers; it aims to account for the ideal genesis of the State; and it makes law the fundamental manifestation of power.' In its place, Foucault proposes,

> One would have to study power not on the basis of the primitive terms of the relation but starting with the relation itself, inasmuch as the relation is what determines the elements on which it bears; instead of asking ideal subjects what part of themselves or what powers of theirs they have

surrendered, allowing themselves to be subjectified, one would need to inquire how relations of subjectivation can manufacture subjects.[76]

This requires adopting a new angle of vision that is necessarily trans-disciplinary. As Deleuze suggests, '[T]he question we should not ask is "What is power and where does it come from?", but "How is it practiced?"'[77] Not only does this require us to question constructs of political endangerment, but also, since it is through the operation of power that political rationalities reveal their distinct preferences for political authenticity and political disqualification, our entire approach to liberalism as a regime of power is invariably transformed:

> Liberalism is usually presented as a principled political philosophy that distinguishes a domain of limited government from a sphere of individual liberty, found and exercised within civil society, which must be respected. However, once we recognize that liberal political rationality might seek to create, work through or utilize freedom, then a set of complementary analytical openings emerge. . . . [In this regard] governing liberally does not necessarily entail governing *through* freedom or even governing in a manner that respects individual liberty. It might mean, in ways quite compatible with a liberal rationality of government, overriding the exercise of specific freedoms in order to enforce obligations on members of the population.[78]

A Foucauldian-inspired critique of liberal terror moves us away from the notion that enlightened truths structure the world through reasoned deliberation. Power produces the truth in order to give legitimate meaning to the prevailing order of things. That is not to deny any truth. Nor is it to refrain from having the courage to speak truth to power whenever we witness horrifying abuse. It is, however, to understand that all truth is the product of power relations. And it is also to appreciate that so-called 'universal normative' claims to truth conceal particular relations of power for the betterment of certain constituencies and the detriment of others. In this regard, our critique of liberal security regimes needs to engage with both 'micro-physics of power' (the political problem of life itself) and 'macro-fields of political formation' (the architectures of life-world systems). For power is always exercised upon bodies as a deliberate strategy so that what it means to be a living thing is always enmeshed in a complex web of techniques for bodily influence. How political projects function in light of its ontological and epistemological assumptions therefore becomes the source of our analytical concern:

> The body – and everything that touches it: diet, climate, and soil – is the domain of the *Herkunft* [descent]. The body manifests the stigmata of past experience and also gives rise to desires, failings, and errors. These elements may join in a body where they achieve a sudden expression, but as often, their encounter is an engagement in which they efface each other, where the body becomes the pretext of their insurmountable conflict.
>
> The body is the inscribed surface of events (traced by language and dissolved by ideas), the locus of a dissociated self (adopting the illusion of a substantial unity) and a volume in perpetual disintegration. Genealogy, as an analysis of descent, is thus situated within the articulation of the body and history. Its task is to expose a body totally imprinted by history and the process of history's destruction of the body.[79]

So what becomes of political agency? It is misguided to argue that technologies of rule lead to the evacuation of all politics as life is simply reduced to the bio-logical fact of being. In his critique of technology, Deleuze shows that technicity is not simply 'machine-like' or purely 'technical'. Neither do technologies of rule precede social assemblages:

'[M]achines are social before being technical. Or, rather, there is human technology which exists before a material technology. No doubt the latter develops its effects within the whole social field; but in order for it to be even possible, the tools or material machines have to be chosen first of all by a diagram and taken up by the assemblages.'[80] Hence, for Deleuze, since our social and technical systems are an expression of our *desires*, what we produce (including systems of social control) is emotionally invested. Human desire is crucial to understanding the links between agency and the biopolitics of security. As Deleuze explains, humans are 'desiring creatures'. We sometimes follow our desires. We sometimes learn to control them. And we can sometimes be manipulated in the most positive ways to desire that which may appear altogether oppressive. As a result, 'there is no such thing as social production on the one hand, and a desiring production that is mere fantasy on the other.'[81] Social production is 'purely and simply desiring production itself under determinate conditions'. This is significant since it forces us to account for our own compromises with power. In doing so, not only can we challenge the manipulation of desire such that we have a better understanding of what is deemed necessary, but we are also able to critique the political implications without resorting to conspiratorial or shadowy theories of power which take place behind the walls of sovereign deliberation.

Desiring subjects focus our attentions on *the active liberation of certain political subjectivities/agencies to the expense of others*. Bypassing, then, the evacuation of politics thesis, what matters is the active politicization of desires to the point of their effective normalization. This exposes the mistaken link between Foucault's analysis of power and the apparent abandonment of political agency.[82] Our problem is not one of de-politicization, if one understands this process to be the full reduction of life to some purely instrumental vision of species-being. Moving beyond the soulless and emotionless narratives of techno-pursuing instrumentalization, what matters are the socially invested power relations which, operating at macro- and micro-specific levels, work by creating generalizable levels of shared affects. So our questions become: How does endangerment affect our political desires? What makes life desire the wilful oppression of its own political freedoms? How do security agencies create the conditions so that we come to desire that which politically appears intolerable? And how is desire manipulated so that certain lives are tolerated while others appear altogether threatening to one's very existence?

– 3 –

Potentialities

Bio-Philosophy of Life

Bob Dylan once intimated that our answers were 'blowing in the wind'. This chorus is perfectly apt for contemporary liberal societies. Everything, it seems, is fleeting – or, to use Zygmunt Bauman's more economically expressive term, 'liquid':

> The solids whose turn has come to be thrown into the melting pot and which are in the process of being melted at the present time, the time of fluid modernity, are the bonds which interlock individual choices in collective projects and actions – the patterns of communication and co-ordination between individually conducted life policies on the one hand and political actions of human collectivities on the other.[1]

Every relationship has been brought into crisis as the organization of life is radically transformed. No longer do we sign up for jobs for life. The idea of a life-long partner for many appears either absurd or at least compromised by the pressures of contemporary living. Many of us would even struggle to identify where our final resting place would be. We have become nomads of a different kind. As Bauman writes elsewhere, 'Progress has turned into a sort of endless and uninterrupted game of musical chairs in which a moment of inattention results in irreversible defeat and irrevocable exclusion. Instead of great expectations and sweet dreams, progress invokes insomnia full of nightmares of "being left behind".'[2] None of this is insignificant. With any foundational sense of being in the world now brought into crisis (Bauman indicates that being itself is now a regressive proposition), we are challenged to look for alternative sources for understanding the human condition which have greater empirical verifiability in relation to the lived experience of our dynamic times.

None of this can be divorced from the advent of complexity thinking and its insistence that movement is defining. Stephen Hawking argued that complexity will be the science of the twenty-first century.[3] Cutting across all the life sciences, 'complexity mirrors the world it would capture'.[4] It denotes a shift away from simple and predictable linear models to a recognition that nothing can be deduced with absolute certainty.[5] Complex systems are therefore seen to be more than the sum of their epistemic parts.[6] As Robert Lewin explains, '[I]ncreased complexity is to be expected as a fundamental property of complex dynamical systems . . . Such systems may, through selection, bring themselves to the edge of chaos, a constant process of co-evolution, a constant adaptation.'[7] Displacing Newtonian thinking, the complexity sciences have not only radicalized our understanding of self-organization, they have also engendered an altogether more powerful bodily trope. At the most basic level, complex life forms appear less rigid and hierarchical, and more adaptive and networked:

Today, . . . we see networks everywhere we look – military organizations, social movements, business formations, migration patterns, communication systems, physiological structures, linguistic relations, neural transmitters, and even personal relationships. It is not that networks were not around before or that the structure of the brain has changed. It is that the network has become a common form that tends to define our ways of understanding the world and acting in it.[8]

Complexity is not simply a useful metaphor for explaining the operations of networked interactions; it provides us with a new science of life. Life resembles its own complex, networked, distributed, and coded system. Bypassing physicality, it is given its own distinct molecular code that inscribes into its body a networked design.[9] Life is quite literally 'full of information'. One only has to look at the advances made in regard to human DNA to recognize these features. Indeed, complex forms of information sequencing are not only mobilizing the life sciences along new biological paths; in the process, they are interfacing life into new complex digital arrangements which are manipulative by design.[10] Code breaking in the twenty-first century is becoming increasingly biological.[11] Life in code therefore means that populations, as with all connectable data-sets, are now considered to be databanks of networked information.[12] They constitute digital samples which are constantly hybridizing – bodies of information continuously *in*-formation.[13] This has a profound bearing on the question of what it means to be a living thing as life is seen to be able to generate beyond itself. So as complexity science inaugurates a new bio-philosophy of life attuned to this new complex age of humanistic discovery, since the liberal subject exhibits complex, adaptive, and emergent characteristics, we are forced to reappraise the ontological meaning of lives.

Complex life, as we have already discovered, exhibits emergent characteristics. This 'notion of emergence', as Lewin explains, is not only the 'principal message of the science of complexity'; it forces 'a reassessment of the way complexity *arises*'.[14] 'Life at all levels' is not simply reducible to 'one damn thing after another'; it is inexorably driven towards 'ever greater complexity'.[15] It is impossible as such to find the origin of things, let alone predict linearity. Everything is always at a point of *intermezzo* (in-between). That is to say, since it is appreciated that things can be 'out of place' – capable of 'becoming other than what they were' – the search for fixed essence is all but abandoned.[16] This is crucial to our understanding of life and its potential to bring about change: that is, the problematic creation of the conditions of the new. As Richard Doyle explained in his groundbreaking work, '[L]ife is no longer confined to operations'; what matters is the 'events associated' with its 'operations of coding, replication, and mutation'.[17] Fixed identity is seconded by 'the events of life', which forces a shift from '*localized agents* to an articulation of living systems as *distributed events*'. So as the Newtonian mechanistic subject that was once deemed capable of being prodded into linear action is fully displaced by a post-industrial subject who displays all the hallmarks of the radically interconnected emergent times, so adaptation, transformation, and change become the source of new potential and altogether more problematic for the very same reasons.[18] As two distinguished managerial scientists once put it, '[T]he most critical knowledge in our real world is not what "is", but how various elements of the universe relate and interact.'[19] What concerns us is the coming-into-being of 'macropatterns that depend on [continuously] shifting micropatterns'.[20]

Strategic thought has been fully rejuvenated by the challenge that emergence poses: that is, to model and mediate the affects *of those radically undecidable singularities whose emergent nature originates at the most microspecific level*.[21] This proposes a distinct epistemological and ontological tension – what could be termed a *liberal paradox of potentiality*. On the one hand, emergent life is understood to bring wonderful benefits. As Friedrich von Hayek foretold, life which embraces emergence has been economically and hence politically liberated.[22] Indeed, removed from the shackles of the former disciplinary regimes whose strict regimentation once so perturbed Foucault, not only is the individual ability to enhance one's own capacities for power, knowledge, and the freedom of opportunity assumed to increase exponentially, so too are its possibilities to occasion profit. The risk-takers are, after all, the serious money-makers. And yet, as we have already discovered, since the problem of emergence allows for forms of freedom which are ambivalent by design – that is, one cannot know the nature or the design of that which is to come – emergent life presents a clear epistemological crisis inasmuch as ontologically emergent features cannot be reduced to knowable intrinsic causal capacities. Onto-logical emergence cannot be neatly contained within systems of prediction since it is, by definition, that which is truly uncertain in a world of radical interconnectivity:

> A property of an object or system is epistemologically emergent if the property is reducible to or determined by the intrinsic properties of the ultimate constituents of the object or system, while at the same time it is very difficult for us to explain, predict, or derive the property on the basis of the ultimate constituents. Epistemologically emer-gent properties are novel only at the level of descrip-tion. . . . Ontologically emergent features are neither reducible to nor determined by more basic features. Onto-logically emergent features are features of systems or wholes that possess causal capacities not reducible to any of the intrinsic causal capacities of the parts nor to any of the (reducible) relations between the parts. Ontological emergence entails the failure of the part–whole reduction-ism in both its explicit and mereological supervenience forms.[23]

There is an important qualification to add here. Emer-gent life is not to be confused with a becoming that is politically different. Nor is it to be confused with the embrace of positivist ontology as promoted by prominent post-structural thinkers. For the liberal subject, everything changes so that everything remains politically the same. This brings us directly back to the idea of resilience, which was the dominant theme at the various sites of remembrance throughout New York in September 2011. Commemorating the tenth anniversary of the fateful attacks, the media set the tone as they grappled with the need for memorialization along with the desire to outlive the trauma of 9/11. *Newsweek* was unequivocal in mapping out the road to recovery. Featuring an image of a passenger jet against a cloudless blue sky, it headlined with ever-increasing font size 'Ten Years of Fear: Grief: Revenge: Resilience'.[24] The image used was painfully reflective in its normality. While New Yorkers were deeply traumatized by the scarred Manhattan skyline – haunted by the spectre of seeing what was no longer there – on this occasion the visibly animate invoked a tragically normalizing complementarity between past memory and yet business as usual. *Time* magazine was equally reflective: its 'Beyond 9/11' cover, designed by Julian LaVerdiere and Paul Myoda, co-creators of the original 'Tribute in Light' memorial, afforded more than a touch of divine transcendental quality to the idea of resurrection, the impetus being, as manager editor Richard Stengel noted, to represent 'something that literally and figuratively moved beyond 9/11'. Meanwhile, *People* magazine's emotional tribute, 'Legacy of Love – The Children of 9/11: Portraits of Hope', showed photographs of those whose 'fathers died on that terrible day, before they were born', its sub-head then going on to say: 'Today, these 10 kids and their moms have triumphed over tragedy.' All sense of time therefore collapses here in these moments of media aestheticization as our sense of immanence is disrupted. As the *New York Times* simply put it: 'Reflect, Remember, Carry On.'

Battery Park in Lower Manhattan was scene to a remarkable staging of the logic of survivability. Surrounding Fritz Koenig's partially disfigured *The Sphere*, which was formerly located at the Austin H. Tobin Plaza (the area between the Twin Towers), 3,000 whitened flags which featured the names of the deceased symbolically memorialized the past all the while celebrating the fact that it was possible for certain things to emerge if slightly transformed in design, meaning, and political resonance. *The Sphere* itself became a living symbol of resilience as it provided an optimistic centre for reflection in a sea of tragic memory. Perhaps, however, it was Marco Grob's exhibition 'Beyond 9/11: Portraits of Resilience', which was displayed in the Milk Gallery and various additional public spaces across Manhattan, which proved most revealing.[25] In this exhibition, featuring stark black and white photographs of the forty faces said to encapsulate the spirit of recovery, resilience was ubiquitously framed by politicians, the major, the admiral, the general, the military hero, the CIA covert operative, along with the CEO, New York fire fighters, artists, and everyday survivors. The messages here were poignant: resilient life was fully inclusive, it made no distinction; catastrophe had strengthened resolve; we learnt more about ourselves by living through the terror; shared experience of trauma brought a people together. Despite vast differences in lifestyles (not to mention wealth), the resilience was universal. Life, however, can be captured only for a moment. Momentarily reflective, we owe it to the victims to face up to the challenge that society must emerge from the ashes and continue its normality apace. With the individual compliant subject therefore becoming the locus for a moment of attention that was delicately poised between past memory and future possibility, so past and future impress upon the present the need to live through the emergency and come out more knowledgeable, adaptive, resolute, and yet politically unscathed.

Subjects of Crises

Benedict Anderson provided the definitive framework for understanding identity in the age of national rivalry. He conceived of the nation as 'an imagined political community – and imagined as both inherently limited and sovereign'.[26] Anderson's terms of engagement are crucial here since they denote a reality that is more constructed than based on the individual's lived experience: '[The nation] is imagined because the members of even the smallest nation will never know most of their fellow-members, meet them, or even hear of them, yet in the minds of each lives the image of their communion.' Despite the fact that Anderson was writing at a time when his very object for study was unravelling before his eyes, he nevertheless made an important contribution. As he insisted, there was nothing self-evident or natural about any identity formation. Identity is always *constructed*. Indeed, while state theorists take constitutional declarations as being the formative event, as Anderson noted, 'the style in which they are imagined' is 'particularistic' and 'indefinitely stretchable'. Importantly for Anderson, however, while the onset of these particular communities was less messianic than in earlier social forms, the resulting tensions they produced actually allowed for the creation of systems of allegiance that were characteristically more violent by design:

> [The modern nation] is imagined as a community, because, regardless of the actual inequality and exploitation that may prevail in each, the nation is always conceived as a deep, horizontal comradeship. Ultimately it is this fraternity that makes it possible, over the past two centuries, for so many millions of people, not so much to kill, as willingly to die for such limited imaginings. These deaths bring us abruptly face to face with the central problem posed by nationalism: what makes the shrunken imaginings of recent history (scarcely more than two centuries) generate such colossal sacrifices?[27]

While the myth of national unity was propagated at every stage of the subject's development (i.e. birth, school, church, industry, culture, media, etc.), the experience of

war was a key ingredient in maintaining allegiance. As
George Orwell would famously declare,

> By nationalism I mean first of all the habit of assuming
> that human beings can be classified like insects and that
> blocks of . . . [t]ens of millions can conveniently be labelled
> 'good' or 'bad'. . . secondly – and this is much more
> important – I mean the habit of identifying oneself with a
> single nation or other unit, placing it beyond good or evil
> and recognizing no other duty than that of advancing its
> own interest.[28]

Foundational approaches to security therefore share an
intimate relationship to war and violence:

> [S]ecurity is a package which tells you what you are as it
> tells you what to die for; which tells you what to love as
> it tells you what to defend (*dulce et decorum est pro patria
> mori*); and which tells you what is right as it tells you what
> is wrong. Its cognates consequently include individual and
> collective identity, evil, goodness, and justice.[29]

Thus, as Schmitt insisted, sovereign power was all about
deciding upon the *exception*. Adjudicating between the
'inside' and the 'outside', enmity proceeded on the basis
that the homeland was to be defended from 'Others'
who simply didn't belong. War as such became highly
'disciplined', 'regimented', 'industrialized', and 'territorial'. Friends and enemies could be clearly identified.
Positions of authority followed hierarchical management
structures as witnessed throughout societies more generally. Soldiers wore military fatigues which were colour-
coded. Battles benefited from distinct temporalities in
which it was possible to work to either negotiated settlement or surrender on account of near total annihilation.
And the antagonists (in theory at least) evidenced some
respect for the rules of warfare as first espoused by
Clausewitz with his idea of the chivalric code between
identifiable warring factions.

Not only are contemporary wars between nations the exception to the rule, soldiers now go to war protecting those who routinely question familiar sovereign terms of engagement. The displacement in 2011 of Muammar Gaddafi's regime in Libya offers but a recent example. War, if there is to be one, must be for a *post-national cause*. While this has resulted in the successful privatization of securitization/warfare, it has also effaced the idea of dialectical enmity which once created clear lines of engagement between disputing factions. There is no inevitable Schmittean decision to be made in advance. There is no universal application of a principle that defines the necessary condition. Neither is Otherness primarily determined by geo-strategic classification. What remains is an open field of political formation which, foregrounding the contingency of potentially dangerous encounters, proposes a post-dialectical arrangement that is purely strategic. This proves significant. Since this post-dialectical ordering sets aside the cold sovereign comforts, the laws of war thesis (along with the notion of the indivisible nature of constituted identity more generally) is once and for all exposed. What is more, with violence and power becoming separated from the traditional sphere of politics, Max Weber's once famous monopoly of violence hypothesis is subject to a higher (albeit more dynamic) purpose. As Subcomondate Marcos more critically questioned:

In the cabaret of globalization, the state performs a strip-tease, at the end of which it is left wearing the minimum necessary: its powers of repression. With its material base destroyed, its sovereignty and independence abolished, and its political class eradicated, the nation state increasingly becomes a mere security apparatus in the service of the mega-enterprises which neo-liberalism is constructing. . . . What is to be done when the violence derives from the laws of the market? Where is legitimate violence then? And where the illegitimate? What monopoly of violence can the hapless nation states demand when the free interplay of supply and demand defies any such monopoly?[30]

While the onset of the post-national critique cannot be divorced from these post-colonial influences,[31] it was the postmodern/post-structural turn and the advent of radical feminism in particular which disrupted the inevitability of national affiliation. Developing a meaningful critique of the state which highlighted its naturalizing patriarchal qualities, the myth surrounding the indivisibility of authority and its claims for unconditional allegiance began to crumble under the weight of micro-political challenges and transnational possibilities. Many, of course, pointed out here that the 'return' to ethnicity and religious affiliation was a logical outcome of these developments. If state authority began to wane, so must any conception of security and political agency. People would therefore search for new sense of meaning and belonging by forging new political alliances. Such revivalism was comforting. Displacing one system of foundationalism with another, it allowed for the emergence of new referents for political discussion without bringing into question the security imperative so central to Western metaphysics. Since this narrative therefore reworked the fixed essence to being, the unifying mask which disguises the many conceptual and conflicting personas which make up any political subject (even in the most 'primitive' societies) remained intact. However, the assumption that illiberal or indeed liberal populations for that matter lost all sense of ethnic or religious agency is open to serious question. Indeed, while this approach supports the 'crises of identity' thesis – that is to say, new identities are embraced out of misguided/manipulated choice and the lack of a more secular and progressive variant – the continual history of colonial struggle illustrates how illiberal populations have always contested the sovereign state.

Some will no doubt argue here that national forms of identity still matter – especially in times of crises. We may point, for instance, to the sudden wave of US patriotism that was evidenced in the immediate aftermath of 9/11. While nobody is denying this reality, it would be ridiculous to suggest a uniform experience. Some undoubtedly found a new sense of national meaning in the face of this trauma. Others notably searched for visible signs of religious symbolism and theistic comfort. Our concern is not to offer some definitive truth on identity politics. Identities are multiple. How identity functions liberally is the problematic we have sought to consider. In this respect, to highlight concerns with national affinity we need only point to liberal disquiet with any form of national retrenchment as experienced by far right and left claims for genuine sovereign autonomy from continental Europe and Latin America, and by the more religious claims made by the orthodox religious groups from Israel to Iran. The liberal self is no longer defined in epiphenomenal terms. It has no clear sense of inside/outside. Nor is it content to accept national limits to its notion of community. Subjected instead to a rationality which is premised on outliving the dangerously incomplete political architectures of geostrategic affinity, liberal subjectivity is reformed by confronting head-on the insecure sediment of global existence. As Stuart Hall forcefully argued:

> Since cultural diversity is, increasingly, the fate of the modern world, and ethic absolutism a regressive feature of late-modernity, the greatest danger now arises from forms of national and cultural identity – new and old – which attempt to secure their identity by adopting closed versions of culture or community and by refusal to engage . . . with difficult problems that arise from trying to live with difference.[32]

Contemporary liberal subjectivity reveals all the hallmarks of a post-dialectical figure. It is no longer the case that people are simply born into identities as if they exhibit some singular and unchangeable signature. Leaving behind 'solid' or fixed remnants, the liberal subject is expected to create his or her own biography that is less about life as it merely is, and more about its prospects. Such affiliation eschews life-long subscriptions, preferring instead to

embrace life's continual unfolding without a pre-determined destination. It embraces risk, in spite of the fact that
the chanced encounter increases the precariousness and
vulnerability of every given situation. This is what Frederic
Jameson has termed 'dialectical saturation', in which 'the
hitherto semi-autonomous sub-systems of these various
social levels threaten to become autonomous tout court,
and generate a very different ideological picture of complexity as dispersed multiplicity and infinite fission.'[33] So
despite the commodification of familiar symbolic accoutre-
ments of the state, nothing is naturally 'given' in terms of
the subject's material qualities. Liberal subjectivity defies
the fixed essence to being which once proved so crucial to
maintenance of sovereign forms of allegiance. Neither,
then, is life fated to play out the telluric tensions which so
clearly defined the violence of the twentieth century. With
life outliving wilful capture and continually projecting
itself beyond itself to the creation of lives yet to be lived,
discontinuity, rupture, and breaks become the new norm.
This passing of concrete reality does not in any way represent a shift to hollow abstraction. Although it now
appears that the liberal subject denies any 'natural' or
'timeless' propriety, its fleeting fabric nevertheless proposes
authentic global 'lifestyles' which are deeply politicized:

> The activation of subjectivity, so central to advanced forms
> of liberalism, creates its own challenges. In many countries
> across the globe, individuals are indeed becoming more
> active, their capacities to know and to question enhanced
> by transnational media, the internet and many other com-
> municative technologies whose power, form and penetra-
> tion were difficult to imagine a decade ago. . . . New
> collectivities are forming, some of which are surprisingly
> resolute and local, while others have no regard at all for
> national boundaries. . . . These new collectivizations, often
> termed 'trans-national', particularly when they are more
> formalized and linked to regulatory aspirations, problema-
> tize many technologies for regulation and control that were
> historically territorialized on national political spaces.[34]

So while it has been common across the humanities to write of the 'crisis of subjectivity', liberal subjectivity is not *in* crisis if we understand crises to be the disruptions to fixed modes of being. Openly challenging sedentary imaginaries which once put life in its 'proper place' (politically, intellectually, and territorially), the liberal subject is *the* subject of crises. Forever seeking to transgress its own self-imposed limits, it lives and breathes through the continual disruption to its own static modes of recovery. The work of Kafka is metaphorically striking. If Kafka's 'Metamorphosis' provides a rich and meaningful metaphor for explaining the human desire to enunciate fixed notions of subjectivity, another of his short stories, 'The Burrow', complements this by offering a critique of self-authoring and networked protectorates. Kafka's animalistic metaphors thus allow us (a) to explain the possibility of human transformation/becoming and (b) to critique the anxieties of the security conscious as a full sense of environmental endangerment leads to the creation of ever wider-circuits of habitation. Together these parables offer a perfectly apt contemporary allegory for explaining the predicament of the globally embedded paranoiac subject. As we shall now discover, this brings us to the relationship between biophilosophy and endangerment. With the liberal subject having to endure what has been termed the 'permanent emergency of its own emergence',[35] it is our predisposition to the unknowable contingency of every new encounter – what we may term the contemporary 'event of life' – which now appears to be the strategic entry point for ethical discourses/practices of emancipation and security discourses/practices of human-made catastrophe.

Becoming Dangerous

Aristotle once mused that 'the accident reveals the substance'. That which gives form of life can also be the source of its very undoing. While nothing is dangerous in

itself, everything, therefore, is potentially endangering.
Danger is determined by affective relations and types of
application. What may be dangerous at a certain moment
may actually prove to be life-saving in another. Nuclear
fusion is the most fitting and horrifying of examples. It
offers to vitalize life in ways that are incomparable, while
it also threatens total annihilation. This integral concept
of endangerment has become a truism of twenty-first-
century security discourse. It has had a profound bearing
on our understanding of both gradual systemic change and
its explosive violent shocks. As Michael Shermer explains,

> So powerful are the effects of contingency that a small
> change in the early stages of a sequence can produce large
> effects in the later stages. Edward Lorenz calls this the
> *butterfly effect* and by now the metaphor is well known:
> A butterfly flaps its wings in Brazil, producing a storm in
> Texas. The uncertainty of our past and unpredictability of
> our future created by contingency is what makes this such
> a challenging idea to historians and scientists, whose
> models and laws call for a search for unifying generalities,
> not capricious happenstances.[36]

Here we encounter a veritable landscape of crisis-events in
which the problem posed by the yet-to-be-revealed singular occurrence encourages a universalizing imaginary of
threat that specifically attends to all actual/possible/prob-
able eventful occurrences. As Brian Massumi writes:

> The universal forcefulness of the accident is such that the
> tiniest local ingression of its indeterminacy actualizes the
> *conditions* of system-wide crisis. Whether the event of that
> conditioning amplifies into an actual crisis depends on a
> panoply of co-factors. The potential disruption that already
> makes itself felt with the strike of the accident may be
> absorbed into the system as a perturbation provoking a
> minor, re-adaptive iteration of a subset of system opera-
> tions. In that case, the incipient disruption dissipates into
> a minor reordering that actually feeds the system's positive

evolution. On the other hand, the force of the accident may elude evolutionary capture and grow into a full-fledged systemic or even pan-systemic disruption.[37]

Deleuze uses the term 'the virtual' to describe the potential which exists in every reality: 'The virtual is opposed not to the real but to the actual. The virtual is fully real in so far as it is virtual.' It must be 'defined as strictly a part of the object – as though the object had one part of itself in the virtual into which it plunged as though into an objective dimension'.[38] It refers us to an unrepresentable or unfolding state of affairs that is subject to a process of endless transformation. Potentiality thus becomes synonymous with the ability to give rise to something new by intensively unleashing those forces which are present and yet to be actualized in every given situation. This is what Deleuze would refer to as being the 'plane of immanence', which is by its very emergent nature unpredictable and wholly contingent. Breaking, then, from the establishment of fixed truths, the virtual represents 'the reality of a task to be performed' and a 'problem to be solved'.[39] It is both problematic and problematizing. Potentiality is not, however, a static concept. Indeed, as we have already discovered, the contemporary liberal subject is said to be altogether more empowered on account of the fact that it exhibits emergent characteristics. It is no longer regimented in a highly mechanical or industrial fashion. Freed from the shackles of disciplinary regimes with their static hierarchical modes of operation, so life offers a more powerful expression as it is opened to a new field of potentiality that multiplies what is possible in any given situation.

We have never been so full of potentiality. Deleuze and Guattari once observed that,

> we know nothing about a body until we know what it can do, in other words, what its affects are, how they can or cannot enter into composition with other affects, with the affects of another body, either to destroy that body or to

be destroyed by it, either to exchange actions and passions
with it or to join with it in composing a more powerful
body.[40]

While the contemporary body has no fixed essence, it is
notably defined by its intensive speeds and radical interconnections. We have become distributed subjects within
globally expansive technologically enabling networks that
render the slow pace of life and concept of the outside
altogether incoherent. For the liberal subject, everything is
potentially accessible and nothing is beyond the boundaries of engagement. And there is no time like the present
to realize it. Indeed to draw away or retreat is a sign of a
failure of the humanistic impulse to know the world and
live as such. Movement has therefore not only become a
defining characteristic of modern life as sedentary imaginaries are displaced by a nomadic sensibility;[41] it is now
seemingly impossible to make universal/timeless commit-
ments as the contingency of life demands more intensive
consideration. Standing still is no longer an option. To
merely hold onto what you have is to sound a defeatist
retreat. Simply 'being in the world' is a preposterous assertion. While this promises to be remarkably enriching as
our life experiences are opened to all the more unknowable
encounters, it comes with a formidable burden as everything we say or do affects lives with a potent immediacy
and a global range that a few generations ago seemed
unimaginable.

We have never been so dangerous. It only takes the
actions of a very small number of nameable individuals to
create the image of a global security crisis. This was one
of the real novelties of 9/11. No standing army. No high-
tech weaponry specifically made for the purposes of mass
slaughter. No military fatigues and conventional weapons
training. No territorial demands. No attempts to capture
the sovereign seat of power. Simply what takes place is
an asymmetric relationship of the most terrifying kind.
For Baudrillard, the increased potential brought about by

technological proliferation has permanently eroded the possibility of lasting signification:

> At one time the body was a metaphor for the soul. . . . Today it is no longer a metaphor for anything at all, merely the locus of metastasis, of the machine-like connections between all its processes, of an endless programming devoid of any symbolic organization or overarching purpose: the body is thus given over to the pure promiscuity of its relationship to itself – the same promiscuity that characterizes networks and integrated circuits.[42]

Schmitt as such becomes increasingly irrelevant. As Michael Dillon and Julian Reid explain, '[T]here is no Schmittean existential enemy defined, in advance or by what Schmitt calls the miracle of the decision, by its radical otherness. No such epistemic comfort is available to the shifting challenges and dilemmas with which liberal strategists are confronted.'[43] What takes its place is a 'continuously open and changing field of formation and intervention: the very continuous and contingent emergency of emergence of life as being in formation; *becoming-dangerous*'. This notion of becoming is crucial. Becoming is emergent. Becoming is eventual. Becoming is unknowable. Becoming is non-identifiable. Becoming is post-dialectical. Becoming is pre-epistemic. Becoming is unknowable in advance. And becoming is largely unstoppable.

We have never been so (in)secure. The idea of security (in principle at least) is meant to make the world safer – not simply as an empirical reality of a present lived condition that is free from personal harm and vulnerability, but as a relation of bodily affects which profoundly shapes our thoughts, perceptions, and behaviours. Yet despite arguably living in the most secure of times, perhaps best evidenced by increasing life-spans, dramatic reductions in mass-casualty warfare, and our abilities to continue to live through illnesses that once wiped out entire populations, the liberal subject of the prosperous metropolitan districts of the world seemingly faces new forms of endangerment on a daily basis. Whether it is the threat of another devastating terrorist attack, some newly discovered air-borne virus, a natural disaster, or unexpected catastrophe, our desire to securitize everything has rendered all things potentially terrifying. There is always something that is going to kill you. It will catch up with you in the end. This is the fateful paradox of contemporary liberal rule. The more we seek to secure, the more our imaginaries of threat proliferate. Not only does this, paradoxically, heighten the stakes, since the internalization of threat paves the way for a recombinant logic that connects all things connectable, it also stakes out new political arrangements in which the very idea that one could remain 'outside' the endangered zone is fully denied. Political allegiance as such is no longer ideologically determined. It is centred on a politics of catastrophe which judges life as it comes face to face with the potentially tragic event-to-come. As Peter Sloterdijk writes:

> Everyday dwelling in latency is more and more anxious. Two kinds of sleepers then start to appear: there are the sleepers in the implicit, those who continue to seek security in ignorance; and there are the sleepers in the explicit, those who are aware of what is planned on the front and await the call to action. . . . It turns some into collaborators of the explicit and by the same token agents of structural terror on constantly shifting fronts, albeit one that is rarely active, against the underlying conditions produced by nature and culture; while the others [are] turned into inner aborigines, regionalists, and the voluntary curators of their own untimeliness.[44]

We have never been more ambivalent. Life, like all things vital, reveals what are now commonly termed 'posthuman' qualities in which the animate is imbued with an agency of its own that is deemed multi-potent. As Robert Pepperell observed, 'If it is the case that the long-held separation between brain and body, or between the mental and the physical, is being eroded as the tide of contemporary ideas runs against it, then we might be gradually drawn to the conclusion that our minds, our bodies and the world are continuous.'[45] Since all things vital are subject to a change in their form and hence their capacity to affect, so whatever holds the potential to impact can be the source of the most joyous affirmation or terrifying despair. Nothing in itself therefore appears malignant or benign. Subject to the laws of transmutation and hence trans-valuation, the natural equilibrium of the times is remarkably disequilibriated. This is fully in keeping with the demands of capitalism, in which the authentic subject (as Bush was so eager to remind us in the immediate aftermath of the 9/11 attacks) unashamedly consumes its freedom wilfully:

> [He] who responds systematically to modifications in the variables of the environment appears precisely as someone manageable, someone who responds systematically to systematic modifications artificially introduced into the environment. *Homo oeconomicus* is someone who is eminently governable. From being the intangible partner of *laissez-faire*, *homo oeconomicus* now becomes the correlate of a governmentality which will act on the environment and systematically modify its variables.[46]

The response to sovereign power is unequivocal:

> This is what the man of right, *homo juridicus*, says to the sovereign: I have rights, I have entrusted some of them to you, the others you must not touch. . . . *Homo oeconomicus* does not say this. He also tells the sovereign: You must not. But why must he not? You must not because you cannot. And you cannot in the sense that 'you are powerless'. And why are you powerless, why can't you? You cannot because you do not know, and you do not know because you cannot know.[47]

Life, then, is no longer born dangerous on account of the fact that it just so happens to be geo-politically framed. It becomes dangerous on account of a radical transformation in character that bears little relation to territoriality. Endangerment as such is bound to the unleashing of a potential that is altogether contingent on particular circumstances. Therefore, while some still try to resurrect the conventional utility of force in order to provide hegemonic comfort (militarily and intellectually), contemporary security agencies show their order of priorities as they focus intently on emergent phenomena that are radically interconnected in design:

> The Cold War model of civil defence – focused on a single, monolithic threat, managed top-down by central government in secret and restricted to a small community – has gone. In its place has come a model better suited to a modern network society with its increased connections and interdependencies bringing with them greater vulnerability to external shock. The new model addresses a wide range of security risks, from terrorism through accidents to natural disasters.[48]

Not only does this strengthen the conviction that humankind advances through catastrophe as we become more knowledgeable and hence more prepared to face the insecure sediment of existence, since the catastrophic is the product of our positive ambivalence, from the perspective of securitization, Derrida's remarks appear more resonant than ever: 'The future can only be anticipated in the form of an absolute danger. It is that which breaks absolutely with constituted normality and can only be proclaimed, *presented*, as a sort of monstrosity.'[49]

Radical Uncertainty

All bodies matter. They matter most, however, when they are *radically undecidable*.[50] Once it is recognized that ontological emergence cannot be reduced to part–whole relationality, i.e. it is *beyond* epistemic calculations, then the real basis for all potential emergencies can be given scientific validation. *Exceeding* the secure limits of modern systems of power and knowledge, ontological emergence becomes the basis for all emergencies by directly challenging the entire ontological and epistemological foundations of biopolitical security practices. 9/11 unquestionably gave these concerns political impetus. Baudrillard, for instance, argued that 9/11 was a 'world event' which constituted a direct 'setback for globalization itself',[51] whereas Wendell Berry, somewhat prophetically, argued in agreement that

> [t]he time will soon come when we will not be able to remember the horrors of September 11th without remembering also the unquestioning technological and economic optimism that ended on that day. This optimism rested on the proposition that we were living in a 'new world order' and a 'new economy' that would 'grow' on and on, bringing a prosperity of which every new increment would be 'unprecedented'.[52]

While the shocking and awful (to borrow Susan Sontag's expression) implications of that day have been rightly critiqued, 9/11 also changed our sense of perception by illustrating how the ability to violently alter the conditions on earth no longer required mass mobilization. *Catastrophic individuals* were now capable of authoring their own *micro-pocalyptic* tale. As Brian Jenkins observed,

> The 9/11 terrorist attacks fundamentally altered perceptions of plausibility. With box cutters and mace, terrorists turned commercial airliners into guided missiles that brought down skyscrapers. People feared that al Qaeda would try to launch more 9/11-scale attacks if it could, or perhaps even more-ambitious attacks. Terrorist scenarios that had been deemed far-fetched before 9/11 became operative presumptions after 9/11. In this environment, no terrorist scheme could be dismissed.[53]

The US Government's *Joint Inquiry into Intelligence Community Activities before and after the Terrorist Attacks of September 11, 2001* follows a similar logic. Confronting the obvious question 'Why?' the report's authors provide a background narrative of the nineteen terrorist individuals in order to 'find out everything [they can] about the hijackers and how they succeeded'.[54] From the attempts to explain how the event unfolded, it becomes clear that security efforts must become more adaptive as the nature of threat is more marginal. The British Government's official report into the subsequent London attacks followed the same script, once again describing globally dangerous marginal life. The report begins by setting out the localized scene of the event: '7 July began unsettled, with heavy showers in places. The early morning rush in London started as *normal*.'[55] Starting from this everyday condition of normality, the report then chronologically outlines the crisis-event, before assessing the immediate aftermath. Significantly, while the document gives a thorough account of 'what' happened, outlining in remarkable detail the *action-of-the-event* in terms of 'where and when', there is a notable absence of all power relations. The report's primary concern is with tracing the movements which are seen to exist within the normal space of flows. Thus, when trying to account for the question: 'Why did they do it?' the report investigates the 'backgrounds' in order to try to identify the moment that 'radicalization' or 'indoctrination' occurred. This is referred to in the appendix as the 'Timeline of the Four Individuals'. Particular emphasis is given to their place of birth, family life, economic status, local deprivations, past behaviour patterns, and social life. Aware of the multi-cultural stakes, the report attempts to paint a picture of four radicalized terrorists who finally became 'out-of-place' (thus possibly holding the key to future singular displacements) not only within British society, but amongst their own Islamic communities:

> As for the process of radicalization, there are a number of factors which have, in the past, contributed. Attendance at a mosque linked to extremists may be a factor. This will

normally have nothing to do with the official mosque hierarchy, but rather extremists identifying potential candidates for *radicalization on the margins*. However, evidence suggests that extremists are increasingly moving away from mosques to conduct their activities in private homes or other premises to avoid detection.

Such reversion to a linear cause/effect methodology proves meaningless. As the report openly admits:

> What we know of previous extremists in the UK shows that there is not a consistent profile to help identify who may be vulnerable to radicalization. . . . Some have been well-educated, some less so. Some genuinely poor, some less so. Some apparently well integrated in the UK, others not. Most single, but some family men with children. Some previously law-abiding, others with a history of petty crime. In a few cases there is evidence of abuse or other trauma in early life, but in others their upbringing has been stable and loving.[56]

These ambivalent findings are to be expected. Newtonian cause/effect methodologies are completely inadequate for appraising what are understood to be highly complex and adaptive phenomena. Nevertheless, this approach is politically expedient since power relations are effectively removed from the analytical area. To put it another way, if one followed the lessons of complexity thinking – that is, interrogating the emergence of complex phenomena through an analysis of their movements, interconnections, relations, speeds, frictions, and affects – the inquiry would need to have accounted for each and every power relationship that could contribute to the event. This would no doubt be problematic since our complicities need to be taken into consideration. Consequently, in its place, what is presented is a simple reaffirmation of a pre-determined theorem which, sidestepping the problem of power relations, merely exposes the reality of bad/ dangerous forms of global circulation. Hence, as the report indicates, the only truth which can be established with any certainty is that the investigation will be 'very much a live one' with the prospect of 'further information' certain to 'emerge'.[57]

Infinite Endangerment

Following the assassination of Osama bin Laden in May 2011, many New Yorkers took to the streets to celebrate an important chapter in the war effort. Applauding the moment, Jonathan Haidt answered 'Why We Celebrate a Killing' by arguing, 'I believe that last week's celebrations were good and healthy. America achieved its goal – bravely and decisively – after 10 painful years.'[58] Haidt justifies his response by drawing upon the affective dimension to politics: 'People who love their country sought out one another to share collective effervescence. They stepped out of their petty and partisan selves and became, briefly, just Americans rejoicing together.' 'Briefly' is the key word here, as the affective dimension soon began to target more familiar emotions. Commenting on the significance of the events, the British Prime Minister, David Cameron, for instance, remarked, 'This news will be welcomed right across our country. Of course, it does not mark the end of the threat we face from extremist terror – indeed we will have to be particularly vigilant in the weeks ahead.' The Foreign Secretary, William Hague, reiterated this stance by adding,

> We must remember that this is not the end of being vigilant against al-Qaeda and associated groups, and, in fact, there may be parts of al-Qaeda that will try to show that they are still in business in the coming weeks, as indeed some of them are. So I have already this morning asked our embassies to review their security, to make sure that vigilance is heightened – and I think that will have to be our posture for some time to come.

The Home Secretary, Theresa May, meanwhile pointed out that this was 'an important and significant development in the struggle against global terrorism', but since there was still a 'real and serious threat', there was a 'continuing need for everyone to remain vigilant and to report any suspicious activity'.

Discourses on terror are rife with contradictions. The United Kingdom's *National Security Strategy* (2010) offers a poignant example. As the report begins,

> Britain today is both more secure and more vulnerable than in most of her long history. More secure, in the sense that we do not currently face, as we have so often in our past, a conventional threat of attack on our territory by a hostile power. But more vulnerable, because we are one of the most open societies, in a world that is more networked than ever before.[59]

The problem of vulnerability is crucial here. All systems have their points of vulnerability. Indeed, the more complex the society (i.e. the more it is radically interconnected), the more points of vulnerability that society faces. What the British Government calls its 'Age of Uncertainty' equates vulnerabilities with the openness the society enjoys: 'The networked world provides us with great opportunities. But Britain's very openness and deep engagement with the world means that we can be particularly vulnerable to overseas events.'[60] Britain is therefore both a beneficiary and a victim of '[g]lobalization in all its forms', which has made 'the world more interconnected both through technology, travel and migration and through the global trade in goods, services and capital. This means that it is much harder to isolate the UK from shocks occurring outside our own territory, whether they are economic or geopolitical.'[61] While this connectivity demands a National Security Strategy that is aware of present risks, it offers no real lasting comforts: since 'the risk picture is likely to become increasingly diverse . . . achieving security will become more complex'.[62] This requires some acceptance on our part that the ambition of perfect security belongs to a bygone era:

> We cannot be complacent. The world will change. Our National Security Strategy needs to position us for the future as well as the present. We must scan the horizon, identify possible future developments and prepare for them. We must be prepared for alternative futures based on key trends, building in the adaptability to respond to different possibilities. . . . Our national interest can be threatened by natural disasters, man-made accidents and by malicious attacks both by states and by non-state actors, such as terrorists and organized criminals. . . . We must do all we can, within the resources available, to predict, prevent and mitigate the risks to our security. For those risks that we can predict, we must act both to reduce the likelihood of their occurring, and develop the resilience to reduce their impact. . . . But we cannot prevent every risk as they are inherently unpredictable.[63]

As Massumi points out, when threat becomes indiscriminate to the environment – that is to say, when the infinitely possible becomes the source of infinite endangerment – 'opposition is no longer generally tenable and cannot be taken as a starting point.'[64] Instead, a 'base redefinition of nature is required outside any categorical opposition to the cultural, social or artificial' – or, to borrow Agamben's terms, everything enters into a 'Zone of Irreducible Indistinction'. While this has many implications as conventional referents lose their identities, the most troubling has been the gradual militarization of civic space. It is well documented that President George W. Bush tried to instil a military spirit into the civilian bodies of American citizens. As he once famously declared, 'Every American is a soldier, and every citizen is in this fight.' While some may explain this in terms of the logic of 'exceptional times', it does not account for the more normalized practices of cultural embeddings of militarism into the daily functioning of contemporary societies. As George Chesterton observed, 'The only place you could be sure of seeing a British soldier used to be outside a pub in a garrison town at chucking-out time. Now there are soldiers on talent shows, parading in sports stadiums and singing on daytime television.' From soldiers dancing on television screens, the rewarding of garrison towns with royal patronage, to the effective militarization of London as part of the 2012 Olympic Games, '[w]e have turned the reality of war into an emotionally nourishing theatre . . . [which] serves an ideological and financial function.'[65] None of this was lost on Massumi, who sees the gradual militarization of civic space as being the logical outcome of a full-spectrum mindset, through which the vulnerabilities exposed by the infinitely possible translate into the infinitely dangerous becoming of our life-world system:

Full-spectrum paramilitary power enters the co-conditioning fray with the mission to act as a synergy dampener: to stanch perturbatory amplification and its intersystem propagation. It continually toggles from one pole of its civil–military operational continuum toward the other, settling preferentially on a setting in between. It moves in lock-step with incursions of threat potential, adopting forms as generically-singularly charged, and as proteiform in their eventual determinations as those of threat itself. It aspires to the singular-generic. It aspires to supercharge itself with a force of indeterminacy determined to be eventfully determined, as a counter to the accident. Its vocation is to be the *anti*-accident. The most visible form full-spectrum power takes in pursuit of its anti-accidental vocation is in the role of 'first responder'. This is power going out to meet the accident in rapid response, at the first flush of an eventfulness setting in. In this role, it takes many forms. The fabled first responder is the most visible figure of the hero in the 'waging of peace' against indiscriminate threat.[66]

– 4 –

On Divine Power

Moral Economy of Truth

We live in the age of liberal reason. This has resulted in the collapse of the space-time continuum that once held modern politics together. Power and politics have in fact been largely separated as the fundamental decisions which affect human lives take place beyond the participatory frameworks of national governments. Not everything, however, is completely novel. Contemporary liberal power in fact reveals a number of key 'remnants' (to borrow Giorgio Agamben's term) that allow us to gain real insight into the singularity of liberal rule and its defining transcendental principle. As Agamben intimates,

> [O]ur concept of history has been formed according to the theological paradigm of the revelation of a 'mystery' that is, at the same time, an 'economy', an organization, and a 'dispensation' of divine and human life. . . . [What is more,] from the beginning theology conceives divine life and the history of humanity as an *oikonomia*, that is, that theology is itself 'economic' and did not simply become so at a later time through secularization.[1]

This particular remnant is compelling. Transcendentally conceived, it can be argued, the early liberal humanist aspiration of creating a 'religion for humanity' was therefore not primarily about some inalienable commitment to rights. After all, this does not square empirically with the violent history of the liberal encounter. It found a more potent expression through an economizing force that could be morally universalizing as an internalizing proposition yet contingently applied without contradiction. If it is possible to deal with the problem of evil which has become so integral to discourses surrounding human-made catastrophe in the post-9/11 moment, this must be achieved by questioning the singular onto-theological expression of liberal power which is manifest in the mysterious workings of a divinely ordained economy of the living.

When George W. Bush declared that he wanted to 'rid the world of evil', not only was he making a confident claim about the eventual historical record; more profoundly still, he was making a philosophical declaration – a statement of truth – which made evil to be part *of this world*. Beyond the obvious ecclesiastical bearing this has upon the political, it necessarily followed that something in the order of the divine (unquestionable truth, goodness, justice) equally *belonged to this world*. As Baudrillard observed, despite the apparent disappearance of God, 'evil has not ceased to exist. On the contrary, it has grown, and sooner or later it explodes. Not evil as seen from a moral point of view, but something in reality itself which contradicts the operationalization of the world.'[2] While Baudrillard detected a progressive/regressive onto-theological schematic, in the immediate aftermath of 9/11 the use of the term set up rather superficial Manichaean divisions in which the world was neatly separated between the righteous and the wicked. As Bush himself once declared,

> We who stand on the other side of the line must be equally
> clear and certain in our convictions. We do love life, the
> life given to us and to all. We believe in the values that

uphold the dignity of life, tolerance, freedom, and the right of conscience. And we know that this way of life is worth defending. There is no neutral ground – no neutral ground – in the fight between civilization and terror, because there is no neutral ground between good and evil, freedom and slavery, life and death.[3]

This sentiment was not just a testimony to the value of life. Neither was it simply a testimony to the necessity for violence. It was a testimony to the onto-power of faith.

Bush was not alone in his troubles. 'Since Plato,' Charles Mathewes notes, 'what the West has called "philosophy" can be understood as an extended meditation on the implications of our experience of the tragic dimension of evil, for it reveals basic metaphysical problems inherent in the relation of human agency in the world.'[4] *Unde malum* – whence the evil? It is common to suggest that during the period of Christian rule the problem of evil was simply tied to God's will. While this is partly true, many contemporary philosophers have nevertheless noted how, long before enlightenment praxis, Saint Paul used theological concepts to instigate earthly change.[5] This built on the Augustinian tradition, which left a lasting impression by proposing that evil could never actually be eradicated *from* the world. Christianity thus provided the grounding for the organization of existential faith, which, as a matter of orthopraxis, anathematized those who did not share certain *ideals* and did not follow certain *practices*. While secularism undoubtedly had a significant impact by reworking the biblical story of the fall (see below), the secularization of the world has nevertheless been less convincing than secularists claimed. As Leo Strauss observed, 'What presents itself as the "secularization" of theological concepts will have to be understood, in the last analysis, as an adaptation of traditional theology to the intellectual climate produced by modern philosophy or science both natural and political.'[6] If modern concepts of evil needed to break with the natural accounts of evil, there is therefore nothing to say that secularism doesn't retain onto-theological tendencies or indeed drivers. That is to say, while ideas of original sin were an anathema to the modern sensibility, which placed the human central to objective scientific deliberations, the idea of responsibility for one's actions retained the possibility for its conceptual reworking. As Susan Neiman further explains, 'The problem of evil can be expressed in theological or secular terms, but it is fundamentally a problem about the intelligibility of the world as a whole. Thus it belongs neither to ethics or metaphysics but forms a link between the two.'[7]

No recent text has broached the problem of evil with more force than Hannah Arendt's *Eichmann in Jerusalem*. Certainly the most widely quoted among Arendt's conclusions from this study was the succinct verdict of the 'banality of evil'. This was a troubling thesis. While Nazism may appear monstrous, the trouble with Albert Eichmann lay precisely in the fact that according to psychological assessments he (alongside so many of his companions in crime) was not a monster or a sadist, but frighteningly normal: 'Half a dozen psychiatrists had certified him as "normal" – "More normal, at any rate, than I am after examining him", one of them was said to have exclaimed, while another had found that his whole psychological outlook, his attitude towards wife and children, mother and father, brothers, sisters and friends was "not only normal but most desirable."' Hence, the trouble with Eichmann was 'precisely that so many were like him, and that the many were neither perverted nor sadistic, that they were, and still are, terribly and terrifyingly normal. From the viewpoint of our legal institutions and our moral standards of judgment, this normality was much more terrifying than all the atrocities put together.'[8] This was not lost on Theodor Adorno, whose famous study into the 'Authoritarian Personality' suggested that the forms of self-selection so evident in the case of the Nazi experience were determined more by natural than by nurtured predispositions of individual character.[9] This proved to be challenging. If the likes of Eichmann were normal, anyone of us, given the 'right conditions', would be capable of acting in a way that thoughtlessly engages with violence. The question therefore appeared to be less about psychopathic genes or demonic characteristics. Instead we should be troubled by the conditioning of situations so that calculated violence becomes normalized and routine.

Arendt's 'Banality of Evil' hypothesis complemented her wider criticisms of modernity more generally as put forward in *The Human Condition*.[10] As she observed, when 'life processes' become synonymous with the 'necessity' of labour and consumption, life itself becomes a technical function (*teche*) that is stripped of political action (*vita activa*). Life is thus reduced to what Arendt terms the *animal laborans*, so that work simply corresponds to the fabrication of an *artificial* world of things, inasmuch as contemporary life is caught up within an instrumentalist vision of being. The social world, in this regard, appears like one giant laboratory that leads humanity to desire ever more power and control over the world of *physis*. This resonated with Arendt's understanding of the Nazi experience. She understood that the 'supreme ends' of fascism were not simply defined by mass slaughter, but, more pervasively, what was truly abhorrent was the 'ghastly experiment of eliminating, under scientifically controlled conditions, spontaneity itself as an expression of human behaviour and transforming the human personality into a mere thing'.[11] This is what she meant by the phrase 'everything is possible'. By subsuming politics within a technologized vision of species-being, it is possible to dominate the subject to the evacuation of the political sphere within the remit of law.

Arendt's concept of evil was troubling. While she proclaimed in 1945 that 'the problem of evil will be the fundamental question of post-war intellectual life in Europe', as Richard Bernstein noted, 'most post-war intellectuals avoided any direct confrontation with the problem',[12] a

lack of engagement that was arguably in part driven by a
form of intellectual policing that wanted to deal with
Nazism through the simple frame of regime theory.
However, 9/11 brought the concept back with a venge-
ance. What is more, inverting the Arendtian problematic,
this event had all the hallmarks of a post-industrial nihilism that demanded rescuing something out of the horrors
of rule so critically questioned. 9/11 represented a 'historical turning point' that would change our discussion of evil
since it resurrected a philosophical problem that had been
largely dormant for some considerable time.[13] Central to
Neiman's explanation was the nature of the catastrophe.
She believed that this event was comparable to the succes-
sion of earthquake, fire, and flooding that engulfed Lisbon
in 1755 and marked the beginning of the modern theory
of evil: 'The parallels are undeniable. The suddenness and
speed of the attack resembled natural catastrophe. There
was no warning. There was no message.' Since the event
was therefore blind to any meaningful form of political
justice, it 'created the kind of fear that made most of us
know we had not, until then, understood the meaning of
the word terror. Like earthquakes, terrorists strike at
random: who lives and does not depends on contingencies
that cannot be preserved or prevented.'[14] If Lisbon therefore led Voltaire and Rousseau to debate the value of
onto-theological explanations for evil in the world,
Neimann sees theology making a forceful re-entry as it
comes to terms with global catastrophes of epic proportions. In this sense, as William Connolly explains, evil
comes to designate some 'lived experience' that unsettles
what is taken for granted: 'Evil surprises; it liquidates
sedimented habits of moral trust; it foments categorical
uncertainty; it issues in a fervent desire to restore closure
to a dirempted world; and it generates imperious demands
to take revenge on the guilty parties.'[15]

It would be somewhat easy to critique Bush's demands
for revenge by drawing attention to his well-documented
religiosity. This would allow us to map out a simple cosmic

narrative of war in which clear distinctions between the righteous and the wicked could readily be established. While this conveniently resurrects familiar Schmittean lines of argument, albeit in a more problematic onto-theological way, there is no attempt to question how the concept of evil has been assimilated into the contemporary liberal sensibility in a more sophisticated progressive fashion. That is to say, while the with us/against us narra-tive evidences familiar structural modes of engagement, this architecture conceals a far more radical account which is more suited to our complex, adaptive, dynamic, and radically interconnected times. John Gray argues that '[m] odern politics is a chapter in the history of religion.'[16] Fully invested in the inevitability of universal progress, we retain a 'belief that history must be understood not in terms of the causes of events but in terms of its purpose, which is the salvation of humanity'.[17] As Christian eschatology returns in the form of universal emancipation, so we turn to a temporal problem of earthly conditions, not some final spiritual judgement: 'Theories of modernization are not scientific hypotheses – but theodicies – narratives of providence and redemption presented in the jargon of social science.'[18] Evil as such becomes integral to purist notions of human progress, setting out in the clearest terms that human life is forever burdened with the guilt of its own (un)making. The Nobel laureate speech given by Barack Obama – tragically ironic yet most revealing in its award to a wartime liberal President – provides a wonder-fully fitting account:

> Violence never brings permanent peace. It solves no social problem: it merely creates new and more complicated ones. As someone who stands here as a direct consequence of Dr King's life work, I am living testimony to the moral force of non-violence. . . . But as a head of state sworn to protect and defend my nation, I cannot be guided by their examples alone. I face the world as it is, and cannot stand idle in the face of threats to the American people. For make no mistake: *Evil does exist in the world*. A non-violent movement could not have halted Hitler's armies.

Negotiations cannot convince al Qaeda's leaders to lay down their arms. To say that force may sometimes be necessary is not a call to cynicism – it is recognition of history; the imperfections of man and the limits of reason.[19]

These connections between 'evil' and 'the imperfections of man' provide some insight into the onto-theological dimensions to liberal rule. It is not that people are born evil. Evil is accounted for by the actions/events which accompany the person. Evil, in other words, is *productive* and *performative*. This approach certainly resonated with Tony Blair, whose 'faith in humanity' was invoked on numerous occasions to justify the War on Terror. As he insisted when addressing the Labour Party conference in October 2001: 'There is no compromise possible with such people, no meeting of minds, no point of understanding with such terror. Just a choice: defeat it or be defeated by it.'[20] For Blair, however, there is something much more at stake here than the mere defence of things. Humanity is realized only by the wars which are fought in its name:

> Our ultimate weapon is not our guns but our beliefs. . . . Ours are not Western values. They are the universal values of the human spirit and anywhere, anytime, ordinary people are given the chance to choose, the choice is the same. Freedom not tyranny. . . . The spread of freedom is the best security for the free. It is our last line of defence and our first line of attack.[21]

Evil, along with the potential catastrophe it promises, is an integral part of the human condition. It is therefore no mere term of Manichaean dialectic. It is a living and breathing entity which is an infectious part of this world. Something of the 'mystery', however, still remains. As Zygmunt Bauman explains, 'Disasters brought about by human actions arrive from an opaque world, strike at random, in places impossible to anticipate, and escape to defy the kind of explanation which sets human actions apart from all other events: explanation by *motives* or *purposes*. Above all – the evil caused by the immoral actions of humans appears ever more unimaginable *in principle.*[22] Evil from this perspective still therefore defies *pre facto* intelligibility.

The Transcendental Principle

Ever since Hobbes wrote his *Leviathan*, the concept of sovereignty has been aligned with the unification of life. Wonderfully depicted in the famous illustration which accompanies his manifesto, the body of the sovereign always presumes the given unity of the body-politic. Security, then, if there is to be any, insists upon this imagined or transcendental figuration. What confirms political wholeness, the unity of the authentic political subjectivity, infers a completion in the order of things, so that oneness becomes the natural and intended condition proper to politically qualified life. While many contemporary theorists point to the sovereign contract as marking a distinct break with the *Ancien Régime*, the idea that the practice of sovereignty still reflects a powerful Christian eschatology is compelling. Schmitt is a key thinker here. As he explained, 'All significant concepts of the modern theory of the state are secularized theological concepts'.[23] Hence, for James Martel,

> Carl Schmitt articulates exactly how this notion of a break itself disguises the crucial (and theological) continuities with medieval and Christian notions of sovereignty. . . . In this way, modernity has a new 'political theology', one that serves to disguise both the more traditional Christian inheritance of the modern state as well as the fact that the modern sovereign, like the Christian God, continues to decide upon the exception.[24]

Derrida is famed in equal measure for expressing similar sentiments. Sovereignty, he argues, evidences a kind of 'ipsocentric[ism]' which points to a 'long cycle of political theology that is at once paternalistic and patriarchal, and thus masculine, in the filiation of father–son–brother'. Such ipsocentricism is 'revived or taken over' by a newer version of itself, moving from the overtly religious and monarchic forms of sovereignty to 'the unavowed political theology . . . of the sovereignty of the people, that is of democratic sovereignty'.[25]

While authors like Wendy Brown have rightly pointed out that the sovereign system which developed out of the Treaty of Westphalia (especially in its theological form) is facing lasting crises (hence its openly aggressive theological expressions) as it faces limitless and uncontrollable forces beyond any measure of control,[26] it is arguable that these processes have been slowly unravelling for some considerable time. We could in fact argue that the sovereign project as invested in the absolute myth of the nation could not be resurrected out of the ashes of the Second World War. We are reminded here by Max Ernst's surreal *Europe after the Rain II*, whose violent-scape brilliantly captures the scene of sovereign abandon. Nothing remains except the beastly figures who are haunted by the scars of war and the memories of a once distant past that is impossible to reclaim. None of this was lost on Arendt. While it would take a number of decades before traces of the Westphalian critique were common across many academic disciplines – that is, the now familiar concerns such as 'crises of democracy', 'crises of identity', 'crises of meaning', 'crises of belonging', and so on – she fully understood in 1958 that the world was beginning to be transformed in ways that would leave a lasting political impression:

> Only now has man taken full possession of his mortal dwelling place and gathered infinite horizons, which were temptingly and forbiddingly open to all previous ages, into a globe whose majestic outlines and detailed surface he knows as he knows the lines in the palm of his hand. Precisely when the immensity of available space on earth was discovered, the famous shrinkage of the earth began, until eventually in our world each man is as much an inhabitant of the earth as he is an inhabitant of his country. Men now

live in an earth-wide continuous whole where even the
notion of distance, still inherent in the most perfectly
unbroken contiguity of its parts, has yielded before the
onslaught of speed. Speed has conquered space.[27]

So how is the transcendent field conceived if sovereign
power alone can no longer unify the species? And what is
the unifying principle for humanity if we assume that the
imperfections of man will always stand in the way of universal togetherness? This requires a return to Kant, whose
relevance to the contemporary global imaginary is not in
any doubt. 'These days,' Bauman writes, 'it is a hard task
to find a learned study of our most recent history that
would not quote Kant's Universal History as a supreme
authority and source of inspiration for all debate of world
citizenship.'[28] Kant's ideas express the kind of optimism
that has inspired the minds of all modernist visionaries,
and is seen by the advocates of 'liberal peace' to outline
the only credible conditions of possibility for global security in the twenty-first century.[29] Michael Doyle, for
instance, has argued that 'the importance of Kant' is not
only that he makes us appreciate that we cannot study
'systemic relations in isolation', but since 'he anticipates
for us the ever-widening pacification of a Liberal pacific
union', he outlines the necessary preconditions so that
'perpetual peace will have been established'.[30] From this
perspective, Kant becomes the intellectual icon for a world
of radical uncertainty. It is not a case, therefore, of questioning whether or not Kant is relevant to the contemporary situation. If Kant troubles, it is precisely because his
work is significant. While the debates concerning how best
to achieve his vision sharply divide liberal internationalists
and cosmopolitan theorists in terms of the grand structural
design for juridical power, very little attention is paid to
the ontological debt owed to his legacy. Too many people
are content to call themselves Kantian cosmopolitans
without ever questioning the ontological significance of
this claim in light of his wider intellectual corpus. As Mary

Midgley succinctly put it, the prevailing 'tendency' when dealing with Kant is to 'treat a few quotations from the rather dramatic opening sections of the *Groundwork* as his last words on individuality and freedom'.[31]

Kant is unrivalled in the *greatness* of his ideas. Even his most vocal critics, such as Gilles Deleuze, who condemn him for being 'completely stifling' still recognize him to be one of the 'great philosophers' whose capacity for creating new concepts was 'absolutely frightening'.[32] Kant's *Critique of Pure Reason* tends to be signalled out for particular attention. This pivotal text was, according to Deleuze, a 'tremendous event in philosophy' in the sense that it effectively created an entirely new temporality which truly radicalized the way we think and relate to the world. Kant's successful opposition to the classical dogmatic modes of theological subjugation would shatter for the very first time the disjunctive coupling (appearances/essences) which served to bind life to cosmological time. Thus, following Copernicus, the Kantian Revolution of the mind not only placed man at the centre of the universe, it effectively enabled us to be liberated from the world of heavenly destiny by installing in its place a more immanent form of critical thought. Thus for Deleuze, it was Kant, not Descartes, who was the first to instigate a revolution in the way the modern problem of *immanence* was actually posed. Foucault expressed similar sentiments:

> The question which, I believe, for the first time appears in this text [*What is Enlightenment?*] by Kant is the question of today, the question about the present, about what is our actuality: what is happening today? What is happening right now? And what is this right now we are all in which defines the moment at which I am writing? . . . In Descartes, you will not find a question like: 'What precisely is this present to which I belong?' Now it seems to me the question Kant answers, that he in fact is prompted to answer, because someone had raised it, is another question. It is not simply: what in the present can determine this or that philosophical decision? The question is about the

present and is, at first, concerned with the determination of a certain element of the present that needs to be recognized, distinguished, deciphered, among others. What is it in the present that now makes sense for philosophical reflection?[33]

The familiar Kantian narrative suggests that the unifying principle for humanity is located in its juridical commitment to rights and justice. Advocates turn here to Kant's thesis on 'Perpetual Peace' along with his idea on the 'Kingdom of Ends' in order to propose new political architectures. Humanity, from this perspective, makes itself real on account of its commitment to those constituted forms of allegiance which reason human togetherness to be the natural order of things. While this structural approach to Kantianism is upheld by a formidable school of intellectual thought, some have pointed out that this frightening juridical architecture effectively undermines Kant's entire critical endeavour. Michael Hardt and Antonio Negri, for instance, argue that 'the leitmotif of Kantian philosophy' is the 'necessity of the transcendental, the impossibility of every form of immediacy, the exorcism of every vital figure in the apprehension and action of being'. Kant therefore 'throws us back into the crisis of modernity with full awareness when he poses the discovery of the subject itself as a crisis, but this crisis is made into an apology of the transcendental as the unique and exclusive horizon of knowledge and action. The world becomes an architecture of ideal forms, the only reality conceded to us.'[34] While these critiques of Kant's idealism are justified, our contemporary concerns with his legacy need to move beyond the structural and turn to the completion of his intellectual corpus: namely with a return to the ontological problem of evil. This is a crucial ontological step. If it can be said that Jean-Jacques Rousseau was the first to question philosophically whether it was possible to have a modern concept of evil by directly connecting human suffering with the realm of human action, Kant replaces sovereign theology with the *eschatology of life*.

Kant faced a terrible crisis in his work. Having put forward his thesis on 'A Perpetual Peace', he subsequently came to the conclusion that it was impossible to achieve. This in many senses is reminiscent of his account of the universal, for while Kant insisted that we needed metaphysics in order to think, nevertheless he lamented that the world was always going to be inaccessible to us. Humans are not omnipotent. Neither can we access what is universal to thought. Like the universal, perpetual peace was therefore an ideal that was continually undermined by the limits of our reason. 'Kant's Shame' was, however, crucial to the progressive imaginary since the aporetic character of life demanded continual working. Kant therefore made sense of life's dangerous (in the sense that it prevents universal completion) and ultimately irresolvable (in the sense that there is no lasting solution) imperfections by introducing the concept of 'radical evil'. This was significant, if not controversial. It would, after all, present a different reading of his earlier *Critique* which sought to displace God's will with that of the human subject. How can we explain this? It is, of course, true that Kant remained deeply religious throughout his life. This turn to the problem of evil can therefore be partly explained by his Christian affinities or at least a desire to reaffirm his theological values. To rest upon this religiosity, however, misses the point entirely. Kant's account of radical evil is actually fundamental to his lasting intellectual corpus since it binds the subject to the world in such a way that the governance of life assumes a moral imperative. In doing so, Kant shows his appreciation for the needs of modern power, so that his thesis of the infinite ideal (everything is possible) can also be translated into a rationality of government (everything is dangerous). So while Kant is rightly famous for criticizing traditional theistic arguments, he prepared the way for a more authentic way of rationally affirming some divine existence.

Kant puts forward his concept of radical evil in *Religion within the Limits of Reason Alone* by displacing 'original sin' with an account of human imperfection that is nevertheless innate to the human condition: '[W]hatever man may have done in adopting a good disposition, and, indeed, however steadfastly he may have persevered in conduct comfortable to such a disposition, *he nevertheless started from evil*, and this debt he can by no possibility wipe out.'[35] Evil, in other words, was 'rooted in humanity itself'.[36] Hence, while humanity by nature has a 'good predisposition', this is infected by an 'evil propensity'. Crucially, here, the term 'propensity' does not necessarily point to some universal orientation. Neither does it accept that evil reveals timeless qualities (Kant, after all, didn't provide any categorical framework to test the evil hypothesis). Propensity is always a propensity *towards*. It is a call to action. This is central to Kant's theory. As he further suggested, 'We cannot start from an innocence natural to us . . . we must begin with the incessant counteraction against it. Since this only leads to a progress, endlessly continuing.'[37] Importantly, given that the imperfections of life meant that life alone was incapable of mastering its own destiny, Kant turned to the theological concept of 'grace' as being capable of providing 'divine assistance'. Kant takes this up specifically in Book 2 of *Religion within the Limits of Reason Alone*, in which he critiques the concept of 'grace' as it is understood through the sacrifice of Jesus Christ. Kant's criticism here is that the symbol of eternal suffering prevents the believer from seeking his or her own *self-improvement*. This proves significant. As Martin Matuštík observes, Kant 'keeps open the metaphysical access of even corrupted free will to moral repentance, as if grace always and already sustained progress and transformation of the human race'.[38]

Since Kant's concepts of evil and grace are fully aligned to a progressive imaginary – that is, they reveal an *enduring presence* – both require abandoning the search for eternal *origins*. Evil has no fixed 'essence' or related static mode of 'being'. Neither is there a 'beginning in time' for evil, except that which resides in the subject's free will. It emerges as we unleash our human potential. It is therefore altogether anthropocentric (a question of agency) since the ambivalent body enables things to go terrifyingly wrong. This is not, however, a source of lament. It conditions actually what is necessary: 'We can already anticipate that this duty will need the presupposition of another idea, namely, of a higher moral being through whose universal organization the forces of single individuals, insufficient on their own, are united for a common effect.'[39] Understanding the nature of this unity of the singular through 'common effect' is crucial for it begins to map out relations between moral evil (innate propensity) and historical forms of development (divine intervention). The regenerative type of dangerous agency Kant puts forward must be matched by a system behind the self (what we may term 'the principle behind the principle' of humanity) that is capable of dealing with emergent potentials. As Sharon Anderson-Gold writes:

> Kant's claim that evil was the 'character of the species' was itself foundational for the way in which the moral life of the individual should be understood. . . . Since historical progress is an attribute of the species, the source of this progress must be in some moral attribute of humanity that, for judgements of moral development, is the functional equivalent of the good will. . . . Kant identifies the human predisposition to morality as a historical operative cause. . . . That radical evil affects the entire species binds the destiny of each to all both as a matter of global interdependence and as a matter of historical legacy. . . . This means that genuine solutions to the problem of evil will require international institutions dedicated to intergenerational economic justice and eco-logically sustainable development.[40]

Kant's concept of 'radical evil' enjoys a privileged position in our contemporary understanding. This is understandable given its relevance to all universalizing modernist narratives. As Kant maintained, moral evil cannot be divorced from global progress since it tells us something fundamental about the character of human life. It certainly resonates with Obama's account of the 'imperfections of man'. In this respect, Kant provides a 'cognitive framework appropriate to the special status of human action as both an empirical phenomena and a manifestation of transcendental freedom'.[41] He provides us with the moral imperative to act towards specific historical goals. While it is common for these goals to assume juridical qualities, as Kant insinuated, something above and beyond structural arrangements would be necessary if any semblance of lasting peace was to be established. It is not without coincidence that Kant shifts his attention in Book 1 of *Religion within the Limits of Reason Alone* away from the individual to 'the species'. As Allen Wood noted, while Kant's notion of evil invariably links human action to the transcendental level, it also functions 'systematically by means of an examination of the sources, extent, and limits of human capacity'.[42] Moving beyond structural explanations, Kant's transcendental principle is what we may therefore term 'The Divine Economy of Life'. It proposes a human–divine partnership through which salvation is tied to moral (re)generation. This is not simply grand theorizing; it reflects the empirical reality of the world in which liberal theorists and policy practitioners have been reworking the concept of rights on more progressive socio-economic lines for some considerable time. This non-foundational metaphysics evidences the more purposeful legacy of the Kantian project, for whenever we say that something is 'unnecessary', we are stepping directly towards the Kantian problem of 'radical evil' in which the transcendental principle for rule gracefully intervenes with its own enduring presence. And like all transcendental principles, its inaccessibility to us still ensures that it retains something of the mystery of a divine supplement:

Even the hypothesis of a *practical* application of this idea [of grace] is wholly self-contradictory. For the employment of this idea would presuppose a rule concerning the good that (for a particular end) we must ourselves *do* in order to accomplish something, whereas to await a work of grace means exactly the opposite, namely, that the good (morally good) is not our deed but the deed of another being, and that we can therefore achieve it by doing nothing, which contradicts itself. Hence we have to admit a work of grace as something incomprehensible.[43]

Fallen Freedom

Kant effectively offered a reworking of the biblical story of the fall. It is not that people are born evil; however, from the moment they enter into the world, they are burdened with the guilt of their own (un)making. As Kant would write, '[W]e may presuppose evil to be subjectively necessary to every man, even the best.'[44] Gordon Michalson Jr captured the implications of this tremendous moral burden majestically with the title *Fallen Freedom*. As Michalson explains, 'Kant's disturbing account of the way the free will turns against its own best interests suggests that each of us carries a malevolent stowaway that could come to life at any moment.'[45] This evidences 'the terrible paradox that our fallenness is our own doing – terrible, because within the Kantian framework this amounts to reason virtually turning against its own best interests, and freedom freely producing its own most severe debility'.[46] This has a profound ontological bearing. As Michalson fully appreciates, this concept of the fall is premised on an account of life that is forever moving between points of potential pro/regress: 'Kant must ultimately show that, in the course of moral regeneration, the "self" that is saved or regenerated is the same "self" that had fallen – for otherwise there would be no moral symmetry to the salvation process.'[47] Crucially, despite universal protestations, not only does this symmetry deny us the ability to specifically identify any timeless qualities to goodness/evil, but the fallen body also paves the way for continual vigilance and intervention on account of the fact that the human condition forever remains dangerously unfulfilled:

> In Kant's handling of the problem of moral regeneration, we have the confluence of a characteristically modern concern for the autonomy of the moral subject and the biblical tradition's preoccupation with divine action exercised for the sake of the salvation of a fallen humanity. . . . Kant is delicately walking a fine line between autonomy and grace, free will and providence, appealing to the human dimension so as to have the result be a truly *moral* regeneration, while referring in vague but substantive ways to divine action so as to underwrite the possibility of what radical evil seems to make possible.[48]

It is often said that Kant was buried for two hundred years only to be rediscovered. That Kantianism has been revived with such formidable force therefore tells us something about Kant's relevance to contemporary understandings of power and governance. This brings us to the Kantian problem of the 'infinite', which correlates with the contemporary ontology of life in which spatial and temporal limits have succumbed to an order of infinite enclosure. Kant famously divided the universe into phenomena and noumena. The former relate to what we can intelligibly access. The latter are beyond all contemporary understanding. Importantly, for Kant, while we are necessarily imperfect on account of our phenomenological capabilities, nevertheless things remain spatially and temporally accessible. This refers us to Kant's 'infinite ideal'. While there is a concept of space-time that it is purely inaccessible (hence purely infinite), there is also an infinite horizon of earthy possibilities which, although existing beyond current epistemic guidance, is nevertheless open to encounter. As Adrian W. Moore explains, '[T]he Kantian starting point [is] that we are, epistemologically and in a metaphysical sense, finite. We find ourselves merely part of a world which is completely independent of us and which, in its own self-contained totality, is infinite.' Hence, in order 'to know anything about it', we must 'become responsive to what surrounds us'.[49] This brings us directly to the heart of Kant's metaphysical project, which, in the process of inserting the infinite into a measurable totality (hence making it phenomenologically accessible), proposes an alternative form of infinity that is based upon one's capacity/propensity to act within the realms of lived perception. The following passage is worth quoting at length:

> Two things fill the mind with ever new and increasing admiration and awe, the more often and the more steadily they are reflected upon: the starry heaven above me and the moral law within me. . . . The first begins at the place which I occupy in the external world of sense, and broadens the connection in which I stand into the unsurveyable magnitude of worlds beyond worlds and systems of systems, and moreover into the limitless times of their periodic motion, its beginning and continuation. The second begins at my invisible self, my personality, and depicts me in a world which has true infinity. . . . The first view of a countless multitude of worlds annihilates as it were my importance as that of an animal creature, which must give back to the planet (a mere speck in the universe) the matter of which it was formed, after it has been provided for a short time (we know not how) with vital power. The second, on the other hand, infinitely raises my worth as that of an intelligence by my personality, in which the moral law reveals to me a life independent of animality and even of the whole world of sense, at least as far as can be inferred from the destination assigned to my existence by this law, a destination which is not restricted to the conditions and limits of this life, but reaches into the infinity.[50]

While Kant offers an important distinction in terms of conceptualizing infinity both in a phenomenal and a noumenal sense of the term, the infinite still points to an ambivalent space of possibly. Ironically, then, while Kant is presented as a universalist, his starry eyes reveal 'an expression of his sense of the sheer contingency of things'.[51] Everything needs to be possible or else free will is actually constrained *in principle*. As Moore further explains, 'When he [Kant] acknowledges a regulative use of our Idea of the world and denies a constitutive (non-regulative) use of it, he is surely saying something very like what is said by those who affirm that the world is potentially infinite (and to that extent exists) but deny that it is actually infinite.'[52] The infinite, in other words, can be infinitely good (infinite progress) or infinitely dangerous (infinite regress). From the perspective of the earthly fall, of course, it is the latter which underwrites the former. As Michalson further detects, 'Kant depicts the fall into radical evil: perversely, freedom seems to have more leeway in the direction of the fall than in the direction of moral recovery.'[53] Human effort thus necessarily requires some form of divine assistance in order to deal with the weight of its own innate capacities to act against its better outcomes. While this may appear contradictory to claims of secularization, it actually proves completely compatible with a system of rule which needs an innate concept of dangerous imperfection to condition the possibility for a universal mission. In this regard, 'Kant is not closing off an era with his equivocal and unstable account of the relation between human capacity and divine aid, but inaugurating a new one', for in order to take the problem of moral evil seriously, 'there is a need to place limitations on human autonomy, inasmuch as autonomy seems incapable of saving itself.'[54]

There is an important caveat to address here. While nobody is exempt from the propensity to act with evil intent (even though we may not know that our actions will be judged in such terms), it was easier to attribute the fall to groups of beings acting in unison. For Kant, the surest way to counter the fall was through the progressive unification of the species. Logically inverted, the surest evidence of the fall is exhibited when lives act in a way that challenges the normative standard. Culture is therefore absolutely central to the Kantian moral economy. It proposes the maxim that to arise from the fall (hence countenance evil in the process) we must *collectively produce something better*. While the Kantian cosmopolitan vision is therefore fully bound up with concerns about culture and its development, it is equally concerned with issues of cultural backwardness. This brings us to a more controversial legacy. Many of the familiar key figures of the 'enlightenment' have been rightly criticized for their racist tendencies.[55] Kant, however, tends to escape this criticism since his ideas can be associated with the promise of rights. This is completely fallacious. While writing upon the conditions of non-white peoples extensively in his anthropological studies, for instance, Kant was completely silent on the visible reality of the slave trade. Contemporaneously this is perhaps comparable to a leading political philosopher of justice having nothing whatsoever to say about the violent and exploitative trade in prostitution which savagely exploits women and children on a global scale. Kant's silence, however, wasn't incidental. He laid the intellectual foundations for moralizing forms of biopolitical rule which, offering a sophisticated racial assay of the species, (dis)qualified life in terms of the way it circulates as a self-organizing, politically differentiating, culturally enriching, productive entity.

Let's return for a moment to a more familiar reading of the Kantian project. In his *Metaphysics of Morals*, Kant articulates a more acceptable postulate of contemporary moral philosophy that 'every man is born free since he has *not yet* committed a crime'.[56] This 'original freedom' is said to be common to all peoples upon entering the world. There is, however, an important caveat to this account of freedom. Having committed no crime is declared only since *no action* is yet assumed to have taken place. A person is free from crime without having acted upon the world. What original freedom Kantianism proposes is therefore pre-subjective. Indeed, as we have already discovered, since this pre-subjective freedom is actually more defined by its 'propensity to evil' (i.e. until one acts in a manner which illustrates the good, then life is burdened and evil triumphs), Kantian ontology opens life to the most continual of progressive assays. There is nothing hidden from us here. While Kant disputed the idea that bondage should be passed down ancestral lines – 'Even if [an individual] has become a *personal* subject by his crime, his subjection cannot be *inherited*, because he has incurred it only by his own guilt'[57] – his anthropological writings nuance this inheritance by shedding more light on the purity of origins, which he explicitly accuses of being 'darkened' over time.[58] Since 'whiteness', in other words, is the standardizing 'stem genus' from which all other races descend, progressive social formations also reveal relative degrees of decay: '[T]he colour of humans goes through all the shades of yellow, brown and dark brown until it becomes black in the hot parts of the earth.'[59]

Free Market Morality

The idea that the economy reveals a transcendental morality allows for a considered genealogy. Adam Smith's 'invisible hand', for instance, has obvious theological connotations as the market is seen to be guided by benevolent divine laws which illustrate providence at work.[60] As Smith famously explained,

> As every individual . . . directing that industry in such a manner as its produce may be of the greatest value, he intends only his own gain, and is in this, as in many other cases, led by an invisible hand to promote an end which was no part of his intention. Nor is it always the worse for society that it was no part of it.[61]

While Smith evidently gestures towards the biblical, Max Weber made the theological connection more explicit in his landmark *The Protestant Ethic and the Spirit of Capitalism*. The question which occupied Weber in particular was simple and yet fundamental. How is it possible to account for our allegiance to transcendental forms of power which condition the possible unreservedly? For Weber, the answer was to be found in a Calvinist 'calling' which, unlike the passive reception of the pious Lutherinian subject, understood production to be a *spiritual end* in itself. The 'spirit of capitalism' is 'an historical individual: a complex of elements associated in historical reality which we united into a conceptual whole from the standpoint of their cultural significance'.[62] The Christian subject therefore glorifies God in life by demonstrating social achievement. Since labour appears to be a theological means and end in itself, the lack of a work ethic is symptomatic of the lack of grace. Importantly, for Weber, material aesthetics (in terms of acquisition, the measure of quality, and the justification for mass accumulation) is crucial to this process. There needs to be a materialization to the glory. Providential purpose needs to evidence qualitative and quantitative results for it to capture the imagination of the hard-working subject.

Agamben's genealogy exposes more fully the connections between modern political economy and the eschatological. In his *The Kingdom and the Glory*, he sets out to establish 'the reasons why power in the West has assumed the form of an *oikonomia,* that is, a government of men'.[63] For Agamben, the notion of a divine economy can actually be traced back to a decisive moment in the history of Christian theology in which questions pertaining to the Holy Trinity found practical meaning. It is therefore possible to derive from Christian theology a 'political theology, which founds the transcendence of sovereign power on the single God, and economic theology, which replaces this transcendence with the idea of an *oikonomia,* conceived as an immanent ordering – domestic and not political in a strict sense – of both divine and human life'.[64] From this perspective, the economy is a 'synonym for the providential unfolding of history according to eschatological design'.[65] Such a divinity does not propose any natural foundation for being. It overcomes the history of being as a metaphysical praxis. What is therefore commonly termed biopolitics, Agamben believes, especially today, remains concerned with the 'divine governance' of peoples according to some divine plan for earthly salvation. As he writes elsewhere, 'Rather than the proclaimed end of history, we are, in fact, witnessing the incessant though aimless motion of this machine, which, in a sort of colossal parody of theological *oikonomia*, has assumed the legacy of the providential governance of the world, this machine (true to the original eschatological vocation of providence) is leading us to catastrophe.'[66]

For Negri, this attempt to bring economy, political theology, and biopolitics into close relation is significant. It enables Agamben to nuance (hence move beyond the structural limitations of) his own juridical paradigm, 'showing how economy becomes a simple agency of theological-political power: an exercise, thus, in the worldly reproduction of social life'.[67] Echoing Agamben, what therefore becomes 'the true problem' is 'not sovereignty but government, not the king but the minister, not the law but the police force, that is, the state machine that they form and keep in motion'.[68] In order to do any justice to Agamben's claim that modernity has carried on the theological project via providential *oikonomia*, it is now necessary to understand how the economy has become indelibly tied to the global problem of unnecessary suffering. This brings us to the legacy of the Second World War. While Kant inaugurates the moral imperative underwriting modern forms of biopolitical rule, the horrors of Nazism justified this imperative's imperative. The spectre of the Third Reich both haunts and conditions the liberal imaginary to the extent that its occurrence has subsequently given sure moral purchase to the attempts at strategizing planetary life. Nazism could not then be seen to be a tragedy that happened to European Jewry alone; it has become the model against which all human imperfections (political, economic, social, cultural, or otherwise) could be ultimately judged.[69] This has had a lasting political impact. Not only has the refrain 'never again' been used to create protective enclaves for endangered peoples (a policy in itself which reveals the highly contingent application of the liberal responsibility to protect); it has also been deployed to sanction forms of interventionism that have ultimately led to the collapse of the Westphalian pretence. While the trauma associated with Nazism therefore destroyed the very idea of humanity as a concept the moment it seemed to be gaining widespread political currency, it has nevertheless become the liberal condition of possibility par excellence. That is to say, while the Holocaust in particular categorically denies any meaningful philosophical intelligibility – especially if one takes the original task of the *philos* to be the order of friendship – every shameful lasting memory it provides resurrects humanistic impulses out of the ashes of its most troubling episode.

With many of the inter-war problems – not least the rise of Nazism – being attributed to socialist orientations, the scene was set for a revival of liberal thought in which the free play of economic forces became synonymous with the political war against totalitarianism in all its forms. Critical to this revival in liberal fortunes were the intellectual contributions provided by the Austrian and Chicago schools of economic thought. The work of Friedrich von Hayek in particular struck a precise chord. In his influential work *The Road to Serfdom*, not only did he offer a damning indictment of socialism by equating it with the rise of fascist power, he also managed to revive the largely dormant moral argument for economic design, while rescuing the theory of the state inasmuch as it was recognized to provide a necessary regulatory and policing function essential to the secure functioning of the market economy.[70] Indeed, for Hayek, not only was the free market the best possible model for dealing with the economic problems of more efficient production and fairer distribution, more pressing, since it was inextricably bound with individual freedom and liberty, was the fact that it came equipped with its own moral and political armoury.[71] In short, for Hayek, given that the political problems the world faced could be reduced to a matter of economic organization, the economic question is by its very nature a question of moral importance and political persuasion:

> The so-called economic freedom which the planners promise us means precisely that we are to be relieved of the necessity of solving our own economic problems and the bitter choices which this often involves are to be made for us. Since under modern conditions we are for almost everything dependent on means which our fellow men provide, economic planning would involve direction of almost the whole of our life. There is hardly an aspect of it, from our primary needs to our relations with our family and friends, from the nature of our work to the use of our leisure, over which the planner would not exercise his 'conscious control'.[72]

The crux of Hayek's argument here is quite straightforward. Quite simply, since the false tyrannical promises of 'planning for freedom' had been followed, then, in the process, societies had fundamentally abandoned the truly enlightened liberal ideal of man as a free economic and political animal who was capable of mastering his own moral destiny through considered choice. This abandonment had disastrous consequences in the sense that it was the dangerous seduction of central planning that had taken us on an amoral detour which constrained the intellectual and creative potential inherent to a free market society. The liberated subject was, in other words, being suffocated beneath the bureaucratic and oppressive weight of planned institutionalism. Hayek thus called for a return of key principles of laissez-faire liberalism, which, attending specifically to the freeing up of economic activity, led to the emancipation of the political subject on a planetary scale. As Hayek explains: '[I]n no other field has the world yet paid so dearly for the abandonment of nineteenth-century liberalism as in the field where the retreat began: in international relations.'[73] Through Hayek, not only, then, was a conscious call made to challenge the traditional political integrities enshrined in the principles of Westphalia since they actually stood in the way of global emancipation, but in the process of replacing this with a truly effective global political economy there was also an intellectual obligation to settle the political at all costs:

> We must make the building of a free society once more an intellectual adventure, a deed of courage. What we lack is a liberal Utopia, a program which seems neither a mere defense of things as they are nor a diluted kind of socialism, but a truly liberal radicalism. . . . Unless we can make the philosophic foundations of a free society once more a living intellectual issue, and its implementation a task which challenges the ingenuity and imagination of our liveliest minds, the prospects of freedom are indeed dark. But if we can regain that belief in power of ideas which was the mark of liberalism at its best, the battle is not lost.[74]

Milton Friedman, in his landmark text *Capitalism and Freedom*, added further intellectual weight to this cause. Noting the etymological misappropriation of the term 'liberal', he sought to emphasize both its political and economic heritage. Thus, running counter to those highly reductionist approaches to liberal power which simply attended to the political concerns with freedom and rights, Friedman noted how the most enlightened and influential liberal luminaries, including Immanuel Kant, Jeremy Bentham, John Locke, Jean-Jacques Rousseau, Montesquieu, Thomas Paine, David Hume, and John Stuart Mill, were also profound thinkers of economy. It would therefore be a mistake, he argued, to stay true to this tradition without dealing with the problem of economy. Importantly, for Friedman, while it is important to acknowledge that the species has the capacity to bring about its own political salvation, it is also important to recognize that autonomous life is dangerously unfulfilled: 'The liberal conceives of man as imperfect beings. He regards the problem of social organisation to be as much a negative problem of preventing "bad" people from doing harm as of enabling "good" people to do good; and of course, "bad" and "good" people may be the same people, depending on who is judging them.'[75] Importantly, for Friedman, then, while economic transformation is the most important catalyst for political change, it must be recognized that there is always a marked distinction between the political equality of rights/opportunities and the economic material equality of life: '[The liberal] may welcome the fact that a free society in fact tends towards greater material equality than any other yet tried. But he will regard this as a desirable by-product of a free society, not its major justification.'[76] In other words, while it is true that liberals believe in virtues of global security, political freedoms, and juridical rights, belief in these virtues should not be confused in any way with egalitarianism.

Capitalization of Peace

It is common currency within liberal discourse to equate capitalism with peaceful political settlement. The work of Michael Doyle here has been crucial as he developed his now popularized 'liberal peace' thesis. Doyle pointed out that foundational to a liberal peace are democracy, equality before the law, along with private property and market mechanisms for the allocation of scarce resources.[77] For Doyle, this happy marriage between law and political economy illustrates classical liberalism at its best. This is not controversial. John Locke's *Two Treatises on Government*, for instance, directly linked private property to individual liberty. Such is the link that, for Locke, it is the absence of material wealth which is the surest evidence of despotic government. The same idea was put forward by

Smith, who argued that 'commerce and manufacturers gradually introduced order and good government, and with them, the liberty and security of individuals, among the inhabitants of the country, who had before lived almost in a continual state of war with their neighbours, and of servile dependency on their superiors'.[78] Meanwhile for Montesquieu, writing in the *Spirit of the Laws*, 'the natural effect of commerce is to lead to peace'.[79] This adds further moral and righteous weight to the onto-theological nature of political economy. As Patrick McDonald explains, what is commonly termed the free market is arguably better termed 'The Invisible Hand of Peace', since its operation is integral to the creation of peaceful relations amongst the world of people:

> Political scientists have traditionally focused on 'political' institutions as critical sources of individual liberty. Although competitive elections expand political participation and force governments to be more responsive to the demands of citizens, state and society interact in multiple institutional settings outside of elections. . . . Society can be empowered through the market to limit abuses of government authority. . . . The democratic peace may really be a liberal peace in which the peace is jointly created by multiple domestic institutions that protect civil liberties, ensure competitive markets, and widen political participation. This possibility suggests another theoretical implication. The peace among democratic states may really be caused by liberal economic institutions. Just as respect for private property and relatively laissez-faire economic policies promote democracy, they could simultaneously promote peace.[80]

In a landmark lecture poignantly titled 'The Struggle for the Soul of the 21st Century,' former US President Bill Clinton offered a reworking of Doyle's geo-strategic conception of the 'peace dividend' by making it applicable to internal conflict and the global security terrain. For Clinton, not only did 'abject poverty' lead to 'accelerated conflict', but in the post-9/11 world it is clear that it also 'creates recruits for terrorists and those who incite ethnic and religious hatred'. This in turn necessarily fuels a 'violent rejection of the economic and social order on which our future depends'. To combat this, Clinton spelt out a four-point plan which claimed that every person who belonged to the international community could profit from conditions of peace:

> I think victory for our point of view depends upon four things. First we have to win the fight we're in, in Afghanistan and against these terrorist networks that threaten us today. Second, we in the wealthy countries have to spread the benefits of the twenty first century world and reduce the risks so we can make more partners and fewer terrorists in the future. Third, the poor countries themselves must make some internal changes so that progress for their own people becomes more possible. And finally, all of us will have to develop a truly global consciousness about what our responsibilities to each other are and what our relationships are to be.

Clinton's prognosis here is perfectly clear. Given that September 11 represented the 'dark side of this new age of global interdependence', fighting the terror requires a positive humanistic approach through which the problem itself must be attributable to our systems of power and rule:

> [I]f you don't want to live with barbed wire around your children and grandchildren for the next hundred years, then it's not enough to defeat the terrorist. We have to make a world where there are far fewer terrorists, where there are fewer potential terrorists and more partners. And that responsibility falls primarily upon the wealthy nations, to spread the benefits and shrink the burdens.

Such responsibility does, however, come at a formidable price: '[T]his is a fight we have to make everywhere.'[81] This thinking has had a profound bearing on policy. As Jonathan Goodhand and David Hume explained,

> Changes in the nature of violent conflict, and the contexts within which it is set, have required changes in the concepts that are used to aid the understanding of contemporary conflict. Analyses that focused on the relationships between states, on military capacities and strategies, on predicting who would win and who would lose and on international political economy have increasingly been replaced by social and cultural analyses that recognize complexity and contingency and that question the feasibility of prediction.[82]

The notion of the 'complex political emergency' has been significant here. Coined by the United Nations Development Program, the term marked a significant departure in the sense that it required practitioners to look for the root causes of social dislocation. As Bridget Byrne contended, it centred 'on struggles over power and resources' and how 'men and women are caught up in different ways in this struggle, through their different identities' and 'differential access to and control over resources'.[83] Moreover, as Joanna Macrae and Nicholas Leader argued, while the term was initially presented as a 'neutral metaphor for civil war', it became increasingly apparent that 'aid' was 'no longer a substitute for political action'.[84] Providing relief to endangered populations gradually became 'the primary form of international policy at the geo-political periphery'. Globalization thus becomes a solution to dangerous localized forms of regression. In the words of Tony Blair:

> The issue is not how to stop globalization. The issue is how we use the power of community to combine it with justice. If globalization works only for the benefit of the few, then it will fail and will deserve to fail. But if we follow the principles that have served us so well at home – that power, wealth, and opportunity must be in the hands of the many, not the few – if we make that our guiding light for the

global economy, then it will be a force for good and an international movement that we should take pride in leading.[85]

Such calls are once again at the policy fore as the global war effort shifts towards creating lasting forms of peaceful settlement. Nowhere has this been more forcefully articulated than with the findings of the United Nations sixteen-member High-Level Panel on Threats, Challenges, and Change, which was established by Kofi Annan to assess new dangers facing international security.[86] Part of this panel's remit was to recommend measures to strengthen the international basis of security. Central here was the very conceptualization of the term 'security', which was to be defined in the broadest (planetary) and deepest (human) of terms. In 2004, following the panel's initial consultations, they put forward a report titled: *A More Secure World: Our Shared Responsibility*. According to this report, since threats were now 'without boundaries' and 'no State can act alone', it was essential to promote a 'new vision of collective security' which was both global and developmental:

> The case for collective security today rests on three basic pillars. Today's threats recognize no national boundaries, are connected, and must be addressed at the global and regional as well as the national levels. No State, no matter how powerful, can by its own efforts alone make itself invulnerable to today's threats. . . . We [therefore] begin with development because it is the indispensable foundation for a collective security system that takes prevention seriously. It serves multiple functions. It helps combat the poverty, infectious disease, and environmental degradation that kill millions and threaten human security. It is vital in helping States prevent or reverse the erosion of State capacity, which is crucial for meeting almost every class of threat. And it is part of a long-term strategy for preventing civil war and for addressing the environments in which both terrorism and organized crime flourish.[87]

This 'capitalization of peace' is not without its critics. It also disrupts familiar narratives of war/peace, which tend to be tied to the cessation of hostilities. Foucault already denounced the illusion that 'we are living in a world in which order and peace have been restored'. He set out to disrupt the neat distinctions between times of war/military exceptionalism and times of peace/civic normality:

> At this point we can invert Clausewitz's proposition and say that *politics is the continuation of war by other means* . . . while it is true that political power puts an end to war and establishes or attempts to establish the reign of peace in civil society, it certainly does not do so in order to suspend the effects of power or to neutralize the disequilibrium revealed in the last battle of war.

What, in other words, occurs beneath the semblance of peace is far from politically settled:

> [P]olitical struggles, these clashes over and with power, these modifications of relations of force – the shifting balances, the reversals – in a political system, all these things must be interpreted as a continuation of war. And they are interpreted as so many episodes, fragmentations, and displacements of the war itself. We are always writing the history of the same war, even when we are writing the history of peace and its institutions.[88]

In addressing NATO as the then Foreign Secretary of Britain's Labour Government, David Miliband, without evidently appreciating the full political, cultural, and philosophical implications, appeared to subscribe to the value of this approach, albeit for an altogether more committed deployment:

> NATO was born in the shadow of the Cold War, but we have all had to change our thinking as our troops confront insurgents rather than military machines like our own. The

mental models of 20th century mass warfare are not fit for
21st century counter-insurgency. That is why my argument
today has been about the centrality of politics. People like
quoting Clausewitz that warfare is the continuation of
politics by other means . . . we need *politics to become the
continuation of warfare by other means.*[89]

Miliband's 'Foucauldian moment' should not escape us.
Inverting Clausewitz on a planetary scale – hence promoting the collapse of all meaningful distinctions which once
held together the fixed terms of Newtonian space (i.e.
inside/outside, friend/enemy, citizen/soldier, war/peace,
etc.) – he firmly locates the conflict amongst the *world of
peoples.* The destiny of humanity as a whole is therefore
wagering its success on its own political strategies. This is
what the RAND Corporation terms 'war by other means'.[90]
In this setting, it is no coincidence to find authors like
David Kilcullen – a key architect in the formulation of
counter-insurgency strategies in Iraq and Afghanistan –
arguing for a global insurgency paradigm without too
much controversy.[91] Placing the managed recovery of maladjusted life at the heart of military strategies, what is
required is a joined-up response in which sovereign/mili-
taristic forms of ordering are matched by biopolitical/
developmental forms of progress.[92] There is an important
point to add here. While terrorists used to be discursively
cast off as external to the political realm, they now become
an extreme yet integral part of this wider security terrain.
Once the capacity for evil is placed within the operative
daily fabric of all non-Western populations, the productive
economy of life begins to assume divine earthly ascriptions
in that the war to relieve insurgent populations from the
scourge of underdevelopment also retains the task of
removing evil from the world. This was made clear by
General David Petraeus, who argued in his 2010 counter-
insurgency guidance to the International Security Assistance Force deployed to Afghanistan: 'We can't win without

fighting, but we also cannot kill or capture our way to victory.'

While contemporary forms of liberal interventionism purport to address threats which emerge from 'within' the social order, it would be a mistake to infer that the Global War on Terror has been localized to specific geographical sites and to particular national struggles in the Middle East (Iraq, Afghanistan, Pakistan) and Africa (Somalia, Sudan). Over and above the attention paid to the apocalyptic nihilism of Al-Qaeda, there is much talk today about the humanitarian costs of sectarian divisions and 'ethnic' rivalry. And similarly, what was once simply articulated as an epic struggle in defence of the liberal values against the forces of evil is now articulated through the quagmire of civil war. Here the language of international 'assistance' takes on a new vogue, by which the crisis at hand is claimed to be foremost the responsibility of the fledgeling transitional governments or the rogue regimes of fragile states. Yet interestingly enough it is this very localization of the conflict which demonstrates the most universal liberal excessiveness. What can be detected by this emphasis on the localization of conflict is, in fact, a broadening of the lines of warfare. As the humanitarian costs of conflict are laid at the feet of local actors for their apparently internally derived problems, the life of the population renders any claim to national sovereignty superfluous. While providing subsequent legitimacy to a more enduring political relationship of long-term occupation, the biopoliticization of war stakes out a new strategic paradigm in which once familiar sovereign integrities are now secondary to the integrity of life itself. Life therefore informs territorial divisions, not vice versa. As Christopher Paul has noted:

> Whether fighting terrorists or insurgents, a strictly 'kinetic' (combat-oriented) solution does nothing to address the underlying popular motives that lead to terrorist or

insurgent movements in the first place. These unaddressed motives remain as impetuses for new terrorist or insurgent recruits and for those who support them. The challenge is to fight the physical battles and to engage the broader population at the same time. But we know that it works, and we know how it is done. For US military units in Iraq, success often arose when commanders were able to simultaneously employ multiple mutually reinforcing lines of operation. . . . Security *and* economy. Democracy *and* development. Legitimacy *and* pacification. Influence *and* direct action.[93]

– 5 –

A New Leviathan

General Crisis Environments

While the problem of underdevelopment threatens localized catastrophe, the 'dangers' of the environment promise
to bring the experience of ruination that is altogether
apocalyptic. Norman Meyer's work has been crucial here.[1]
He first raised the issue in the 1970s in relation to deforestation, soil erosion, and population growth in the Ethio-
pian highlands which caused heightened tensions with
neighbouring Somalia. Meyers suggested that the changing
environmental conditions were crucial to understanding
the ensuing violence. Having made this connection, he
then elaborated his theory by directly linking environmental degradation, war, and insecurity. For Meyers, the conscious destruction of the environment during times of war
merely adds to this reasoning. While the total destruction
of the Second World War in particular destroyed built
environments, the Vietnam War witnessed a conscious
policy of rural destruction through the use of various
chemical agents. The most controversial was the continued
targeted use of Agent Orange by the United States as
the favoured method for dealing with the 'inhospitable

environment'. As a direct result of this conscious and excessive biospherical militarism, an amendment to Protocol I of the 1949 Geneva Convention on the Protection of Victims of International Armed Conflicts (1977) was introduced, thereby internationalizing environmental concerns.[2] At stake here was the issue of 'human well-being', which Meyers defined as 'not only protection from harm and injury but access to water, food, shelter, health, employment, and other basic requisites that are due of every person on Earth. It is the collectivity of these citizen needs – overall safety and quality of life – that should figure prominently in the nation's view of security.'[3]

The UN World Commission on Environment and Development developed these concerns by directly linking security and environmental governance in its influential Brundtland Report titled *Our Common Future* (1987). As the report states, 'Humankind faces two great threats. The first is that of a nuclear exchange. Let us hope that it remains a diminishing prospect for the future. The second is that of environmental ruin world-wide and, far from being a prospect for the future, it is a fact right now.' This report did not, however, simply suggest that the environment was a biospherical problem. It directly equated 'environmental ruin' with political, social, and economic collapse. As the report explained, since 'poverty, injustice, environmental degradation and conflict interact in complex and potent ways', the threat posed to the environment 'can only be dealt with by joint management and multilateral procedures and mechanisms'.[4] Calling, then, for a holistic approach to environmental security, thereby framing all societal problems within a generalizable framework for biopolitical engagement, the report increasingly moralized the environment as the potential for localized violence became synonymous with a catastrophic topography. In order to combat this, the report argued, liberal market states would have to take the lead in creating a new global architecture for political change:

The integrated and interdependent nature of the new challenges and issues contrasts sharply with the nature of the
institutions that exist today. These institutions tend to be
independent, fragmented, and working to relatively narrow
mandates with closed decision processes. Those responsible for managing natural resources and protecting the environment are institutionally separate from those who are
managing the economy. The real world of interlocked economic and ecological systems will not change: the policies
and institutions concerned must.[5]

Robert Kaplan popularized these concerns by suggesting that the environment had far-reaching implications
beyond the sanctuary of any single sovereign power. Environmental degradation was not simply a problem for the
global poor; it could potentially affect us all. 'The Coming
Anarchy' (1994) spelt out in apocalyptic prose what catastrophes await: '[T]he political and strategic impact of
surging populations, spreading disease, deforestation and
soil erosion, water depletion, air pollution, and possibly,
rising sea levels – developments that will prompt mass
migration and, in turn, incite group conflicts – will be the
core foreign-policy challenge in the twenty-first century.'[6]
These politically compelling ideas have found a receptive
audience. The United Nations High-Level Panel on Threats,
Challenges, and Change, for instance has argued: 'Rarely
are environmental concerns factored into security, development or humanitarian strategies. . . . International institutions and States have not organized themselves to address
the problems of development in a coherent, integrated
way, and instead continue to treat poverty, infectious
disease and environmental degradation as stand-alone
threats.'[7] This has been further echoed in the United
Nations Development Programme's 2007 Human Security
Report, *Fighting Climate Change: Human Solidarity in a
Divided World*, which offered a comprehensive reflection
on the inter-related problems of security, development, and
climatic conditions: 'In the long run climate change is a
massive threat to human development and in some places

it is already undermining the international community's efforts to reduce extreme poverty.'[8] Meanwhile, in his Nobel laureate speech, Barack Obama insisted that:

> It is undoubtedly true that development rarely takes root without security; it is also true that security does not exist where human beings do not have access to enough food, or clean water, or the medicine they need to survive. It does not exist where children cannot aspire to a decent education or a job that supports a family. The absence of hope can rot a society from within. And that is why helping farmers feed their own people – or nations educate their children and care for the sick – is not mere charity. It is also why the world must come together to confront climate change. There is little scientific dispute that if we do nothing, we will face more drought, famine and mass displacement that will fuel more conflict for decades. For this reason, it is not merely scientists and activists who call for swift and forceful action – it is military leaders in my country and others who understand that our common security hangs in the balance.[9]

The World Bank acts for greater policy coherence. Its 2010 World Development Report, *Development and Climate Change*, attends to the inter-related problems of governing underdevelopment and climate change. As the report indicates, 'Left unmanaged, climate change will reverse development progress and compromise the well-being of current and future generations.' This demands a fully integrated approach: 'Better application of known practices and fundamental transformations – in natural resource management, energy provision, urbanization, social safety nets, international financial transfers, technological innovation, and governance, both international and national – are needed to meet the challenge.'[10] What the Bank calls 'Climate-Smart Development' implies that bad stewardship of local resources is not only wasteful, but also increasing the probability of localized forms of violence that can have an impact beyond borders, thus contributing to global instability. This echoes the two central policy themes which have informed the UNDP's position. The first is 'Ecological Interdependence': 'Climate change is different from other problems facing humanity – and it challenges us to think differently at many levels.' The second is 'Climate Stewardship': 'There are many theories of social justice and approaches to efficiency that can be brought to bear on climate change debates.'[11] Taken together, climate steward-ship in an age of ecologically driven biopolitical independ-ence not only places a moral imperative of epic proportions at the heart of all resource management; it also sets the scene in which those who are classified bad stewards instantly become agents of future catastrophe.

As a result of this 'becoming dangerous' of the envi-ronment, what was commonly known as the develop-ment–security nexus has more recently continued to widen its security ambit to include the environment, climate adaptation, and the management of scarce resources. The development–security–environment nexus (Desnex) is therefore now part of a mobilization on all fronts – human and biospheric. As argued elsewhere,[12] the ambition here is no longer simply to police and main-tain the global life-chance divide between developed and underdeveloped lives; it is to forge a new global settle-ment that generalizes biopolitical rule. To cite a recent proclamation by the UNDP:

> Climate change is the defining human development issue of our generation. All development is ultimately about expanding human potential and enlarging human freedom. It is about people developing the capabilities that empower them to make choices and to lead lives that they value. Climate change threatens to erode human freedoms and limit choice. It calls into question the Enlightenment prin-ciple that human progress will make the future look better than the past.[13]

Not only, then, does the prospect of environmental catas-trophe take biopolitical reasoning to its logical territorial conclusion; the ability to divide the world of peoples along highly complex and radically interconnected lines by drawing together political, economic, social, cultural, and micro-climatic conditions firmly entrenches the catastrophic imaginary such that the destiny and very survivability of all life is wagered on the successes/failures of liberal political strategies. As Jeremy Rifkin observed some time ago:

> Unlike geopolitics, which views nature exclusively as strategic resources, biosphere politics views the environment as the irreducible context that sustains all of life and sets the conditions and limits for all other human thought and activity. In the biospheric era, the exploitation of nature gives way to a sense of reverence for the natural world and a sustainable relationship with the environment.[14]

Faith-based politics never lets empirical reality get in the way of a good hypothesis. Liberalism's pseudo-scientific concerns with the potential for the catastrophic are no exception. Just as the connections between conflict and underdevelopment are open to critical question (war is a rather costly business), so the extension of this to incorporate environmental degradation is doubly dubious. The logic proposed here is clear: The global poor are dangerous. Their poverty leads to resentment and violence, which may have global consequences. Environmental catastrophe further intensifies this drama. It forces the global poor to fight over even scarcer resources, such that the Malthusian prophecy is played out with devastating results. So not only is it assumed that the global poor are more dangerous on account of their relative depravation, it is further taken that this potential is exacerbated on account of the fact that they will in all probability act in a dangerous way should the hypothesized series of events come to pass. Interventionism is therefore predicated upon the assumption of a dual hypothesis: that is, should certain conditions pertain, they will act in a certain way. While of course the nature of the potential catastrophe is altogether different, there are logical similarities here with the justification for intervention in Iraq (continued onto Iran). If Saddam Hussein had Weapons of Mass Destruction, we can be sure that he would have used them. Hypothesis upon hypothesis! Nobody is suggesting here that we shouldn't have a more considered ethics towards the environment. However, having liberal societies take the lead when they have contributed the most to the problem is similar to having the United States lecture on nuclear proliferation when it remains the only nation to have experimented with its horrifying potential.

Homo Homini Lupus

A New Leviathan is being created. Not in the Hobbesian sense in which the Leviathan's transcendent power is predicated upon the sovereign right to impose order. A new divinity is being formed which is justifying its presence in the terms of *global strategies for species survival*. Global security therefore inevitably becomes a liberal regime of bio-power as the catastrophic imaginary becomes 'all-inclusive'. It proceeds by conducting a sophisticated assay on the planetary body as a problem to be solved. It promotes vital elements, while weeding out that which threatens to upset the healthy vision of earthly paradise. While this attempt to profoundly shape the world in order to realize more peaceful habitation is altogether modern, what is novel today are the ways in which security governance is tied to *the conservation of all that is living*. To be expected, since conservation sanctions new forms of interventionism and moral trusteeship, not only does it force us to believe in the possibility that the ultimate expression of Kantian evil – the human species' unnecessary extinction – could be realized, but also liberal rationality is indelibly tied to the lasting security of humanity as a whole – or alternatively its ruination. As Ulrich Beck puts it:

> Thomas Hobbes' political theory of sovereignty is based on the formula *homo homini lupus*, man is wolf to man. The political theory of risk society, by contrast, takes an adaptive version of this principle as its starting point: *humanity is a wolf to man*. The 'predatory character' referred to by Hobbes is attributed here not to individual people but to humanity as a whole. Humanity is at once the subject and object of its own endangerment. It is not a nation-based 'faith in the community' that creates legitimacy, but rather a *belief that the risks facing humanity can be averted* by political action taken on *behalf* of endangered humanity.[15]

Importantly, for Beck, jeopardizing the future of the entire species cannot be anything other than an unnecessary evil:

> Humanity's potential suicide can never be a voluntary death, as when an individual takes their own life (out of despair, pain or loneliness). It is necessarily the involuntary 'murder' of all – collective murder as the unintended side-effect of scientific, technological, military, and political action; a 'murder' that originates nonetheless in individual acts and in a system of acts that has become autonomous.[16]

Beck is fully aware that this collective suicide is a matter of both *perception* and *anticipation*. As he explains, '[T]he global perception of global risks is not tied to the objectivity of risks. Its omnipresence needs to be implanted into people's hearts and minds through global information and global symbols, regardless of such objectivity.' There is a sense here that 'humanity is wolf to humanity' is also a call to think the world anew; that species endangerment conditions the possibility for a new beginning: 'Humanity's foremost priority is the timeless principle of self-preservation. Death is the first amongst all evils. At the individual level,

it cannot be avoided, but not so at the level of humanity.'
For Beck, then, the implications are clear:

> Since the national sovereign is unable to guarantee internal
> and external security to protect the lives of his citizens any
> longer, the citizens' duty of obedience *becomes null and
> void.* . . . The social contract can no longer be grounded
> in the anarchy of separate, individual states. Instead, it
> needs to create an inter-state order that draws its cosmo-
> politan legitimacy from preventively combating the threat
> to humanity.[17]

Such legitimacy invariably rewrites the rules of the political game as humanity begins to wage the destiny of the
entire human species on the success/failures of its own
political strategies.

Each catastrophe serves only to strengthen Beck's thesis
that we live in a 'world risk society' marked by inescapable
dangers that cannot be managed by prediction or measures
of control. As Beck explains, 'Uncontrollable risks must
be understood as not being linked to place, that is they are
difficult to impute to a particular agent and can hardly be
controlled on the level of the nation-state.' They appear
'beyond rational calculation', pushing us further 'into the
realm of unpredictable turbulence'.[18] This logic has certainly resonated. It has, for instance, been echoed in the
literature of contemporary security studies for the Western
context which proposes 'reflexive' thinking to replace outdated modes of strategic thought.[19] It also lends itself to
the liberal notion that societies should actively invest in
their own risk management strategies to ensure healthy
living and longevity beyond the here and now. As Beck
further explains, 'Risk is a modern concept. It presumes
decision making. As soon as we speak in terms of "risk",
we are talking about calculating the incalculable, coloniz-
ing the future.' Crucially, for Beck, while it is clear that
the idea of risk has always been part of modernity's master
narrative, what marks a new departure in the logic is the
effective *de-bounding* from any sense of space and time:

'This de-bounding is three-dimensional: spatial, temporal and social. In the spatial dimension we see ourselves confronted with risks that do not take nation-states, or any other boundary for that matter, into account. . . . Similarly, in the temporal dimension, the long latency period of dangers . . . escapes the prevailing procedures used when dealing with industrial dangers.'[20]

This has a profound bearing on our sense of security, political belonging, and human togetherness by disrupting the inviolable claims to total sovereignty. As Zygmunt Bauman explained in reference to 9/11,

> There is some grave symbolic importance in the fact that the terrorist force that took it upon itself to call the bluff of the self-reliance and invulnerability of the most self-reliant and least vulnerable state in the world acted from a territory which has long since ceased to be a state, having turned into an incarnation of the void in which global power flows.[21]

These new 'imagined communities' therefore appear like all fears of the global since they are 'formed against the state, its territoriality, its claims to total sovereignty, its inborn tendency to draw and fortify borders and impede or arrest border traffic'. Indeed, evidencing the real frailty of boundaries long since theorized by post-structural thinkers, one of the consequential effects of any attack is to

> show that the verdict of confinement has its loopholes, that confinement is ineffective as an instrument of disempowerment, that blows can be delivered far beyond the limits of confinement – and that, despite the advantages drawn from the speed they command and their freedom to float, the powerful adversaries have their Achilles' heel where they can be hit and wounded – not mortally perhaps, but painfully all the same.[22]

An important consequence of this has been to pose a limit to the utility of understanding politics today in terms of sovereignty.

Nodal Sovereignty

So what becomes of sovereignty? Our principal concern here is the problem of *indivisibility*. As Hans J. Morgenthau once wrote, '[S]overeignty over the same territory cannot reside simultaneously in two different authorities, that is, sovereignty is indivisible.'[23] This was certainly the opinion of Hobbes, who argued that

> [a] Common-wealth is said to be Instituted, when a Multitude of men do Agree . . . that to whatever Man, or Assembly of Men, shall be given by the major part, the Right to Present the Person of them all . . . every one . . . shall Authorise all the Actions and Judgements, of that Man or Assembly of men, in the same manner, as if they were his own, to the end, to live peaceably amongst themselves, and be protected against other men.

'The Essence of Soveraignty' is therefore 'incommunicable and inseparable'.[24] Capturing these concerns succinctly, Jens Bartelson argues that

> [t]he fact that our way of perceiving the political world has been conditioned by a peculiar reading of Plato's *Parmenides* that made the One prior to the Many does not make that world any easier to change, but it might help explain why this has been so difficult. If the above analysis is correct, the relocations of sovereignty from God to kings, from kings to particular peoples, and then from these peoples to humanity as a whole have been made possible by the underlying assumption that the nature of political authority remains essentially the same irrespective of its source and locus, and this precisely by virtue of its inherent indivisibility.

Yet for Bartelson, even though our conception of sovereignty situates the One prior to the Many in a form of symbolic ordering which presupposes political authority to be indivisible, 'the findings of modern political science have almost invariably testified to its actual divisibility. . . . [T]he only thing that has led us to believe otherwise [that Many come before the One] is the violent imposition of that form upon the world.'[25]

Conventional approaches to sovereignty which privilege the singular over the multiple always failed to reflect the reality of political power, which has always been multilayered and prone to contestation of unified sources of authority and identity. As Derrida wrote, '[E]ven in politics, the choice is not between sovereignty and nonsovereignty, but among several forms of partings, partitions, divisions, conditions that come along to broach a sovereignty that is always supposed to be indivisible and unconditional.'[26] Although sovereignty therefore never quite matched the theoretical grandeur its advocates claimed, contemporaneously, there is now a need to face the implications of the Westphalia dissolution. As Wendy Brown explains, 'While weakening nation-states yoke in their fate and legitimacy to God, capital, the most desacralizing of forces, becomes God-like: almighty, limitless, and uncontrollable. In what should be the final and complete triumph of secularism, there is only theology.'[27]

Even though sedentary ways of thinking still dominate orthodox political traditions, the reason why certain disciplines are becoming increasingly irrelevant (except for their own audiences) is because they fail to come to terms with the empirical complex reality of the world. Sedentary imaginaries still offer neat intellectual comforts untroubled by a differential ontology that casts doubt upon the entire methodological tradition. This, however, puts them at odds with the significant advances made in the human and physical sciences that have necessitated the study of radically interconnected forms of life in circulation. Michael Hardt and Antonio Negri have already offered a timely challenge, arguing that contemporary power 'does not rely on fixed boundaries or barriers. It is a *decentered* and *deterritorializing* apparatus of rule that progressively incorporates the entire global realm within its open, expanding frontiers.' It works by managing 'hybrid identities, flexible hierarchies, and plural exchanges through modulating networks of command'.[28] While orthodox ideas of sovereignty therefore maintain their commitment to forms of juridical structure, the New Leviathan is driven by biopolitical ambitions so that bounded forms of ordering become purely contingent. Sovereignty thus is territorially exposed, so that law features as a tactical measure in the production and maintenance of particular relations of power:

> In the modern world the old Clausewitz adage that war is a continuation of politics by other means represented a moment of enlightenment insofar as it conceived war as a form of political action and/or sanction and thus implied an international legal framework of modern warfare. . . .When we reverse the terms, however, and war comes to be considered the basis of the internal politics of the global order, the politics of Empire, then the modern model of civilization that was the basis of legalized war collapses. We are still nonetheless not dealing with a pure and unregulated exercise of violence. War as the foundation of politics must itself contain legal forms, indeed must construct new procedural forms of law. . . . Whereas war previously was regulated through legal structures, war has become regulating by constructing and imposing its own legal framework.[29]

None of this is unexpected. Liberalism emerged as a critique of too much government. From its inception, its advocates promoted a certain set of inalienable ideals, all of which were deemed necessary to ensure that sufficient autonomy was granted to maximize productive economies. These included a belief in the individual, freedom of choice, market security, laissez-faire, and minimal government. Through these ideals, liberalism could be presented to be the champion of individual freedoms and political autonomy. Liberalism has never, however, been a political philosophy which promotes certain inalienable values.

Working on the basis of its effects, it offers to calculate productive relations of power which in essence are 'value-free'. Being directly concerned with the 'political problem of population', it bears little resemblance or at least gives secondary importance to issues concerning freedom, democracy, and rights.[30] This is supported by Mitchell Dean, who observes, 'The emergence of a liberal rationality of government is dependent on the discovery of the government of processes found in the population, the economy, and society. It introduces the Liberal problematic of security in the form that security must take hold of these "non-political" processes on which government will depend.'[31] It is, as Foucault puts it, a 'practice or "way of doing things" orientated towards regulating political life by means of a sustained reflection'. And it is through this sustained reflection that it becomes a 'principle and a method of rationalizing the exercise of government, a rationalization that obeys – and this is its specificity – the internal rule of maximum economy'.[32] Liberal regimes thus have always demonstrated *de-bounding* tendencies. They have always revealed ambitions beyond the limits of any given nation-state. They have consistently shown willingness to undermine neighbouring sovereign integrities for the purposes of capitalization and regime change. And they have continuously undermined their own territorial integrities and limits for the purposes of progress and development.

This brings us back to Philip Bobbit's state theory. While not subscribing to a linear teleology that is clearly present in all times and places, Bobbit's transformative narrative is nevertheless compelling. For Bobbit, the state has moved through a number of phases, which include 'princely states', 'kingly states', 'territorial states', 'nation-states', and the contemporary 'liberal market state'. While each state project has its own unique source of authority which determines forms of allegiance, liberal market states derive their authority from the market as it empowers citizens. The liberal market state therefore solves the contemporary 'crisis of legitimation' (as evidenced, for instance, by its inability to offer meaningful protections to subjects) by 'redefining the fundamental compact on which the assumption of legitimate power is based'.[33] So, rather than lamenting the shift towards the private provision of state services, for Bobbit it reflects a more efficient and effective way to provide security and govern populations. There is, however, an important caveat. Our understanding of law needs to adapt to reflect the reality of a system no longer predicated upon the outdated virtues and soverign integrities enshrined in the Treaty of Westphalia. So while Bobbit's vocal criticism of certain abuses of the executive privilege in the conduct of the War on Terror attracted public attention, he demands a more nuanced tactical mindset in order to facilitate the creation of a more responsive 'rule of law' that is adequate to our time of war. Sovereignty is thus conceived not in terms of absolutist or universal constructs but as systems of ordering which exhibit decentralized and dynamic characteristics:

> At some point in the twenty-first century a new constitution for the society of states will come into being that reflects the emerging constitutional order of the market state. By varying the degree of sovereignty retained by the people – an idea that is itself incompatible with the conventional conception of sovereignty as equal, indivisible and complete – states will develop different forms of the market state, resulting in a pluralism that the constitution of the society of market states will necessarily reflect. This new international law will be built out of radical devolutionary ideas of sovereignty, including markets in sovereignty.[34]

We gain a real sense of this emerging networked order by analysing the power invested in International Zones. What these zones illustrate (from Green Zone protectorates, international airports/airspace, to the increasingly fortified compounds of major multinational corporations, international governmental organizations, and agents of

global governance) is an emergent archipelago of power
that is premised on providing secure passage and temporary habitat for the world's political, economic, financial,
cultural, and military elites. It also allows for the creation
of a system that is complemented by the erection of temporary and/or permanent barriers to contain populations
without contradiction. In certain respects, this is reminiscent of the shift Deleuze detected from 'disciplinary societies' to 'societies of control'. As Nikolas Rose explains,

> In disciplinary societies it was a matter of procession from
> one disciplinary institution to another – school, barracks,
> factory . . . each seeking to *mould* the conduct by inscrib-
> ing enduring corporeal and behaviour competences, and
> persisting practices of self-scrutiny and self-restraint into
> the soul. Control society is one of never-ending modulation
> where modulation occurs within the flows and transactions
> between forces and capacities of the human subject.[35]

Network theory proposes an understanding of complex,
dynamic, and emergent systems by drawing our attention
to 'nodal' points of intersection. Connections between
nodes are represented by solid lines of intersection which
denote possible flows between fixed points. Nodes are
what we may refer to as being territorial stop-gaps or sites
of solidification in a system of dynamic fluidity. Liberal
sovereignty conforms to this nodality. Solidified in fixed
safe zones around the globe which connect the global
metropolis to the dangerous borderlands, it proposes an
unbound topography of power that is being continually
adapted. Some nodal points are evidently remarkably
entrenched, i.e. the Global Cities. Others remain altogether contingent, i.e. Green Zones at new points of inter-
vention/crisis. This attempt to gain a tangible purchase on
sovereignty as a networked system of rule represents an
important departure. Firstly, it makes it perfectly clear that
sovereignty and biopolitics are not strategically opposite:
sovereignty refers to the militarization and policing of

liberal space so as to permit good forms of global circulation and eliminate bad forms of global circulation. Secondly, since political empowerment is tied to the subject's ability to move around the system, nomadism opens up a new terrain for emancipation ethics. To put it another way, if people are being violated, it is not because inalienable rights (as law defines them) are being denied; it is because their movements are restricted. Thirdly, what marks out conceptions of citizenship (i.e. circulatory compliance) is less about national affiliation than about the differences between 'insurable' and 'non-insurable' lives. The former are seen to pose minimal risk to the operative logic of the system, while the latter provide no factual basis for epistemic comfort. And fourthly, within this topography of power it is no longer possible to simply forge out clear territorial distinctions between 'First' and 'Third' world enclaves. Insurable and non-insurable lives inhabit most settings (most notably the urban), carving out new microphysical geometries of power that reveal how the local interfaces with the global *in lieu* of a truly dynamic temporality.

One of the obvious counters against a global biopolitics is the continued existence of borders between states. It all, however, depends upon the way we approach frontiers. Borders conventionally understood appear to be highly structured and preventative measures. We can think here of razor-wire fences, surveillance cameras, border security, along with the meticulously regimented systems of entry in which the border attendant appears to represent the capillary ends of the sovereign encounter. This, however, is just a matter of perspective which validates familiar accounts of sovereignty based on the continuing existence of bordered structures. By contrast, let's imagine the border from its primary referent – namely the body itself. Borders would, after all, have no meaning whatsoever unless the frontier encountered the human (including its activities). From this biological perspective, borders signify a more complex corporeal arrangement that is all about regulating the flows of life. They inhibit intelligent and biopolitically determined characteristics which allow certain types of entry while denying the passage of others. Borrowing from William Walters, we may call these 'biopolitical borders'.[36] They are corporeal frontiers which exhibit sophisticated asymmetrical traits (passage/blockage) on account of the subject's biological profile, or 'code', to use the more familiar digital expression. It is important to point out that while fixed essences or generalizable profiles (notably, ethnic or religious marks of distinction) undoubtedly prefigure in terms of marking out certain characteristic behaviours and probabilities, final deliberations are not tied to these essentialist character traits. Nobody is categorically denied entry in principle, just as nobody is exempt from the complicity test. So what becomes the surest guarantee of smooth entry (i.e. to flow without friction or resistance) is the capability to evidence compliance in *advance* of the proposed journey. Here security is completed virtualized – not only in the digital sense of the term as border crossings are fitted with the very latest surveillance technologies, but in a way that the right to passage can be virtually guaranteed.

Nomos as Circulation

Writing a decade after the Second World War, Schmitt forewarned that the European juridical model for world order – the *jus publicum Europaeum*, whose centre of gravity was the sovereign state – was facing a lasting crisis. The European solutions to the ordering of the world that were taking shape through 'the dualism of East and West' were 'only the last stage before and ultimate, complete unity of the world – the last round, the final step, so to speak, in the terrible rings to a new nomos of the earth'.[37] Showing considerable foresight, Schmitt envisaged the possibility for a new configuration of power that would force us to encounter 'the earth, the planet on which we live, as a whole, as a globe, and to seek to understand its global division and order'.[38] These analytical demands have invariably excited followers. Agamben, more than any other, has pursued this task in a way that has proven to be highly influential and equally provocative. Focusing in particular on the lasting experiences – or what could be termed 'remnants' – of fascist modernity, Agamben has sought to draw our attentions to the relations which exist between 'giving forms to life' and the conditions of life in 'the camp'. Since one of the most 'essential characteristics' of modern biopolitics is to constantly 'redefine the threshold in life that distinguishes and separates what is inside from what is outside', for Agamben utmost attention should be given to sites that 'eliminate radically the people that are excluded'.[39] The camp is therefore the *defining paradigm of the modern* inasmuch as it is a 'space in which power confronts nothing other than pure biological life without any mediation'.[40] It epitomizes when 'politics becomes bio-politics and the *homo sacer* becomes indistinguishable from the citizen':

> The birth of the camp in our time appears as an event which decisively signals the political space of modernity itself. It is produced at the point at which the political system of the modern nation-state (which was founded on the functional nexus between a determinate localization [land] and a determinate order [the State] and mediated by automatic rules for the inscription of life [birth or the nation]) enters into a lasting crisis, and the State decides to assume directly the care of the nation's biological life as one of its proper tasks. If the structure of the nation-state is, in other words, defined by the three elements of land, order, birth, the rupture of the old *nomos* is produced . . . in the point marking the inscription of bare life (the birth which thus becomes nation) within two of them. Something can no longer function within the traditional mechanisms that regulated this inscription, and the camp is the new, hidden regulator of the inscription of life in the order – or rather the sign of the

system's inability to function without being transformed into a lethal machine.[41]

Agamben's analysis is forced to give priority to modernity's intractable and lasting lethal crisis in order to substantiate his claims. This is essential to his methodology, for it then enables him to retain the assertion that it is the exception which serves to enforce the rule – that which is outside constitutes the inside. In this way, not only can Agamben remain faithful to the first principle of sovereign power, i.e. abandonment, he is then permitted to widen its application by including those new sites of abandonment that exist outside the 'normal' remit of international juridical order and which come to constitute the formative spaces of global modernity. From this position, it is argued, since the definitive rupture of the old territorial *nomos* has opened up the planetary domain, this has necessarily permitted the creation of new extra-juridical sites from which the state of exception can become a new condition of global spatial order. Thus understood, the 'camp as *nomos*' is seen to work on two very distinct levels. There are local sites of confinement whose modes of abandonment produce a wide array of differing bare life forms. From refugee camps, mega-city ghettos, temporary holding cells for non-criminal migrants, to the increasingly confined transitory spaces occupied by the last remnants of non-sedentary living, the habitudinal reality is one of a life that is biologically reduced to its 'bare essentials' and thus deprived of any onto-theological status that would be necessary to qualify that life worthy of living. This is more broadly inserted within a new global configuration of power, which, yet to be supported by a complementary juridical architecture or framework, witnesses the creation of extra-juridical sites which constitute the new basis for global emergency.

Guantánamo Bay is often cited as evidence of this paradigm. For Agamben, the physical location of this site has a juridical purpose by situating the inhabitants outside the regular territory of the 'civilized world'. This enables the full separation of the combatants from any normal legal procedures and constitutional rights. The 'unlawful combatants' are therefore reduced to 'the object of a pure rule' which ensures they are subjected to a detention 'entirely removed from the law'.[42] What is more, since Guantánamo is seen to be the exemplary site of contemporary exceptionalism, a permanent extra-juridical site that is absolutely necessary to maintain the protection of global order, it produces 'a situation in which emergency becomes the rule, and the very distinction between peace and war . . . becomes impossible'.[43] In this context, the significance of Guantánamo is not simply whether or not its inmates are being denied recourse to international legal obligations, but rather the way in which it reveals the disintegration of the entire basis of legality which traditionally served to separate the state of exception from the state of rule. With the global exception becoming the global rule, any commitment to law is suspended indefinitely as the contemporary 'biopolitical threshold' which serves to mark out the distinction between biological life and political life thus enters a 'third space' – a planetary 'zone of indistinction' where the ability to separate the life that is worth living and that which is disposable is fully abandoned.

Agamben's modelling of the *nomos* is defined by its modes of separation and inclusion along with its fixation and fluidity. On the one hand, at local levels it still retains an allegiance to Schmitt's notion of a 'fundamental localization' or a spatial orientation which 'does not limit itself to distinguishing what is inside from what is outside but instead traces a threshold (the state of exception) between the two, on the basis of which outside and inside, the normal situation and chaos, enter into those complex topological relations that make the validity of the juridical order possible'. And yet, on the other hand, these localized cases are recognized to be subsumed within a wider order that is 'without localization': that is to say, a political system which 'no longer orders forms of life and juridical rules in a determinate place, but instead contains at its very centre a *dislocating localization* that exceeds it and into which every form of life and every norm can be virtually taken'.[44] Agamben is therefore still committed to the Schmittean structure of exception which is founded upon the existence of an order based within a fundamental relation between the juridical-political domain and territory: that is, to the '*nomos* of the Earth' in its original gesture, the founding spatial ontology that binds every juridical-political order to a concrete territory, to the '*sense* of the Earth'.[45] Agamben, however, takes this localization to serve as the principle which then decides its global (dis) application – the camp as permanent space of exception. In this sense, the real crisis we face is not just the disruption caused to the sedentary distribution of the world, but the shattering of the entire nomological order in which determinable forms of territoriality and distinct juridical forms of order were capable of effectively mediating the rules which gave form to all life.

While Agamben's betrayal of Foucault's biopolitics should be valued for the way it rigorously pursues the depoliticizing nature and inner violence inherent to the biopolitical, it is a mistake to give total allegiance to the spatial figuration of the camp. Not only does this limit our understanding of the more positive biopolitical relations that create communities through the active promotion of life, but giving iconic reverence to the camp is tantamount to sounding a retreat back into the familiar geo-strategic modes of analysis which, contrary to our findings, once again prioritize sovereign modes of power over the biopolitical. A shift in perspective is needed. This does not require an outright rejection of Agamben's biopolitical analysis, nor does it need us to dismiss the miserable and politically suffocating conditions of encamped life. It does, however, require a different emphasis. Instead of taking geo-political abandonment to be the constitutive function of inclusion, the biopolitical *nomos* foregrounds the problem of planetary *circulation*. As Michael Dillon phrases it:

> As a *dispositif de securité*, biopolitics not only functions through mechanisms that elevate contingency into a dominant field of formation for western societies as a whole, it similarly also opens up an entirely different spatial configuration of security. If distribution is the spatial figuration that characterizes traditional geopolitical rationalities and technologies of security, circulation is the spatial configuration that characterizes the biopolitics of security. Whereas distribution signals a world understood to be divided between sovereign territorial political subjects and their competing hegemonies, circulation concerns a world understood in terms of the biological structures and functions of species existence together with the relations that obtain between species life and all of its contingent local and global correlations. If geopolitically driven imperialism seeks to control the distribution of territory and resources, biopolitically driven imperialism seeks to control circulation as such.[46]

With the political terrain having phase-shifted from the sovereign recovery of unified order towards the securitization of life for its progressive unification, the question no longer concerns some apparent juridical transgression or de/re-subjectivization through law. For while exceptional politics led to the abandonment of fixed norms in order to ultimately rescue those precise conventional referents out of the conditions of disorder (something which is, however, altogether contingent upon the next event), the contemporary condition witnesses the proliferation of threat so that governments can foreground a socio-economic account of maladjustment in order to reaffirm a commitment to the problem of life necessity. This is a thoroughly liberal problematic which is immeasurably greater than any juridical remedy. With legitimate sovereign recovery restored, what reveals the reawakening of the liberal sensibility is the heightened focus given to ameliorating all global problems – of which terror is one – within the remit of global security discourses and practices. The prevailing rationality underwriting this complex commitment to life necessity is not tied to limit conditions. Problems of life necessity in fact take the form of (in)calculable risks which, bound to the world of statistical measure, imagine a world already foreclosed.

So how can we square this with any commitment to natural rights and universal laws? Universal normative standards are seen by liberals to guarantee reasonable relations amongst peoples so as to guarantee security, justice, and peace for the global citizenry. Once these guarantees are met, it necessarily transpires that the subject is free from fear, hence emancipated from the negative threats which bring into question his or her autonomous existence. This provides the framework for a formidable architecture of juridical power which, holding true to the belief that humanity's greatest expression is found in its universal proclamations, proposes an account of law which is both political (i.e. law is politics) and ultimately incontestable (i.e. to question the universal aspiration is to act unreasonably in principle). Here we encounter a substantive conception of the universal wherein the universal appears to be a progressive process that is constituted by the actions of rational political actors working towards the humanitarian ideal. To reason therefore already presupposes a given universality such that the universal claim and the rational process appear co-extensive. If we reason universally, we reason on behalf of humanity. Questions of individual desire, self-interest, and political difference then become evidential traits of a characteristic fall which is deemed inherent to an account of freedom forever haunted by the propensity to act against what is universal to reason. This, however, is temporally compromised. Since this invariably presupposes a political frame which seeks to encapsulate all contingency while nevertheless appreciative that this is beyond the realms of lived experience (as Kant understood all too well), what is universal appears to be an 'impossible necessity'. Judith Butler offers a compelling critique of this incommensurability which, taking the universal as a heuristic point of departure, theoretically constructs a meta-dogmatism:

> The claim to universality always takes place in a given syntax, through a certain set of cultural conventions in a recognizable venue. Indeed, the claim cannot be made without the claim being recognized as a claim. But what orchestrates what will and will not be recognizable as a claim? Clearly, there is an establishing rhetoric for the assertion of universality and set of norms that are invoked in the recognition of such claims. Moreover, there is no cultural consensus on an international level about what ought and ought not be a claim to universality, who may make it, and what form it ought to take.[47]

Following Butler's incisive intervention, we can argue that there are by definition no universal, all-embracing, value-neutral, timeless *a priori* norms which occupy some purified and objective existential space waiting access by the learned justices of the peace. There is no absolute convergence point to human reason. Every norm is simply the outcome of a particular power struggle. Since the norm is therefore fully invested in the biopolitical decision of what must live and what must die for the universal good, it is possible for de-politicization to occur when life is being primed for its own betterment: that is, *within* the remit of humanitarian discourses and practices. This offers an alternative reflection on Agamben's bare life. Bare life for Agamben is seen to be a product of the sovereign encounter. Life, in other words, becomes bare since it is abandoned from the law – hence the juridical protections which normally guarantee the subject a place in our moral and political universe of obligation. What the '*nomos* as circulation' hypothesis, however, suggests is that the bare life of the biopolitical encounter is the product of a different logic. No longer banished from the realm, life is denied its political quality as the 'bare essentials' for human survival take precedence. No longer then rendered inactive to the society it endangers, life is stripped bare of its pre-existing values on the basis that those precise qualities impede its potential productive salvation. Hence, while the bio-political subject is assumed to be *without* meaningful political quality – albeit in this instance because of some dangerous lack of fulfilment (what we have termed Fallen Freedom) – exceptional politics are nevertheless displaced by the deeply politicized *bare activity* of planetary species survival.

Policies of Containment

Without question, the 9/11 attacks in New York and Washington and the 7/7 bombings in London helped to re-enforce the narrative that trans-border movements are potentially dangerous. The British media in particular made significant play of the fact that three of the London suicide bombers were former refugees. Though not hidden or clandestine, they nevertheless originated from *else-where*. As a result, gaining entry into Europe on the whole has increasingly become far more difficult for those ordinarily seeking refuge from intolerable local conditions.[48] The tragic irony of this should not escape us. Not only are those seeking refuge by far more likely to come into contact with forms of political terror, the War on Terror itself has through various military incursions created its own forced displacements.[49] This is not, however, a radically new departure. Liberal regimes have been fully active in thwarting the possibility of mass migration from zones of political crises for some considerable time: formal attempts to control immigration began with decolonization, while the metaphor 'Fortress Europe', for example, entered common usage in the late 1980s.[50] Such concerns evidently came to the fore during the 1990s along with the advent of the so-called 'complex political emergency'. Although seeing conflict as a multi-causal process which affected all aspects of society proved to be the catalyst for a new-found humanitarian interventionism, it was nevertheless also driven by a concern with the displacement and the exodus of populations in and from zones of crisis.

The restrictive European response to the break-up of the former Yugoslavia proved significant in this respect. Despite the premising of interventionism on humanitarian grounds, it was clear that the 'refugee problem' focused the attentions and galvanized the political response of European leaders. Such concerns have more recently been expressed with the prospect of fleeing refugees from Libya into Italy and onto mainland Europe. At the same time, we would also do well to remember that many so-called 'humanitarian' agencies decided to intervene in the Rwandan crisis only when international borders had been crossed.[51] While this was undoubtedly a disastrous ethical and policy failure, Rwanda is not, however, an exception. The problem of underdeveloped life has been routinely and systematically *contained* to better manage the life-chance divide separating the global North and South. Containment in this regard has become the unwritten truth of the development–security nexus. For while it is a truism of the post-Cold War period that *you cannot have development without security, and security without development is impossible*, so you cannot have *either* development *or* security without the *containment* of those deemed threatening to the continuation of liberal ways of living. The environment once again promises to generalize this. As Kevin Grove shrewdly appreciates:

> Far from being apolitical and 'technical', institutional discourses on dangerous climate change extend the project of earlier environmental security discourses – specifically, the attempt to secure Western ways of life against the effects of environmental change. Discourses on dangerous climate change put biopolitical technologies of risk management to work alongside and through geopolitical technologies of security to sustain the exclusion and containment of

underdeveloped populations, and the mobility of the global elite, that characterize contemporary practices of 'development.' Insuring 'our common future' – to borrow the title of the Brundtland Report that put sustainable development on the map – here involves transfers of risk management knowledge, technologies and resources to underdeveloped states, which strengthen their ability to contain and manage their populations in an emergent socio-ecological setting.[52]

Containment is altogether biopolitical as questions of entry reveal a distinct allegiance to social, economic, and political compliance/fitness. As Manuel Castells previously intimated, the Fourth World is part of a new global topographical arrangement that no longer benefits from clear geo-strategic distinction; instead it is locatable at the dynamic margins of every metropolitan homeland. New Orleans provides sufficient testimony to the fact that liberal democracies are more than willing to contain poor populations from roaming elsewhere. Within a few days of Hurricane Katrina striking the city, attentions quickly turned to what the *Wall Street Journal* famously dubbed 'the storm after the storm'. As Nicole Gelinas from the Manhattan Institute wrote:

> [O]n a normal day, those who make up New Orleans' dangerous criminal class – yes, likely the same African-Americans we see looting now – terrorize their own communities. . . . [F]ailure to put violent criminals behind bars in peacetime has led to chaos in disaster. . . . Now, no civil authorities can re-assert order in New Orleans. The city must be forcefully demilitarized, even as innocent victims literally starve.[53]

Here we have the clearest of indications how it becomes possible to render an entire people inhospitable as a result of their character deficiencies, which, although manifest in their conditions of social backwardness, become a reality through the experience of an environmental catastrophe

that intensified a dangerous potentiality that was waiting
to erupt. It simply required a certain change in local conditions to allow that which was potential to become actualized. As this example shows, endangerment is not only
already *pre-supposed* despite any claims of objective neutrality; ideas concerning environmental inhospitability
(actual or potential) actually reveal *already existing* concerns about political inhospitability before any catastrophic
event takes place. We only have to contrast this to the
dignified liberal response to environmental catastrophe as
represented in popular culture such as the movies *Deep
Impact* (1998) or *The Day After Tomorrow* (2004) to
appreciate prejudice and crude assumptions about hypo-
thetical endangerment.

Securing environmental displacement through policies
of containment undermines any claims to political justice.
Here the case of Palestine strikes with critical force. As
Bauman has acutely observed, Palestinian refugees
embody the *sans papiers* in a world that is otherwise full.
Numbering today some three million, they are neatly
contained in various refugee camps throughout the
Middle East in a condition which can only be described
as 'frozen transience'. Offering no prospect for escape,
their habitual reality is 'permanently temporary': 'The
camps are artifices made permanent through blocking
the exits. The inmates cannot go back "where they came
from" . . . but there is no road forward either: no government would gladly see an influx of homeless millions'.
Outside of their camps, they are out of place, viewed as
obstacles and trouble; inside their camps, they are forgot-
ten. Meanwhile, the walls, the barbed wire, the controlled gates, the armed guards – all ensure the permanence
of their exclusion: 'They do not change places; they lose
a place on earth, they are catapulted into a nowhere'.[54]
While this specific security architecture emerged out of a
novel political disaster, it is now expanding and deepen-
ing with each crises of international circulation that

fronts the problem of unwanted migration globally. According to the Internal Displacement Monitoring Centre, for instance, there are some 25 million victims of forced displacement living in such permanently temporary conditions.[55] Such individuals have no prospect of leaving. As the capitalization of peace therefore continues to demand localized solutions – which in practice means policies of containment – so the possibility that flight can become a meaningful political strategy is denied to those who don't live up to the demands set by contemporary systems of rule.

– 6 –

The Event Horizon

Time of the Event

Let's imagine for a moment the sense of circumstance felt by an employee working on the upper floors of the North Tower of the World Trade Center on the morning of September 11, 2001. The day may have begun like any other. They may have gazed out of their apartment window at New York's beautifully clear skyline on that bright autumnal morning. Lower Manhattan would have been full of the usual hustle and bustle as people started living out another day with familiar routines and ritualistic patterns. The ebb and flow of city life would have evidenced various speeds and intensities as the population went about its daily business. And the newspaper stands would have been full of the usual topical discussions about the successes and failures of political leaders, recent murders in various no-go areas, latest must-see cultural events and sites for social gatherings, along with various commentaries on key sporting occasions. Upon reaching the office, however, any sense of normality would have soon been shattered. Having looked out upon the familiar urban landscape that offered extended views to upper Manhattan and beyond, something unusual would have gradually appeared in the distance. Not unusual in terms of its material form. New York's skies are, after all, constantly full of various types of air traffic. What was unusual was the trajectory. As American Airlines Flight 11 travelled southward, traversing with continual speed the symmetrical lines of this remarkably geometric urban experiment, the familiar three-dimensional topographies would have been punctured by the singularity of a particular line of flight.

As this no doubt terrifying moment unfolded, it is plausible that the witness may have experienced a sense of *disorientation* as the familiar urban topography was unsettled by the unconventional flight; a sense of *untimeliness* as the normal flow of daily life was disrupted by something out of the ordinary; a sense of *distance* as the terrifying object travelled across space at catastrophic speed; and a sense of *duration* as time passed towards the subsequent impact. Borrowing a term from astrophysics with evident resonance to catastrophe theorizing, we may term this period from the moment of intuition to the final point of no return the 'event horizon'. Everything that was going to happen happened. This brings us to two of the more significant concepts in Continental political philosophy, the horizon and the event.

The idea of the horizon was rigorously analysed by the founder of twentieth-century phenomenology, Edmund Husserl. While, previously, it was common to see the horizon as the limit of our perception – hence a space defined by its sense of boundary – for Husserl, our field of intuition does not simply correspond to our fields of perception alone. The horizon is continuously 'penetrated' by 'indeterminate actualities' which constitutes the very reality of things.[1] The horizon is therefore defined as a 'predelineated potentiality' with lines of articulation that 'mystify' or render inaccessible epistemologically grounded lines of segmentation. This offers a distinct departure from simply seeing the horizon as a point of perceptive finitude. For, as Husserl explains, our intuition continually reminds us that what actually appears *on the horizon* is forever haunted by what appears *beyond* the limits of perceptibility. Since the horizon always presupposes new possibilities, openness, and indeterminate determinations, it reveals different temporalities which, although allowing us to locate a fixed positioning, affirm the dynamic fluidity of any given situation. This was appreciated by Derrida, whose reading of Husserl moves us beyond the temporal and empirically grounded notion of the horizon, towards a notion of the horizon which prefigures 'the totality of possible historical experiences':

> Horizon is always already there of a future which keeps the indetermination of its infinite openness intact (even though this future was announced to consciousness). As the structural determination of every material indeterminacy, a horizon is always virtually present in every experience – for it is at once the unity and the incompletion for that experience; the anticipated unity in every incompletion. The notion of the horizon converts critical philosophy's state of abstract possibility into the concrete infinite potentiality secretly presupposed therein. The notion of horizon thus makes the apriori and the teleological coincide.[2]

Derrida forces a return here to our previous understanding of potentiality by allowing us to explain the horizon in terms of an 'open space' or 'supra-sensible plane' (i.e. consisting of both intuition and perception) across which the virtual becomes actualized. This is somewhat reminiscent of what Agamben terms 'the threshold' – the moment when everything becomes possible. What appears solid enters into crisis so that familiar referents occupy a 'zone of irreducible indistinction'. It is at this moment that we become exposed to the sheer contingency of everything. What is previously taken for granted no longer provides comforting reference. Deleuze's notion of the *élan vital* is useful here to designate the moment when the virtual passes the threshold towards its actualization.[3]

Constantine Boundas insists that the '[é]*lan vital* is not an occult power, but rather the name of the force(s) at work each time that a virtuality is being actualized.'[4] It is 'difference passing into action'. What is virtual in this context generate 'disjunctions as they begin to actualize tendencies which were contained in the original unity and composibility'.[5] Since the actual is therefore established prior to any logic of fixed or stable boundaries, it offers no philosophy, if we understand philosophy to be concerned with foundational questions of the real. Indeed, once the virtual is actualized, there is no point of stasis, for every actuality contains within it new virtual potentials which alter our intuitions and perceptions. As a consequence, our orientation changes so that all things have a momentary existence, one whose unquestioned fixity only really comes into focus the moment it starts to disappear from the world.

This brings us back to our concern with the second of our significant political-philosophical concepts, the event. Events have come to define our ways of thinking about problems in contemporary times. As William Connolly explains, 'At The Contemporary Condition we are magnetized by the politics of the event. We strive to dig into it, think with and against it, even sometimes to nudge it in this way or that while it is underway.'[6] This fixation on events, for Connolly, highlights a certain 'mesmerization' which is manifest by the positive ability to 'startle, provoke and energize', along with a profound lethality made through a 'combination of uncertain origins, messy modes of self-amplification, and fateful possibilities'. But what makes an event an 'event'? From what we have already discovered from the complexity sciences, we can argue that there is no 'truth of the event' at the point of its emergence. Creating the world anew (what we may term 'the eventual') in fact requires a certain *infidelity* to the prevailing normative and truthful assumptions. So, rather than attempting to authenticate in vain the true meaning of events, it is more pertinent to ask how events *function* politically. Here we return to Deleuze. Not only did he argue that the sole aim of philosophy was to become 'worthy of the event'; his understanding of ontology puts forward the question of whether we could have a politics or ethics which is adequate to emerging conditions of the new. For Deleuze, however, the concept of the event is far more complicated than forms of mass occurrences which impact upon a significant number of people. While an event may be a revolutionary gathering, an uprising, or even a catastrophic disaster, it can also be a Francis Bacon painting or indeed a manuscript. Events are singular expressions of force which affect and counter-affect lives (singular or multiple) to such an extent that the world is no longer thought, perceived, or experienced the same again by the experiencing subject.

Events mark a rupture in the continuity of one's historical experiences. They are not a thing in themselves. Neither do they have a distinct material form. The event is the actualization of the virtual expressed as force. It is a momentary encounter following which the virtually possible inaugurates a new sense of reality of a different kind. From this perspective, the event has no evident starting-point or terminus. It allows for the creation of new virtualities (infinite condition of possibility) out of the new conditions of the real. While some may be tempted to argue here that the significance of an event must nevertheless be measured in terms of it quantitative dimensions (i.e. how many people are immediately affected), we should not underestimate the importance or the potential force of the qualitatively singular. As the complexity sciences further purport, in complex systems sometimes it is the most minor change within that system which has the most cascading effects. We only have to draw attention here to what we may term 'the event of Rosa Parks' to illustrate how a singular moment can have tremendous force well beyond the laws of quantitative power. Events in this regard have no teleological history. History in fact appears to be a highly reductionist method of recording a series of complex expressions, mishaps, and accidents that defy pre-intelligibility at their point of actualization. As Connolly further writes:

> [E]vents often throw Intelligence experts, media representatives, political leaders in other places, and practitioners of the human sciences into intense bouts of self-doubt and self-scrutiny. 'How come we did not anticipate this?', ask the Intelligence agencies. 'What were our leaders doing?', say media talking heads. 'And what about those of us in the media?' 'How come we did not predict this?', whisper political scientists to each other, before they catch themselves enough to recall that they only promise to predict hypothetical events under conditions in which the 'variables' are strictly specified, not to explain actual events in the messy, ongoing actualities of triggering forces, contagious actions, complex and floating conflicts, obscure purposes, subterranean anxieties, and contending hopes.[7]

Nietzsche's *Thus Spoke Zarathustra* provides a metaphorical way into the ontology of the event by bringing us directly back to the concept of the horizon.[8] Nietzsche draws attention to the horizon when referring to the Greek goddess Eos (whom he terms Lady Dawn). Fascinating owing to her ability to usher in a new day, she reveals the capacity for 'difference' (contingency) within the 'same' environment or dawning sense of renewal (Nietzsche refers to this as the Eternal Return). Eos therefore offers a way into understanding the event horizon. As Frank Stevenson explains,

> [I]n her act of rising (alone, singular) *above* her couch (horizon) Eos represents the pre-existing verticality of the horizon itself as the line marking earth/sky and night/day difference, a line that will momentarily be crossed (transgressed) by the rising sun which, once shining, will cause Eos in her proper sense as 'Dawn' to disappear. The rising Dawn, in other words, reinforces our sense that the horizon of our perception already has a vertical as well as horizontal gap or difference.[9]

It is also important to appreciate, as Stevenson notes, that Nietzsche correlates this concept of the horizon with Eos' sense of the accidental (*Zufall*), chance (*Ohngefähr*), and the experimental spirit (*Übermuth*). Every event of the night becoming-day thus becomes a game of chance – the dice-throw. Deleuze takes this idea of the dice-throw and gives it a distinct metaphysical purchase: 'The dice are thrown against the sky. . . . They fall back to earth with all the force of the victorious solutions which bring back the throw.' Not only is Deleuze proposing here that chance (throw of the dice) actualizes virtual actualization ('[T]he throw of the dice affirms chance every time; every throw of the dice affirms the whole of chance each time'); he is also pointing to the radical openness of all possibilities, so that the horizon assumes a virtual (potential) quality. Hence, for Deleuze, what is at stake here is more than simple rearrangement of epistemic reason. The event of life itself evidences an emergent ontology:

> Ontology is the dice-throw, the chaosmos from which the cosmos emerges. . . . This is precisely what Nietzsche meant by will to power . . . – that dice-throw capable of affirming the whole of chance. . . . If 'being' is above all difference and commencement, Being is itself repetition, the recommencement of being . . . and an origin assigns a ground only in a world already precipitated into universal *ungrounding*. . . . This is the point at which the ultimate origin is overturned into an absence of origin (in the always displaced circle of the eternal return). An aleatory point is displaced through all the points on the dice, as though one time for all times.[10]

This brings us to an important temporal distinction between 'historical time' and the 'time of the event'. Heidegger would have reminded us that all time is preceded by some great or 'historically significant event', so that time assumes a qualitative determination.[11] The ultimate example is 'the Christ event', which serves to give the entire Gregorian calendar content and substance beyond the mere numerical passing of time. History thus conceived is the measure of the flow of life as the eventfulness of existence. Without the event, time is meaningless. Historical time nevertheless still appears to us chronologically. *Chronos* designates the epistemological horizon so that time has an intrinsic significance. Such time refers us to the familiar metric pattern in which time is neatly parcelled and subject to the historical record. It can be measured, chronicled, and re-presented so as to serve as a fixed point of reference. The time of the event, however, is subject to a different temporality. It highlights the aporia of history on account of the inability to appropriate the event. Time can be said to stand ever before us. Borrowing from Nietzsche, this time of the event may be termed *Aion*. It is time 'out of joint',[12] what Nietzsche also referred to as being 'the untimely'. It is the point at which everything has already happened, while everything is going to happen. It is at this precise epistemologically contingent intersection where security agencies now enter. Confronting the time of the event of everything has happened/everything is going to happen, so questions are turned to become 'What has just happened?' 'What is going to happen?'

Pre-emptive Governance

When the practice of security aims to secure us all from each and every form of contingent excess – those micro-specific 'aleatory events' which are now assumed to place our individual destinies into question – then for all our sakes the principal objective shifts to ensure that no subject is exposed to the *alea* of a pure outside. There cannot be any room for the alterior since the unknowable is precisely that which is dangerous in a world of radically interconnected circulation. What is more, since terror is intimately aligned with those aleatory phenomena that complex and adaptive systems necessarily entail, and since the very task of making life live securely insists upon the (im)possibility of securing the potentially limitless or at least unknowable ways in which such terror may be announced, a new micro-specific security conjecture has appeared whose concern with the virtual necessarily places terror at the heart of all possible *event*ualities. Knowing that we don't know about the future therefore reveals the aporia of our times. While ideas of better times ahead are projected onto the future so as to cast doubts on our present, we are also reminded that the ambivalence of the future means that it could be truly terrifying at its point of emergence. As a result, it doesn't really matter whether one is confronting a terrorist attack, a natural disaster, or an unfortunate accident. Reasonable strategic commonality can be established inasmuch as they are all presented to be security concerns which strike out at random, drawing no distinctions between the guilty or the innocent, let alone those lives that are more worthy of living. As the comprehensive precursor to the latest British Government National Security Strategy explained:

> [T]he overall objective of this National Security Strategy is to anticipate and address a diverse range of threats and risks to our security, in order to protect the United Kingdom and its interests, enabling its people to go about their daily lives freely and with confidence, in a more secure, stable, just, and prosperous world. . . . [Threats and risks] are real, and also more diverse, complex, and interdependent than in the past. The policy responses outlined . . ., therefore, are not only individually vital to our future security and prosperity, but also wide-ranging, complex, and, crucially, interdependent. They reflect an integrated approach to developing policy and building capability, intended to deliver results against a number of linked objectives.[13]

Virilio calls this tendency to place all potentially disastrous events within one analytical framework the *Integral Accident*: 'the global accident that integrates, one by one, the whole set of minor incidents along the way that once characterized societal life'.[14] Brian Jenkins, a senior adviser at the RAND Corporation, has long advocated taking such a 'deliberately unconventional, broad, and inclusive approach'.[15] The *Fifth Annual Report to the President and the Congress* ('Fifth Report'), which was presented in December 2003, broke new ground in this respect. Based on the report's recommendations, the advisory panel called for a 'New Normalcy' approach to terror, with the future potential for risk no longer being seen in terms of the exceptional. As Michael Wermuth explains, 'It was the panel members' firm intention to articulate a vision of the future that subjects terror to a logical place in the array of threats from other sources that the American people face every day – from natural disease and other illness to crime and traffic and other accidents, to mention a few.'[16]

What we are encountering here is the onset of an all-hazard spectrum of threat through which every small disruption – man-made or natural – is becoming part of a complex and interconnected system of potentially cataclysmic effects. Little wonder that when a catastrophe first strikes, we are never quite sure as to the nature of the terror being faced. Even if we are encountering what turns out to be an unfortunate accident, we still need to provide the supplementary qualification that 'terrorism can be ruled out'. With this in mind, it is therefore arguable that what 9/11 permitted was to accelerate the convergent process wherein all that threatens the authentic substance of life, each and every accident or potential catastrophe, could find some form of connection. We should not be under any illusions as to the significance of this. What these linkages firmly re-establish (or at least render obvious) is one of the original philosophical fractures which would serve to justify the objective and amoral scientific validity of the modern condition. It has already been noted that the modern notion of evil was premised on the ability to set apart the *randomness* of natural disaster from the *intentionality* of moral evil.[17] The onset of an all-hazard spectrum of threat, however, proposes that *all randomness is potentially evil and all intentionality potentially disastrous.* The Terror of the Event appears in the very possibility of any unanticipated rupture – those surprising but accidental occurrences which remind us of the impossibility of a fully secure existence and yet reaffirm the purpose of our agendas. With terror therefore politically neutralized, all that remains are simply the 'accidents in time' which pose a fundamental challenge to our settled and foreclosed existence.[18] Melinda Cooper explains:

> If the catastrophe event is often presented as something of a paradox of risk-management, it is because it confounds the traditional framework of rational decision-making. Classical risk theory presumes that we can predict the likelihood of a future event, at least in statistical terms. The longer our time-scale and the wider our field of vision, the more accurate our predictions will be. If we feel that we are unable to calculate the probability of an event, we can always wait until more information becomes available before making a decision. Prediction founds the possibility of prevention. At worst, classical risk theory reassures us that, if the accident does occur, we will have been able to insure against it. Catastrophe risk, on the other hand, denies us the luxury of preparation. When and if it happens, it will be by surprise, abruptly, and on a scale that overwhelms all efforts at damage control. What we are dealing with here is not so much the singular accident, as the accident amplified across a whole event-field, a phase transition that may emerge without warning, instantaneously and irreversibly transforming the conditions of life on earth.[19]

Whereas traditional approaches to terror were orientated towards 'actions' (i.e. committing a terrorist act) or 'intentions' (i.e. intending to commit such an act),[20] the problem of emergence shifts the priority to focus on *capabilities*: 'Capabilities-based planning is planning, under uncertainty, to provide capabilities suitable for a wide range of modern-day challenges and circumstances, while working within an economic framework. . . . Capabilities-based planning has the virtue of encouraging prudent worrying about potential needs that go well beyond currently obvious threats. At the same time, it imposes the requirement for responsibility and choice.'[21] Invariably, this model works in a multidimensional fashion. As Brian Jackson explains, given that 'uncertainty presents a particular problem', then 'planning techniques [must] attempt to deal with uncertainty by designing of portfolios of capabilities and testing how the performance of different policy choices might be affected by key uncertainties.'[22] Hence, refining the more traditional concerns with mitigation and resilience, a new approach – 'consequence prevention' – is to be offered whose new strategic calculus can be assessed in terms of 'preventative performance'. Key to this strategy is the merger of two approaches. Firstly, 'given there will likely always be some uncertainty about future terrorist threats, policies that are either less sensitive – or are insensitive – to limits in knowledge would be desirable.'[23] And secondly, given that it is precisely this uncertainty – or lack of clarity about intentions – which troubles security practitioners, then a pro-active response is necessary: '[T]his can be done by constructing alternative futures or using scenario analysis to test how portfolios will perform under different sets of assumptions. . . . [P]reventive portfolios that performed well across a range of possible futures would be judged less sensitive to threat uncertainty – and therefore more attractive given an unknowable future.'[24]

This strategic rethink does not encourage paranoiac entropy. With governmental reason now seeking to actively produce (hence profit from) the future, we enter a new strategic age in which not only does the advent of radical emergence place terror at the heart of all eventualities, but life must also live in a time when the very process of living demands that we exist in the spotlight of dangerous uncertainty. The permanence of terror thus serves to continually reinvest itself, giving sanction to the most terrifying forms of peace – a peace that, although always deferred, is nevertheless continuously self-valorized by rendering dangerous the very account of life it otherwise holds so dearly.

Thus, upon this post-Clausewitzean security terrain, terror is characterized not merely by the blurring of friend and enemy beyond meaningful distinction, nor by the equal blending of organic and inorganic, animate and inanimate. What truly defines terror in today's world is how the infinite now connects to the finitude of existence.[25] Ever since Kant, the modern condition has attempted to give more to the finitude of existence by incorporating life within the structures of the great infinity of ideas. Indeed, as Quentin Meillassoux explains, it was precisely through inaugurating the (in)finite condition, which was shaped no longer by the God–world relationship, but by the infinite possibility of finite beings *in this world*, that the 'necessity of contingency' began to take shape.[26] That today's security-speak talks in such a Kantian-inspired language to position contingency at the forefront of security debates is therefore not incidental. The language of civil contingencies is the necessary product of a situation in which the finitude of life as a biological fact of being is now fully complemented by the infinite becoming of emergent life. As Michael Dillon and Julian Reid argue:

> Not all emergence is good . . . good emergence has to be distinguished from bad, desired emergence from unwanted emergence. In the process, war becomes less a periodic phenomenon than the very optimization of the state of living required by an emergency of emergence – such an emergency determined by the character of life itself rather than the presence, for example, of deadly geo-strategic or even ideological rivals. Emergence is simply a permanent emergence. . . . Monstrosity [thus] arises as much from within as from without. Catastrophe finds a new location. It continues of course to be associated with forces of nature. . . . But it also finds a new site here in the very bio-informatic order as such: the body threatens catastrophe.[27]

When strategic priority foregrounds *what-is-to-come*, power becomes *pre-emptive*. While pre-emption is often associated with the controversial military doctrine of the Bush administration, it has become the 'operative logic of power' which defines our political age.[28] As the shift towards event-based thinking illustrates, security governance is all about securing our tomorrows. This offers a number of significant departures. As Brian Massumi explains, '[P]re-emption is not prevention. Although the goal of both is to neutralize threat, they fundamentally differ epistemologically and ontologically.' With prevention it is necessary to have 'an ability to assess threats empirically and identify their causes'. Causation thus places epistemological demands upon security practitioners in the sense that the ability to establish precise empirical relations between causes and effects lends itself to the formalization of preventative strategies. Prevention as such 'operates in an objectively knowable world in which uncertainty is a function of a lack of information, and in which events run a predictable, linear course from cause to effect'. Pre-emption, in contrast, 'operates in the present on a future threat'. Hence, unlike preventative strategies, which depend upon the ability to verify threat before it is written, the pre-emptive epistemology is 'unabashedly one of *uncertainty*'. While prevention therefore has 'no ontology of its own because it assumes that what it must deal with has an objectively given existence prior to its own intervention', with pre-emption there is an 'ontological premise' that what is dangerous is precisely that which has yet to be formed, what has '*not yet even emerged*'.[29]

Since pre-emption works from the ontological premise that the nature of threat cannot be specified, its battles are directly fought upon the ontological terrain. Its power is unashamedly onto-rationalized. Importantly, however, since pre-emptive actions target that which cannot be epistemologically grounded in verifiable fact, it necessarily affirms a certain faith-based politics which draws exclusively upon the liveliness of the human condition. It operates by having a certain 'sense of the situation' or a feeling that something is untoward. In other words, the perception of threat is not based upon verifiable truth, but relies unashamedly upon received wisdom. Pre-emptive acts cannot therefore be anything other than promissory. Taking the unknown to be its point of departure, not only does the pre-emptive strike derive its legitimacy from claims to be able to shape the unknowable, but its operative fabric relies upon matters of pure faith. Thus the consequential ethics which guided the humanitarian interventions of the late 1990s are taken to their logical extreme by pre-emptive politics. While these missions had already established that the distinction between 'doing something or doing nothing' demanded a certain faith in mission, this tendency to rely solely upon one's senses demands complete faith in the righteousness of the task. To put it another way, since pre-emptive war is ultimately an attempt to wager that which is radically undecidable against that which is radically uncertain, then the only way such actions can be legitimated is to suggest that to deny support for the war effort is effectively tantamount to losing faith in humanity.

Since pre-emptive power takes that which is yet to emerge to be its object, it is fully complicit in manufacturing its own destiny. The only way to deal with a virtual threat is to actually provoke it into action. The exercise of pre-emptive power is therefore *incitatory* in that it 'contributes to the actual emergence of the threat'. The logic which underwrites this is rather simple. Since the most effective way to confront the problem of emergence is to deal with it on your terms, the 'best option is to help *make it proliferate more*'. Indeed the only way an unspecified threat can be dealt with is to 'actively contribute to *producing* it'.[30] This was certainly the logic used in terms of Al-Qaeda in Iraq. The Allied powers reasoned that there was a presence in Iraq, even though there was no verifiable evidence. The intervention took place; Al-Qaeda appeared. This only went to prove that 'the potential' was there from the beginning. No longer do we require epistemological proof. It is all about mastering the open horizon of possibilities. Winning is not therefore simply about perfecting networked forms of organization; it is all about creating the future. The meaning of the content can be worked out after the event. So can the legality of the actions. As illustrated by the recent case of Amine El Khalifi in Washington, DC, it is now even possible for security agencies to openly recruit, indoctrinate, actively train, and subsequently arrest would-be terrorists on account of the fact that they showed the potential for becoming-terroristic. As FBI agents foil their own terrorist plots, so the lines between offensive action and defensive behaviour blur without any clear distinctions.

This future orientation is highly significant when it comes to retrospective deliberation. No consistency can be offered other than simply giving chronological content to the dangerous and disruptive nature of emergent forms.[31] The British Government's report released to provide official insight into the 7 July London bombings proves instructive in this regard. While the document gives a thorough account of 'what happened', outlining in remarkable detail the *action-of-the-event* in terms of 'where and when', and even 'who' was responsible, no explanation whatsoever is offered to 'why'.[32] The report simply traces movements which are seen to exist in another dimension outside the normal flows of daily life. Without any meaningful assessment of the politics of the event, therefore, what was undertaken was a complex mapping exercise so that we can simulate the terrorists' performances and hopefully insert these types of accident within our calculable models for future amelioration. As noted in a joint study by the US National Institute for Occupational Safety and Health and the RAND Corporation:

> Emergency response organizations are the nation's first line of defence when disaster strikes. While their work is inherently dangerous on any scale, it becomes even more perilous in a major crisis, such as a terrorist attack or large-scale natural disaster. With this in mind . . . the exceptional

complexity and scale of major disasters oblige response organizations to rethink their approach to safety management. Safety should be viewed not as an individual concern, with each organization responsible only for the well-being of its own workers, but rather as a collective one, where safety is a multi-agency function and organizations join forces to keep all responders from harm.[33]

Nowhere is this better evidenced than with the *simulations* of the all-too-expected *future* catastrophic events. Training governmental agencies to respond to all forms of potential catastrophe has become an essential activity of government. In particular, designing and staging of mock terror attacks that simulate the next violent event has become a regular urban feature. Setting the trend, on Friday, 12 April 2002, the United States would simulate an aerial attack of pneumonic plague in Oklahoma City that would infect 95 per cent of the population. With local scouts 'playing' the plague-ridden victims, the focus of this scenario was to calculate the number of probable deaths; to assess the responding agencies' effectiveness; to determine the public's resilience; and invariably to remind the public that there was still a danger 'out there' to be faced. During the summer months, another series of attacks would be simulated that imagined 'Iraqi-financed Afghan terrorists were spraying the smallpox virus into shopping centres in Oklahoma City, Philadelphia and Atlanta'.[34] By March 2003, the United Kingdom was following suit, with the then Home Secretary, David Blunkett, noting that these 'future planned exercises' were to cover 'a catastrophic incident in central London', which could range from an attack by a 'toxic agent' to the 'disruption to the national gas supply and flood defences'.[35] While the exact nature of these catastrophes can never be fully predicted, the purpose of these drills is to provide a probabilistic framework for using 'terrorism risk modelling' in a 'break-even analysis'. Risks are therefore expressed in terms of the 'annualized loss' to the status quo, which consists of assessing the damage caused by conveying the 'combined estimates of the consequences'.[36] Beneath the preparatory lines of these future imaginaries, however, we find a sophisticated biopolitical reasoning at work. As Stephen Graham points out in respect to the securitization (what he terms the 'lock-down') of London's 2012 Olympic Games:

> The security preoccupations of Olympics present unprecedented opportunities to push through highly elitist, authoritarian and speculative urban planning efforts that otherwise would be much more heavily contested – especially in democracies. These often work to 'purify' or 'cleanse' diverse and messy realities of city life and portray existing places as 'waste' or 'derelict' spaces to be transformed by mysterious 'trickle-down effects'. . . . During the Games themselves, so-called 'Olympic Divides' are especially stark. In London, a citywide system of dedicated VIP 'Games lanes' are being installed. Using normally public road space, these will allow 4,000 luxury, chauffeur-driven BMWs to shuttle 40,000 Olympic officials, national bureaucrats, politicians and corporate sponsors speedily between their five-star hotels, super-yachts and cordoned-off VIP lounges within the arenas. . . . Far removed from their notional or founding ideals, these events dramatically embody changes in the wider world: fast-increasing inequality, growing corporate power, the rise of the homeland security complex, and the shift toward much more authoritarian styles of governance utterly obsessed by the global gaze and prestige of media spectacles.[37]

The Truth of the Event

Catastrophes (actual or potential) bring into sharp relief what Jacques Lacan called the 'Symbolic Order'. Although Lacan introduced this concept in terms of language, the symbolic also extends to encompass all the great signifiers of social, political, and moral formation. The symbolic therefore represents that which gives concrete meaning to the otherwise abstract imaginary of political communion. As Žižek explains, 'The Symbolic Order is the realm of language, signs, culture, and law. It includes official institutions such as schools, political parties, and Churches; as well as quasi-official institutions like codified and noncodified social norms, i.e. handshakes, winks, etc. The Symbolic Order is a chain of signs that is grounded in the Master Signifier – a sign which grounds itself.' It is what is often termed the 'big other', which 'allows the Symbolic Order itself to become a subject'.[38] National communities have provided us with the most obvious examples of this. While they forever remain imagined constructs in the most abstract and reified sense, their symbolic façades help to materialize a shared sense of belonging by homogenizing life through the regulation and channelling of political desires. National flags and/or presidential palaces, for example, continue to serve as great Oedipal signifiers which, demanding absolute allegiance, concentrate otherwise fragmented and diffuse political desires within any spatialized setting. Such signifiers therefore operate like some 'fantasmic spectre' whose 'presence guarantees the consistency of our own symbolic edifice'.[39] They work by formalizing perceptive belonging and producing a semiotic system of formal content in order to compel obedience. Understanding the importance of these symbols of power is no doubt crucial to our problematic. Not only does it explain why utmost priority is given to protecting symbolic structures for power which are in fact altogether illusionary (a building or a flag, after all, has no intrinsic power in itself since it cannot express its own force); it also explains why counter-violence so often targets the symbolic order of things. Symbolic violence is primarily all about exposing the fragility of the objective illusion of any given imagined community so that it becomes mortally aware of its own finite qualities and fleeting significance.

Ambitions to violence can be understood by questioning the intended audience for the symbolic attack. The audience for 9/11, for instance, was not simply the population of the United States of America. This simultaneous yet slightly staggered attack reveals how the real target was a digitally hard-wired audience which is tuned into the daily functioning of global cities at any given moment. In doing so, we were forced to confront the fragility of our political imaginaries, which relied upon universal narratives in order to promote a post-political settlement that was blind to the contested nature of liberal political rule. We can also learn a great deal about the rationalities and strategic priorities of political projects by analysing the ways in which catastrophes are memorialized in order to leave a lasting political impression. The politics of memorialization can take many different structural and material forms. It is immediately realized through the continual re-running of the event in all the available globally accessible forms of media. It is also consecrated in the creation of new symbolic façades which become lasting shrines to the suffering experienced by the sacrificial victims. Such memorialization is not, however, undertaken simply for the purposes of respecting the tragically fallen. It re-presents the catastrophic moment so that the sense of trauma is harnessed to function politically. This is what Jenny Edkins refers to as being 'the struggle over memory' in which the policy of gentrification promotes a culture of victimhood that 'offers sympathy and pity in return for the surrender of any political voice'.[40] Memory thus serves here to promote a distinct politics of representation in which the contemporary moment is colonized by a catastrophic imaginary to the suffocation of the political. As Maja Zehfuss puts it:

> The unimaginable horror of what happened that day at the World Trade Center has overshadowed not only the other attacks of that day; it has also made it difficult for us to think appropriately about how we should deal with this situation. Nothing is as it was before, we are told. Before anyone really had time to think about what it all means, about what, if anything, we should do, September 11 had

already been turned into a symbol, into a watershed. As such it is an obstacle to critical debate, not only about these specific events, but about fundamental questions of politics, about who we are, about how to address our inevitable vulnerability and our responsibility towards others.[41]

Memorialization is all about ascribing truth to the catastrophic event. 'September 11, 2001 will always be', Bush insisted, 'a fixed point in the life of America'.[42] It is through memorializing that the event is actualized in corporeal terms so as to mark out its lasting significance. This impulse is altogether modern. As Derrida has explained, the experience of a major event 'calls for a movement of appropriation (comprehension, recognition, identification, description, determination, interpretation on the basis of a horizon of anticipation, knowledge, naming and so on)'.[43] Despite the initial bewilderment ('what's happening?'), soon after came the now familiar statements of truth that were made in order to make *sense* of the situation, i.e. 'America under Attack', 'Attack on the Civilized World', 'Attack on Freedom', 'The Day the World Changed Forever', 'An Act of Pure Evil', etc. While the complexity of the situation was all too apparent, such explanations nevertheless still overwhelmingly followed a familiar approach so that the event could be 'neatly broken down into narrative accounts of cause/effect or rational models of independent/dependent variables'.[44] Although these narratives were invariably presented as objectively neutral truths about the event, as David Campbell reminds us, such truths are 'committed to an epistemic realism, whereby the world comprises material objects whose existence is independent of ideas or beliefs about them'.[45] What we may therefore term the 'production-reality' of the event is always subject to a certain truth-telling exercise which glosses over the multiplicity of personal experience in order to offer some universal epistemic surety out of the ashes of catastrophe. As Timothy Rayner explained shortly after the atrocity of the 9/11 attacks:

Ordinarily, when we think of an event, we think of something that takes place within the flow of history. To have
an understanding of 'events' in these terms is to follow
'current affairs' – the kind of everyday occurrences that are
recorded by journalists, and documented in the daily
news. . . . But does this do justice to the event itself? Not
at all. For the most part, this viewpoint elides the event
itself. For here the event is represented as an objective
circumstance – something which takes place 'out there in
the world,' requiring us only to be present on the scene to
capture the moment with our cameras, sum it up in a
sound bite.[46]

What was taking place here was the actualization of the
event so as to constitute a particular 'state of affairs'.
Derrida summarizes this as follows:

With every event, there is indeed the present moment of
its actualization, the moment in which the event is embod-
ied in a state of affairs, an individual, or a person, the
moment we designate by saying 'here, the moment has
come'. The future and the past of the event are evaluated
only with respect to this definitive present, and from the
point of view of that which embodies it.[47]

Such embodiment is essential, for in the process of *trans-
lating* events, i.e. offering definitive *content*, the epistemological basis for counter-actualizations is formed. As
Foucault understood,

[S]ecurity will try to plan a milieu in terms of events or
series of events or possible elements, of series that will have
to be regulated within a multivalent and transformable
framework. The specific space of security refers then to a
series of possible events; it refers to the temporal and the
uncertain, which have to be inserted within a given space.[48]

While this space of security has a distinct territoriality
within the horizon of the event, it also brings dogmatic
force to bear upon the discursive and analytical field in

order to place limits around the acceptable framing of problem-solutions. Deleuze refers to this process as one of 'signification', following which a certain 'image of thought' is resurrected and imposed upon new lines to the closure of political spaces. The implication here is that even before we think, we already have a vague idea of what it means to think, its means and ends.[49] Hence, ascribing truth to the event leads to the promotion of an altogether familiar conception of power that appears to be 'the object of a recognition, the content of a representation, the stake in a competition, and therefore makes it depend, at the end of a flight, on a simple attribution of established values'.[50] This is crucial. Once power is conceived in this way, it is possible to formalize a full spectrum of type-related threats that always refer back to the dominant signifier rather than dealing with the event on its own terms. As Massumi reminds us:

> The singular is exactly as it happens. Other events may follow. Its happening may prove to have been the first in a series of occurrences carrying what may well be considered, under systematic comparison, the 'same' accidents. These cease retrospectively to be anomalies, becoming identifiable traits. On the basis of the shared properties lately assigned to them, the series of occurrences can now be grouped together as belonging to a type: a new type (a new form of content for the propositional system's expression). The event has passed from the status of a singularity to that of a particular instance of a general type: a member of a collection. Propositional systems are type-casting collector mechanisms.[51]

This brings us directly back to the self-depreciating Kantian idea that representations are an essential feature of knowledge since they allow us to move beyond some pre-conceptual horizon. All the while, however, we continue to follow an all too familiar Western metaphysical tendency of focusing upon master signifiers which, applying after-the-event fixed schematics, reveal the finite qualities of our political imaginaries. Derrida terms these master signifiers as being 'the sign' which, 'standing equally for meaning or referent', represents the 'present in its absence. It takes the place of the present. When we cannot grasp or show the thing, state the present, the being-present, when the present cannot be presented, we signify, we go through the detour of the sign. . . . The sign, in this sense, is deferred presence.'[52] While the deferred presence has a performative element expressed in staged acts of remembrance, the symbolic also functions here in such a way that societies can be mobilized in new political directions. What is to be done? Was 9/11, for instance, an act of war? Was the adoption of a war paradigm the logical response? 9/11 here invariably becomes a symbol or a sign in its own right, expressing its own subsequent force that reveals a number of virtual possibilities. Symbolic events in this context appear to be 'problematic and problematizing'.[53] They lead to the 'double question': 'what is going to happen, and what has just happened'.[54] This doubling is crucial since it reconciles the particular event with a universal truth in order to appear as a problem imperative (i.e. a problem that demands action and cannot be left to chance). In doing so, what needs to be done can be forcefully articulated regardless of the particulars of the experience. As a result, a double-articulation or metaphysical structuring of the problem imperative takes place, leading to the creation of catastrophic imaginaries. As Deleuze explained:

> We are led to believe that problems are given ready-made, and that they disappear in the responses or the solution. Already, under this double aspect, they can be no more than phantoms. We are led to believe that the activity of thinking, along with truth and falsehood in relation to that activity, begins only with the search for solutions, that both of these concern only solutions. This belief probably has the same origin as the other postulates of the dogmatic image: puerile examples taken out of context and

arbitrarily erected into models. According to this infantile prejudice, the master sets a problem, our task is to solve it, and the result is accredited true or false by a powerful authority.[55]

While the horrifying violence which followed the attacks of 9/11 was fully dependent upon the memory of suffering, memorialization can also work in more subtle and lasting political ways. The contemporary memorialization of 9/11 is instructive. Although the tenth anniversary launch of the National September 11 Memorial at Ground Zero offered a more sombre reflection than the overt militarism of the previous decade, it still reaffirmed the unflinching commitment to the catastrophic imaginary. Michael Arad's design for the central monument in particular appears remarkably symbolic. Foot-printing the Twin Towers buildings, it draws the past into the present as each of the names of the victims is etched into the granite composite, thus providing lasting unity to the tragically fallen. This is accompanied by a cascading symmetrical flow of water so representative of what Bauman calls the 'liquidity' of our modern times. This differentially repetitive flow of life then descends some thirty feet into a large pool whose centre has a deeper and more prominent darkened void perfectly representative of the black hole phenomenon so often associated with the event horizon catastrophe. Everything is drawn into this inner void. Nothing escapes. Such symbolism is illuminated at night. Then the lighted inner sides of the memorial truly emphasize the epistemic certainties of the trauma by making visible what is no longer there. At the same time, the continuation of the catastrophe paradigm is drawn into sharp relief as the central void, drawing in all the concentrated matter, acts to remind visitors of the event that is forever etched into the collective consciousness. These collective imaginaries, however, remain haunted by the unknowable horrors of the experience, which lies inaccessibly beneath the surface of the memorial's fixed frames.

Thinking Eventually

The event is also at the forefront of contemporary political and philosophical thought. We may even argue that, post-Nietzsche, every political philosopher working out of this tradition connects to the genealogy of the thought-event in one form or another. While this foregrounds the links between subjectivity and the conditions of the new, theorists are sharply divided over the question of the truth of events. This opens up a particular critical and analytical wound that formed the basis of deconstructionism. Gerald Prince's *A Dictionary of Narratology* defines the event as a 'change of state manifested in discourse by a process statement in the mode of *Do* or *Happen*. An event can be an action or act . . . or a happening . . . . Along with existents [subjects and/or objects], events are the fundamental constituents of the story.'[56] While this definition underscores the reasoning that events are the *essential* component of any narrative, whether an event has an essence in itself is open to deep philosophical question. True to our Kantian-inspired metaphysical heritage, it has been common to argue that all events are driven by claims to truth. We seek to access the universal of any given situation. As a result, the politics of the event is always underwritten by the politics of truth so integral to the foundationalism and hyper-structuralism of Western metaphysics. This idea has been developed by the leading contemporary thinker of the event, Alain Badiou, who uses set theory to explain the truth of the event. As Badiou writes in his *magnum opus Being and Event*, '[A] subject is nothing other than an active fidelity to the event of truth.'[57] Hence, for Badiou, since being is explicable in terms of mathematics, it is possible to reconstruct the deconstructive orientation and begin reassessing the deeply structured meaning of 'the logic of worlds'.[58]

Deleuze argued that '[o]ne does not ask how the subject gains its experience, but how experience gives us a subject.'[59] So whereas for Badiou a subject is that which articulates itself in relationship to an event, indeed finds itself in fidelity to that event, Deleuze comes at the problem of novelty by affirming the infidelity to truth. While Badiou therefore affirms hyper-structural metaphysical frames (*Being and Event* can be read as the Cartesian meditations for our time) so that the conditions of the new reveal the truth in the sense of a generic process of subjectivization, Deleuze encourages us to accept that the conditions of the new defy pre-intelligibility at the moment of its emergence. If it can be thought the same, it cannot be new. If it is thought already, it is merely more of the same. This approach resonated with Derrida, who argued,

> The undergoing of the event, that which in the undergoing or in the ordeal *at once opens itself up to and resists experience*, is, it seems to me, a certain unappropriability of what comes or happens. The event is what comes and, in coming, comes to surprise me, to surprise and to suspend comprehension: the event is first of all *that which* I do not comprehend. Better, the event is first of all *that* I do not comprehend . . . – my incomprehension.[60]

This incomprehensibility is compelling. We only have to look at the re-runs of the television broadcasts on 9/11 to evidence a complete lack of understanding such that words failed us. Derrida understood this better than most:

> *Le 11 Septembre* . . . 'To mark a date in history' presupposes, in any case, that 'something' comes or happens for the first and last time, 'something' that we do not yet really know how to identify, determine, recognize, or analyze but that should remain from here on in unforgettable: an ineffaceable event in the shared archive of a universal calendar. . . . 'Something' took place, we have the feeling of not having seen it coming, and certain consequences undeniably follow upon the 'thing'. But this very thing, the place and meaning of this 'event', remains ineffable, like an intuition without concept, like a unicity with no generality on

the horizon or with no horizon at all, out of range for a language that admits its powerlessness and so is reduced to pronouncing mechanically a date, repeating it endlessly, as a kind of ritual incantation, a conjuring poem, a journalistic litany or rhetorical refrain that admits to not knowing what it's talking about.[61]

9/11 showed how imposing a uniform truth on the event represented a profound failure of the political imaginary. Judith Butler accounts for this in terms of the framing of the problem: 'The "frames" that work to differentiate the lives we can apprehend from those we cannot (or that produce lives across a continuum of life) not only organize visual experience but also generate specific ontologies of the subject. Subjects are constituted through norms which, in their reiteration, produce and shift the terms through which subjects are recognized.'[62] Importantly, for Butler, since what matters here is the subsequent production of certain truthful subjectivities out of the ashes of devastation, we must bring into question the framing of life as a seemingly objective ontological and epistemological fact:

> [T]o call the frame into question is to show that the frame never quite contained the scene it was meant to limn, that something was already outside, which made the very sense of the inside possible, recognizable. The frame never quite determined precisely what it is we see, think, recognize, and apprehend. Something exceeds the frame that troubles our sense of reality; in other words, something occurs that does not conform to our established understanding of things.[63]

This call to break with the dominating content of the time is more than an attempt to draw attention to the multiplicity of the experiences of events. It is to open up the space for the political by breaking apart the myth of the universal experience of truth. The value of this approach was shared by Henry Giroux, who, writing on the tenth anniversary of 9/11, added:

> In the hours and days that bled out from the tragic events of September 11, 2001, the unfolding sense of trauma and loss drew us together in a fragile blend of grief, shared responsibility, compassion, and a newfound respect for the power of common purpose and commitment. The translation of such events into acts of public memory, mourning, and memorializing are ambivalent and deeply unsettling. We must recall that they do not only bring about states of emergency and the suspension of civil norms and order. They can, and did, give birth to enormous political, ethical and social possibilities. Yet, such enlightened moments proved fleeting. A society has to move with deliberate speed from the act of witnessing to the responsibility of just memorializing; in other words, to the equally difficult practice of reconfiguring what politics, ethics and civic engagement should mean after 9/11. On the tenth anniversary of that tragic day, our struggle to remember and reclaim those moments in good faith was constantly challenged, and in ways that few of us would dare to have imagined a decade later.[64]

Shared trauma of violence doesn't necessarily translate into discourses of revenge. Counter-violence is simply the option most preferred by certain political ways of thinking. Undoubtedly the history of modern politics has been distinguished by the normality of violence. What the United States and its allies therefore did in the immediate aftermath of 9/11 was not in any way exceptional. An exceptional response would have been a non-violent one. Instead, the chain of events followed the all too familiar conventional norms that through violence justice would be served and future catastrophe would be averted. None of this is, however, inevitable. Indeed, despite this violent weight of historical reasoning, at the human level, it is increasingly clear that the experience of the tragedy was far more complex. As Giroux further explains, 'What 9/11 made clear is that just memory requires those elements of counter-memory that challenge the official narratives of 9/11 in order to recover the most valuable and most vulnerable elements of democratic culture too often sacrificed in tragedy's aftermath.' Hence, for Giroux, to truly honour the victims of 9/11,

> we should not be reluctant to engage also in public dialogue about both the legacy and the politics that precipitated and emerged from the events that took place on that tragic day. . . . Such uncomfortable moments of consciousness provide the basis for a form of witnessing that refuses the warmongering, human rights violations, xenophobia, and the violation of civil liberties that take shape under the banner of injury and vengeance.[65]

Simon Critchley dared to think the 'impossible' and take this a remarkable stage further:

> What if the government had simply decided to turn the other cheek and forgive those who sought to attack it, not seven times, but seventy times seven? What if the grief and mourning that followed 9/11 were allowed to foster a nonviolent ethics of compassion rather than a violent politics of revenge and retribution? What if the crime of the Sept. 11 attacks had led not to an unending war on terror, but the cultivation of a practice of peace – a difficult, fraught and ever-compromised endeavour, but perhaps worth the attempt?[66]

Critchley's provocation offers more than a warning against the political ruination of violent responses. He is challenging us to think how we may have a political ethics adequate to such events. This shift towards a politics of forgiveness is no doubt a remarkable thing to ask for. Perhaps that is the precise point. Ours remains a history marked by a violent humanism so often masquerading in the name of security, peace, and justice. To advocate a politics of forgiveness when faced with such crises would pass for something truly exceptional. Critchley's previous affinity with Derridean ethics is striking here. As Derrida maintained, an act of forgiveness worthy of the name must be offered in the event of something altogether unforgiveable: 'It *should not be* normal, normative, normalizing. It should remain exceptional and extraordinary, in the face of the impossible: as if it interrupted the ordinary course of historical temporality.'[67] The forgiving of unforgivable acts presents itself as an aporia of impossibility. And yet, as Derrida reminds us, it is precisely when the aporetic moment arrives that it becomes both possible and necessary. 'It only becomes possible from the moment that it appears impossible.'[68] The fact that such a proposition still appears altogether impossible is indicative of the violence of liberal humanism. And yet, the normalized alternative, so common to the history of modern life, illustrates with devastating and politically debilitating surety why Nietzsche was insistent that nihilistic behaviour was tied to a spirit of revenge. Once we begin to act out of resentment, so the catastrophic cycle of violence continues, to the evacuation of political alternatives.

Beyond the Catastrophic

Our current tendency to colonize the political imaginary with the prospect of all manner of catastrophic events reveals how hyper-paranoiac contemporary liberal rule has become. It has also been nothing short of politically catastrophic. Anticipating the physical violence of the future, we do a terrible intellectual violence to the present. For while today's security mantra is all about securing tomorrow, the fact that tomorrow defies pre-intelligibility casts terrifying suspicion on the present. While memorialization is therefore crucial as our imaginaries emphasize the worst case scenario, so the intellectual terrain once occupied by theorists often decreed abstract or esoteric on account of their radical alterity now appears fully in keeping with contemporary security discourses. This renders Continental thinking both necessary and yet altogether problematic as far as power is concerned for the very same reasons. As a result, since both security and Continental thinkers take the open horizon of the event to be their emergent object for ideas of freedom, justice, and political emancipation, so the latter's thinking becomes more than a novel curiosity. Continental thinking thus appears at a crucial juncture. Either it seeks conformity to a compromised alliance with this bio-technologizing pursuit or it becomes something that needs to be vanquished at all political costs. Maybe the merger between the radical and the fundamental is already instructive in this regard as political difference becomes increasingly dangerous. As Richard Posner explicitly puts it:

> What if anything should society be doing to prevent . . . catastrophes? 'If anything' is an important qualification. Not all problems are soluble, and we mustn't merely assume that we can do something about the catastrophic risks that cloud the future. We must first try to get a handle on their true gravity, which is a function of both the probability that one or another of them will materialize if we do nothing and the awful consequences if that happens. Then we must weigh up the costs that would have to be borne, and the psychological and political obstacles that would have to be overcome.[69]

There is an important point to be made here. Biopolitical regimes of security governance have always revolved around threats to existence. Not only has this rendered life to be a problem that is forever *irresolvable*; its entire discourse on security is paradoxically underwritten by an appreciation that life can never actually be made fully secure. Biopolitics is always about dealing with the problem of precarious or vulnerable subjects. It is all about dealing with the catastrophic threats posed to life's inevitable

mortality and the finitude of its existence. While this biological rationality has been compensated for by various
eschatological forms of communion, the divine order of
the biopolitical economy of life today promotes subjects
of crisis. Such is the case that this order's emergent characteristics work against the former compulsion to secure
the political subject in any fixed sense. This is not incidental. The liberal subject is the subject of transformative
self-authoring. He or she willingly embraces regulated
choice. Security consumption is an integral part of this. We
buy into various technologies which promise to keep us
safer from harm, just as various lifestyles are promoted on
account of their ability to promise a more vital existence.
While there is a clear economy at work here that profits
from the potential catastrophic encounter, none of these
products ever promise to be 100 per cent secure. Indeed,
as any person who has come into contact with the insurance industry will appreciate, insurance offers safety and
protection to those whose lives are at less risk of the
chance mishap. What security agencies therefore ultimately
seek to insure against has become precisely something
which cannot be secured with any measure of quantifiable
certainty or regulatory application – life most certainly
included.

So where does this leave us politically? And how can
we challenge the liberal biopolitical security arrangements
which now stake the future of planetary existence on their
political strategies? Biopolitics would be hollow and empty
if it reduced life to the mere level of a biological fact of
being. It would not be able to command any obedience.
What we desire to follow must positively induce. While
biopolitics therefore renders life problematic in terms of
its biological capacities, for its system of rule to hold true
there needs to be something in operation which provides
a more seductive bio-philosophical meaning. People
don't just simply desire securitization for securitization's
sake. The free circulation of desires needs to be positively

manipulated for such processes to take hold. Materiality invariably works. Tales of rags to riches (and vice versa) prove rather convincing when encouraging subjects to follow biopolitical techniques for progressive emancipation. Insecuritization invariably works. Linking the subject's everyday ways of living to the possibility of his or her very ruination proves particularly compelling in the desire to securitize all manner of threats. And moralization invariably works. Imposing moral imperatives on a society so that certain productive ways of living become normalized to the point that they are not even questioned is a sure way of embedding secure practices. Such moralization is what allows biopolitical practices to take hold. It also exposes why the transcendental principle for the liberal biopolitics of security is the divine economy of life. Hence it is precisely this particularly humanistic eschatology of the living that the political must draw into question by thinking beyond.

Nietzsche infamously wrote of the death of God. This was more than mischievous on his part. It allowed him to subsequently pose the question of what happens when God is replaced by man. What theological expression does man give to himself once God is deprived of His divine status? What system of rule does this ordain? And what violence does this sanction? History shows that there is no singular eschatology of the times. Yet our times are no less eschatological than those prior to the secularization of modern societies. Nietzsche understood this, to great intellectual cost. While the myth of the nation concentrated eschatological power in the figure of the popular sovereign, liberal humanism offered a biopolitical alternative which proposed a new divinity modelled on the eschatology of the living. While having 'faith in humanity' became the prevailing mantra, so life appeared to be guided by a moral force greater than itself. This was necessary to overcome the imperfections that life posed unto itself. Liberal humanism thus introduced a moral imperative into the very subjectivization of liberal biopolitical rule so that the active promotion of life was continually reminded of its potential for self-ruination. Contemporary bio-philosophy has merely added a new novel twist. With the potential for the catastrophic subjected to life's capacity to regenerate beyond its current formative state, so life's potency has increased exponentially on account of the subject's ambivalence to its radically interconnected situation. We have all become capable of setting off a chain of events without ever possibly being aware of the force of their impact, let alone the lasting impression they may leave. Such is the contemporary onto-theological burden of our fallen account of freedom that Kantianism forced us to inherent. Not only is the contemporary liberal subject now forced to carry the fallen weight of an imperfect world on its shoulders, it is also fearful of that world for it continually thwarts all securable attempts at establishing true morality, true eschatology, and true subjectivity.

Faced with the failures of liberal humanism – which are as much onto-theological as political – we need a new political imaginary that breaks away from the spectre of Kantianism that underwrites liberal attempts at securing life in all its planetary forms. Not only does Kantianism condemn us all to live a temporal purgatory – i.e. life is always guilty of the moral deficiencies of the past, yet incapable in its own right of exorcizing them in the future – but it demands these innate imperfections in order for life to continue to prove its moral and political worth. Humanism as such is forever fated within this schematic to be profoundly suspicious of its principal and justificatory referent: human life. Contemporary bio-philosophy has merely added more urgency to these suspicions by heightening the ontological stakes. With the contemporary liberal subject endowed with infinite potentiality, such that the Kantian regulatory idea brings full governmental force to bear upon the infinitely possible, so a global security imperative becomes morally assured without the need for political qualification. Spinoza's cry that 'we still don't know what a body can do' therefore no longer simply registers as a condition of political possibility. It fully underwrites the catastrophic imaginary of contemporary liberal security governance without exception. Now more than ever we need reasons to start believing in this world. So now more than ever we need a truly exceptional politics that demands the impossible. As the universal delusions of the liberal aspiration are increasingly exposed for their narcissistic qualities, so thinking beyond the terror of liberal humanism becomes the most pressing intellectual challenge for the twenty-first century.

Notes

Chapter 1 Imaginaries of Threat

1 As Benjamin famously noted, 'The tradition of the oppressed teaches us that the "state of emergency" in which we live is not the exception but the rule. We must attain to a conception of history that is in keeping with this insight.' See 'Theses on the Philosophy of History: Reflections on the Temporality of an Emergency', in Walter Benjamin, *Illuminations: Essays and Reflections* (New York: Schocken Books, 1968), p. 257.

2 See William Rasch, *Sovereignty and Its Discontents: On the Primacy of Conflict and the Structure of the Political* (London: Birkbeck Law Press, 2004); Chantal Mouffe (ed.), *The Challenge of Carl Schmitt* (London: Verso, 1999); and Mary Kaldor, *Human Security: Reflections on Globalization and Intervention* (Cambridge: Polity Press, 2007).

3 Carl Schmitt, *The Concept of the Political* (Chicago: University of Chicago Press, 1996).

4 Martti Koskenniemi, 'International Law as Political Theology: How to Read *Nomos der Erde?*', *Constellations*, vol. 11, no. 4 (2004), p. 493.

5 Giorgio Agamben is the notable exception here. Agamben is acutely aware that power is multiple, and it is therefore no

coincidence that the liberal revival in the thought of Schmitt has limited engagement with Agamben's work. Indeed, whilst there are a number of problems with Agamben's commitment to the spatial figuration of the camp, as we shall discover, his work on the bio-political opens a meaningful way by which to reveal its onto-theological connections.

6 Boutros Boutros-Ghali, *Uncommon Opportunities: An Agenda for Peace and Equitable Development* (London: Zed Books, 1994), p. 44.

7 'Blair Terror Speech in Full', 5 March 2004. Online at: *http://news.bbc.co.uk/1/hi/3536131.stm* (accessed 11 June 2012).

8 See in particular Jason Ralph, 'The Laws of War and the State of the American Exception', *Review of International Studies,* vol. 35, no. 3 (2009), pp. 631–49.

9 This analysis offers an extension of Carl Schmitt's ideas on the spatial ordering of global politics. See Carl Schmitt, *The Nomos of the Earth in the International Law of the Jus Publicum Europaeum* (New York: Telos Press, 2003).

10 David Chandler, 'The Revival of Carl Schmitt in International Relations: The Last Refuge of Critical Theorists?', *Millennium: Journal of International Studies*, vol. 37, no. 1 (2008), p. 30.

11 John R. Hall, *Apocalypse: From Antiquity to the Empire of Modernity* (Cambridge: Polity Press, 2009), p. 9.

12 Paul Veyne, *Writing History: Essay on Epistemology* (Middletown CT: Wesleyan University Press, 1984), p. 87.

13 Hall, *Apocalypse*, pp. 211–12.

14 Maurice Merleau-Ponty, *Humanism and Terror* (Boston: Beacon Press, 1969), p. 92.

15 Paul Ricoeur, *Time and Narrative* (Chicago: University of Chicago Press, 1984), p. 208.

16 George Bush Jr, 'The 2004 State of the Union Address', 20 January 2004. Online at: *http://news.bbc.co.uk/1/hi/world/americas/3415361.stm* (accessed 11 June 2012).

17 Mitchell Dean, *Governing Societies: Political Perspectives on Domestic and International Rule* (Maidenhead: Open University Press, 2007), p. 316.

18 Jacques Derrida, 'Force of Law: The "Mystical Foundation of Authority"', in Drucilla Cornell, Michael Rosenfeld, and David Gray Carleson (eds), *Deconstruction and the Possibility of Justice* (New York: Routledge, 1992), pp. 3–67.

19 See also Jacques Derrida, *The Beast & the Sovereign: Volume 1* (Chicago: University of Chicago Press, 2009).

20 Michael Dillon, *The Politics of Security: Towards a Political Philosophy of Continental Thought* (London: Routledge, 1997), p. 20.

21 Drawing reference to the 'allegory of Plato's cave', in which he presents a metaphor of humanity who is but a prisoner watching mere shadows upon a wall, Heidegger notes how this not only instigates a revolution in the Western concept of truth through which the world becomes a suspect imitation, but equally affirms in our political consciousness that political power lies in the control of images. Truth as such is simply reduced to a polemical unveiling. See Martin Heidegger, 'Plato's Doctrine of Truth', in *Pathmarks* (Cambridge: Cambridge University Press, 1998), pp. 155–82.

22 Martin Heidegger, *The Question Concerning Technology and Other Essays* (New York: Harper & Row, 1977), p. 127.

23 Gilles Deleuze and Félix Guattari, *A Thousand Plateaus: Capitalism and Schizophrenia* (London: Continuum, 2002), p. 168.

24 Phillip Bobbit, *Terror and Consent: The Wars for the 21st Century* (New York: Penguin, 2008).

25 Ibid., p. 26.

26 Ibid., pp. 44, 45.

27 John Arquilla and David Ronfeldt, 'The Advent of Netwar (Revisited)', in John Arquilla and David Ronfeldt (eds), *Networks and Netwars: The Future of Terror, Crime and Militancy* (Santa Monica, CA: RAND Corporation, 2001), p. 2.

28 David Ronfeldt and John Arquilla, 'What Next for Networks and Netwars?', in Arquilla and Ronfeldt (eds), *Networks and Netwars*, p. 313.

29 Ibid., p. 312.

30 Arthur Cebrowski and Thomas Barnett, 'The American Way of War', *Proceedings of the US Naval Institute*, vol. 129, no. 1 (2003), pp. 42–3.

31 The RAND Corporation in particular begins its analysis on Netwar by adopting the very same gaming metaphor Deleuze and Guattari use in their chapter 'Treatise on Nomadology', which features in *A Thousand Plateaus*. See John Arquilla and David Ronfeldt, *In Athena's Camp: Preparing for*

Conflict in the Information Age (Santa Monica, CA: RAND Corporation, 1997).

32 John Arquilla and David Ronfeldt, 'Afterword (September 2001): The Sharpening Fight for the Future', in Arquilla and Ronfeldt (eds), *Networks and Netwars*, p. 363.

33 Arquilla and Ronfeldt, 'The Advent of Netwar (Revisited)', pp. 12, 13.

34 Ibid., p. 14.

35 Luis Amaral and Julio Ottino, 'Complex Networks: Augmenting the Framework for the Study of Complex Systems', *The European Physical Journal*, Spring/Summer (2004), p. 147.

36 Ibid., p. 148.

37 Duncan Watts, *Six Degrees: The Sciences of a Connected Age* (New York: Norton, 2002), p. 301.

38 Zygmunt Bauman, *Society under Siege* (Cambridge: Polity Press, 2002), pp. 12, 17.

39 Ulrich Beck, 'The Silence of Words: On Terror and War', *Security Dialogue*, vol. 34, no. 3 (2003), p. 255.

40 Bobbit, *Terror and Consent*, pp. 521, 522.

41 Manuel Castells, *The Informational City: A Framework for Social Change* (Toronto: University of Toronto Press, 1990), p. 14.

42 Paul Virilio, *Speed and Politics* (Los Angeles: Semiotext(e), 1986).

43 Hall, *Apocalypse*, p. 124.

44 Paul Virilio, *The University of Disaster* (Cambridge: Polity Press, 2009), pp. 6–7.

45 Michael J. Shapiro, *Cinematic Geopolitics* (New York: Routledge, 2009).

46 Truls Lie and Jacques Rancière, 'Our Police Order: What Can be Said, Seen, and Done', *Le Monde Diplomatique*, 8 November 2006.

47 This infamous comment was first made by Fukuyama in a paper titled 'Is History Over?' for the Summer 1989 issue of the *National Interest*, p. 4. This was then developed into a more comprehensive treatment in his follow-up volume. See Francis Fukuyama, *The End of History and the Last Man* (Harmondsworth: Penguin, 1993).

48 Slavoj Žižek, *Welcome to the Desert of the Real* (London: Verso, 2002), p. 33.

49 Alain Badiou, *Infinite Thought: Truth and the Return to Philosophy* (London: Continuum, 2005), p. 106.

50 Zygmunt Bauman, 'Reconnaissance Wars of the Planetary Frontierland', *Theory, Culture & Society*, vol. 19, no. 4 (2002), p. 82.

51 Saskia Sassen, *The Global City: New York, London, Tokyo* (Princeton: Princeton University Press, 2001).

52 Paul Virilio, *City of Panic* (London: Berg, 2007), p. 33.

53 Ibid., p. 50.

54 Ibid., pp. 51, 55.

55 Bauman, *Society under Siege*, p. 87.

56 Ibid., p. 90.

57 David Campbell, 'Time Is Broken: The Return of the Past in Response to September 11', *Theory and Event*, vol. 5, no. 4 (2001). Online at: *http://www.david-campbell.org/wp-content/documents/Time_is_broken.pdf* (accessed 26 June 2012).

58 Jean Baudrillard, *The Spirit of Terrorism and Other Essays* (London: Verso, 2003), p. 10.

59 Ibid., p. 97.

60 Susan Neiman, *Evil in Modern Thought: An Alternative History of Philosophy* (Princeton: Princeton University Press, 2002), p. xi.

61 Brian Massumi, *The Politics of Everyday Fear* (Minnesota: University of Minnesota Press, 1993), p. vii.

62 Frank Furedi, 'The Only Thing We Have To Fear is the Culture of Fear Itself', *Spiked Online*, 4 April 2007. Online at: *http://www.spiked-online.com/index.php?/site/article/3053* (accessed 11 June 2012).

63 Gilbert Guillaume, 'Terrorism and International Law', *International and Comparative Law Quarterly*, vol. 53, no. 4 (2004), p. 537.

64 See Paul Virilio, *The Original Accident* (Cambridge, Polity Press: 2007).

65 Virilio, *The University of Disaster*, p. 6.

66 Brian Massumi, 'National Enterprise Emergency: Steps Toward an Ecology of Powers', *Theory, Culture & Society*, vol. 26, no. 6 (2009), pp. 153–85.

67 See Roger Lewin, *Complexity: Life at the Edge of Chaos* (Chicago: University of Chicago Press, 1999); John H. Holland, *Emergence: From Chaos to Order* (Oxford: Oxford

University Press, 1998); and Steven Johnson, *Emergence: The Connected Lives of Ants, Brains, Cities and Software* (London: Penguin, 2001).

68 Stuart Kauffman, *Investigations* (New York: Oxford University Press, 2000), p. x.

69 Melinda Cooper, 'Pre-empting Emergence – The Biological Turn of the War on Terror', *Theory, Culture & Society*, vol. 23, no. 4 (2006), p. 116.

70 Michael Dillon, 'Governing Terror: The State of Emergency of Biopolitical Emergence', *International Political Sociology*, vol. 1, no. 1 (2007), p. 8.

71 As Kauffman writes: 'If you are lucky enough to be in the survivable regime, you can survive by being adaptable.' Kauffman, *Investigations*, p. 240.

72 François Debrix and Alexander Barder, 'Nothing to Fear But Fear Itself: Governmentality and the Bio-political Production of Terror', *International Political Sociology*, vol. 3, no. 4 (2009), p. 441.

73 Zygmunt Bauman, *Liquid Fear* (Cambridge: Polity Press, 2006), p. 7.

74 Didier Bigo, 'The Globalization of (In)security and the Ban-Opticon', in Naoki Sakai and Jon Solomon (eds), *Translation, Biopolitics, Colonial Difference* (Hong Kong: Hong Kong University Press, 2004), p. 109.

75 Stephen Graham, 'Switching Cities Off: Urban Infrastructure and US Air Power', *City*, vol. 2 (2005), p. 169.

76 Ibid., pp. 174, 175.

77 Peter Sloterdijk, *Terror from the Air* (Los Angeles: Semiotext(e), 2009).

78 Virilio, *The University of Disaster*.

79 Massumi, 'National Enterprise Emergency'.

80 Gregory Treverton, 'The Intelligence of Counter-Terrorism', in Brian Michael Jenkins and John Paul Godges (eds), *The Long Shadow of 9/11: America's Response to Terrorism* (Santa Monica, CA: RAND Corporation, 2011), p. 162.

81 See, for example, World Bank and Carter Centre, *From Civil War to Civil Society* (Washington, DC: World Bank & Carter Centre, 1997).

82 Freidrich von Hayek, *Law, Legislation and Liberty* (London: Routledge, 1973).

83 World Economic Forum, *Global Risks 2012* (Geneva: WEF, 2012), p. 10.

84 Mitchell Dean, *Governmentality: Power and Rule in Modern Society* (London: Sage, 1999), p. 177.

85 Ibid., p. 178.

86 François Ewald, 'Insurance and Risk', in Graham Burchell, Colin Gordon, and Peter Miller (eds), *The Foucault Effect: Studies in Governmentality* (Chicago: University of Chicago Press: 1991), pp. 191, 199.

87 Peter Miller and Nikolas Rose, *Governing the Present: Administering Economic, Social and Personal Life* (Cambridge: Polity Press, 2008), p. 100.

88 Frank Furedi, *Culture of Fear Revisited: Risk Taking and the Morality of Lower Expectation* (London: Continuum, 2006), p. xvii.

89 Michael Dillon, 'Underwriting Security', *Security Dialogue*, vol. 39, nos 2–3 (2008), p. 310.

90 Ibid., p. 313.

91 Ibid., p. 314.

92 Ibid., pp. 321, 322.

93 See in particular World Economic Forum, *Global Risks 2012*, pp. 32 and 37 for diagrammatic examples in which 'the Event' is written and displayed centrally.

94 It is, for instance, central to the UK security strategy. Online at: *http://www.cabinetoffice.gov.uk/ukresilience* (accessed 11 June 2012).

95 Crawford Stanley Holling, 'Resilience and Stability of Ecological Systems', *Annual Review of Ecology and Systematics*, no. 4 (1973), pp. 1–23.

Chapter 2 Liberal Security

1 Giorgio Agamben, 'Security and Terror', *Theory & Event*, vol. 5, no.4 (2001) (online).

2 Ulrich Beck, *Power in the Global Age* (Cambridge: Polity Press, 2006), pp. 253–4.

3 Agamben, 'Security and Terror'.

4 See Ken Booth, 'Security and Emancipation', *Review of International Studies*, vol. 17, no. 4 (1991), pp. 313–26; Ken Booth (ed.), *Critical Security Studies and World*

Politics (Boulder, CO: Lynne Rienner, 2005); Bary Buzan, *People, States and Fear: An Agenda for International Security Studies in the Post Cold War Era* (Boulder, CO: Lynne Rienner, 1991); Barry Buzan, Ole Waever, and Jan de Wilde, *Security: A New Framework for Analysis* (Boulder, CO: Lynne Rienner, 1998); Richard Wyn-Jones, *Security, Strategy, and Critical Theory* (Boulder, CO: Lynne Rienner, 1999).

5 Tim Dunne and Nicholas Wheeler, '"We the Peoples": Contending Discourses of Security in Human Rights Theory and Practice', *International Relations*, vol. 18, no. 9 (2004), p. 10.

6 Ken Booth, 'Introduction', in Booth (ed.), *Critical Security Studies*, p. 14

7 Richard Wyn-Jones, 'Message in a Bottle? Theory and Praxis in Critical Security Studies', *Contemporary Security Policy*, vol. 16, no. 3 (1995), p. 301.

8 Richard Falk, *On Humane Governance: Towards a New Global Politics* (Cambridge: Polity Press, 1995), p. 243.

9 Human Security Centre, *The Human Security Report 2005: War and Peace in the 21st Century* (University of British Columbia: Human Security Centre, 2005).

10 Miguel de Larringa and Marc Doucet, 'Sovereign Power and the Bio-Politics of Human Security', *Security Dialogue*, vol. 39, no. 5 (2008), p. 528.

11 Kaldor, *Human Security*, pp. 150, 151.

12 Ibid., p. 152.

13 Steve Smith, 'The Contested Concept of Security', in Booth (ed.), *Critical Security Studies*, p. 27.

14 See in particular US Department of the Army, *Field Manual 3–24: Counterinsurgency* (Washington, DC: Department of the Army, 2006).

15 Barack Obama, 'Remarks by the President on a New Strategy for Afghanistan and Pakistan' (Washington, DC: Office of the Press Secretary, 27 March 2009).

16 Rupert Smith, *The Utility of Force: The Art of War in the Modern World* (London: Penguin, 2006).

17 Robert Kagan, *Paradise and Power: America and Europe in the New World* (London: Atlantic Books, 2003).

18 See Michael Dillon and Julian Reid, *The Liberal Way of War: Killing to Make Life Live* (London: Routledge, 2009);

Brad Evans (ed.), 'Liberal War', *The South Atlantic Quarterly*, vol. 110, no. 3 (2011) (Special Issue).

19 Michael Ignatieff, *Empire Lite: Nation-Building in Bosnia, Kosovo and Afghanistan* (London: Vintage, 2003), p. 19.

20 US Department of Defense, *Quadrennial Defense Review Report* (Washington, DC: Department of Defense, February 2010), p. 20. *http://www.defense.gov/QDR/images/QDR_ as_of_12Feb10_1000.pdf* (accessed 11 June 2012).

21 Martin van Creveld, 'In the Wake of Terrorism, Modern Armies Prove to be Dinosaurs of Defence', *New Perspectives Quarterly*, vol. 13, no. 4 (1996), p. 58.

22 Boutros-Ghali, *Uncommon Opportunities*, p. 55.

23 Mary Kaldor, *New and Old Wars: Organized Violence in a Global Era* (Cambridge: Polity Press, 1999), p. 69.

24 See Manuel Castells, *End of Millennium* (Oxford: Blackwell, 1998), p. 161.

25 Kaldor, *New and Old Wars*, p. 2.

26 For a full versions see Subcomandante Marcos, 'The Fourth World War Has Begun', in Tom Hayden (ed.), *The Zapatista Reader* (New York: Nation Books, 2002), pp. 270–85.

27 William Shawcross, *Deliver Us from Evil: Peacekeepers, Warlords and a World of Endless Conflict* (New York: Touchstone, 2001), p. 324.

28 Ignatieff, *Empire Lite*, p. 19.

29 Mark Duffield, *Development, Security and Unending War: Governing the World of Peoples* (Cambridge: Polity Press, 2007), p. 27.

30 Cited in Mary Kaldor and S.D. Beebe, *The Ultimate Weapon Is No Weapon: Human Security and the New Rules of War and Peace* (New York: Public Affairs, 2010), p. 68.

31 Julian Reid, 'Life Struggles. War, Discipline and Biopolitics in the Thought of Michel Foucault', in Michael Dillon and Andrew W. Neal (eds), *Foucault on Politics, Security and War* (London: Palgrave, 2008), p. 66.

32 White House, *The National Security Strategy of the United States of America* (Washington, DC: White House, 2006), p. 9.

33 Michael Hardt and Antonio Negri, *Empire* (Cambridge, MA: Harvard University Press, 2000); and Michael Hardt

and Antonio Negri, *Multitude: War and Democracy in the Age of Empire* (London: Hamish Hamilton, 2004).

34 Giorgio Agamben, *Homo Sacer: Sovereign Power and Bare Life* (Stanford: Stanford University Press, 1995); and Giorgio Agamben, *State of Exception* (Chicago: University of Chicago Press, 2005).

35 See, in particular, Michel Foucault, *Society Must Be Defended: Lectures at the Collège de France 1975–1976* (New York: Picador, 2003); Michel Foucault, *Security, Territory, Population: Lectures at the Collège de France 1977–1978* (New York: Palgrave Macmillan, 2007); and Michel Foucault, *The Birth of Biopolitics: Lectures at the Collège de France 1978–1979* (New York: Palgrave Macmillan, 2008).

36 As John Protevi has suggested, 'To the (in)famous demand that Foucault provide a normative "standard", we can reply that he does; it's just that he trusts the governed to know when intolerable governance needs resisting without having to wait for a philosopher to bless their resistance by having it match some universal standard.' John Protevi, 'What Does Foucault Think is New about Neo-Liberalism?', *Warwick Journal of Philosophy*, no. 21 (2010), p. 1.

37 Foucault, *The Birth of Biopolitics*, p. 3.

38 Paul Patton, 'Agamben and Foucault on Biopower and Biopolitics', in Matthew Calarco and Steven DeCaroli (eds), *Giorgio Agamben: Sovereignty and Life* (Stanford: Stanford University Press, 2007), pp. 203–18.

39 Beatrice Hanssen, *Critique of Violence: Between Post-Structuralism and Critical Theory* (London: Routledge, 2000).

40 John Marks, 'Michel Foucault: Bio-Politics and Biology', in Stephen Morton and Stephen Bygrave (eds), *Foucault in an Age of Terror* (London: Palgrave, 2008), p. 88.

41 Foucault, *Security, Territory, Population*, p. 10.

42 Ibid., p. 29.

43 Ibid., pp. 29, 45.

44 Michael Dillon and Andrew W. Neal, 'Introduction', in Dillon and Neal (eds), *Foucault on Politics, Security and War*, p. 15.

45 Didier Bigo, 'Security: A Field Left Fallow', in Dillon and Neal (eds), *Foucault on Politics, Security and War*, p.107.

46 Dillon, 'Governing Terror', p. 11.

47 Foucault, *Security, Territory, Population*, p. 65.
48 David Campbell, *Writing Security: United States Foreign Policy and the Politics of Identity* (Minneapolis: University of Minnesota Press, 1998).
49 Foucault, *The Birth of Biopolitics*, pp. 63–4.
50 Dillon and Reid, *The Liberal Way of War*, p. 17.
51 Michel Foucault, *Power/Knowledge: Selected Interviews and Other Writings, 1972–1977* (New York: Pantheon, 1980), pp. 194, 196.
52 I posed the question to Duffield on the deployment of bio-politics in his work. In response he stated: 'You are right about the implicit nod to Foucault in *Global Governance and the New Wars*. This came from two directions. First, an existing appreciation that power is idiomatic and can be derived from its utterances. Second, concerns my meeting Michael Dillon at a conference on "The Politics of Emergency" in the Department of Politics, University of Manchester, May 1997. I'd given a paper on Complex Emergencies in response to which Michael Dillon coined the term "emerging political complexes" as better describing what I was driving at. Out of this began an informal Emerging Political Complexes Group. Myself, Michael, Jenny Edkins, and David Campbell were the main participants. These meetings were kind of like my fieldwork meeting their analytical powers. It certainly shaped the argument in global governance, especially the emergent characteristics of network war. However, regarding the explicit use of the terms biopower/politics, the first reference I can track down is a paper entitled "Emerging Political Complexes" given at a LUCAS Conference on Peasants, Liberation, and Socialism in Africa, Weetwood Hall, Leeds, 3 May 2002. The first published explicit usage was: "Carry on Killing: Global Governance, Humanitarianism and Terror", 2004, DIIS Working 2004/23 (Copenhagen: Danish Institute for International Studies). It has since been a dominant feature of subsequent publications, culminating in the attempt in *Development, Security and Unending War* to understand the biopolitics of under-development in terms of the complementary functions of humanitarian intervention and adaptive self-reliance (and as distinct from dependent forms of developed life).'
53 Duffield, *Development, Security and Unending War*, p. ix.

54 Ibid., pp. 117–18.
55 Rosa Ehrenreich Brookes, 'War Everywhere: National Security Law and the Law of Armed Conflict in the Age of Terror', *University of Pennsylvania Law Review*, vol. 153 (2004), p. 677.
56 Nicholas Wheeler, *Saving Strangers: Humanitarian Intervention in International Society* (Oxford: Oxford University Press, 2000).
57 Human Security Centre, *The Human Security Report 2005.*
58 Andrew Linklater, 'Political Community and Human Security', in Booth (ed.), *Critical Security Studies*, p. 119.
59 Foucault, *Society Must Be Defended*, p. 124.
60 Foucault, *Security, Territory, Population*, p. 20.
61 Hardt and Negri, *Multitude*, p. 20.
62 Eyal Weizman, *Hollow Land: Israel's Architecture of Occupation* (London: Verso, 2007), pp. 106–7.
63 Sloterdijk, *Terror from the Air*, p. 16.
64 Ibid., p. 22.
65 Ibid., p. 25.
66 Ibid., p. 28.
67 Ibid., pp. 95, 23.
68 Kathleen Stewart, 'Trauma Time: A Still Life', in Daniel Rosenberg and Susan Harding (eds), *Histories of the Future* (Durham, NC: Duke University Press, 2005), pp. 321–40.
69 Ibid., p. 325.
70 Ibid., p. 338.
71 Ibid., p. 324.
72 Ibid., p. 325.
73 Brian Massumi, 'Introduction', in Deleuze and Guattari, *A Thousand Plateaus*, p. xvi.
74 Michel Foucault, *The Order of Things: An Archaeology of Human Sciences* (London, Routledge, 2001), p. xxiii.
75 Ibid., p. xxvi.
76 Michel Foucault, *Ethics: Subjectivity and Truth* (New York: The New Press, 1998), p. 59.
77 Gilles Deleuze, *Foucault* (London: Continuum, 1999), p. 60.
78 Dean, *Governing Societies*, pp. 108, 109.
79 Michel Foucault, 'Nietzsche, Genealogy, History', in Paul Rabinow (ed.), *The Foucault Reader: An Introduction to Foucault's Thought* (London: Penguin Books, 1991), p. 83.
80 Deleuze, *Foucault*, p. 34.

81 Gilles Deleuze and Félix Guattari, *Anti-Oedipus: Capitalism and Schizophrenia* (London: Continuum, 2003), p. 29.

82 On this see Jan Selby, 'Engaging Foucault: Discourse, Liberal Governance and the Limits of Foucauldian IR', *International Relations*, vol. 21, no. 3 (2007), pp. 324–45.

Chapter 3   Potentialities

1 Zygmunt Bauman, *Liquid Modernity* (Cambridge: Polity Press, 2000).

2 Zygmunt Bauman, *Liquid Times: Living in an Age of Uncertainty* (Cambridge: Polity Press, 2007), pp. 10–11.

3 *San Jose Mercury News*, 23 January 2000.

4 John S. Dryzek, 'Complexity and Rationality in Public Life', *Political Studies*, vol. 35, no. 35 (1987), p. 425.

5 Ilya Prigogine, *The End of Certainty* (New York: The Free Press, 1997).

6 Herbert A. Simon, *The Sciences of the Artificial* (Cambridge, MA: MIT Press, 1981), p. 195.

7 Lewin, *Complexity*, p. 149.

8 Hardt and Negri, *Multitude*, p. 142.

9 See in particular Lily Kay, *Who Wrote the Book of Life? A History of the Genetic Code* (Stanford: Stanford University Press, 2000).

10 The Human Genome Project refers to this as being 'bio-infomatics': 'a term coined for the new field that merges biology, computer science and information technology to manage and analyse the data, with the ultimate goal of understanding and modelling living systems'. Human Genome Project, *Genomics and Its Impact on Society* (US Department of Energy Office of Science, 2006), p. 4.

11 Alan Michelson and Martha Bulyck, 'Biological Code Breaking in the 21st Century', *Molecular Systems Biology*, vol. 2 (2006) (online).

12 As Deleuze explains, '[M]asses become samples, data, markets, or *banks*.' Gilles Deleuze, 'Postscript on Control Societies', in *Negotiations: 1972–1990* (New York: Columbia University Press, 1995), p. 180.

13 See Howard Rheingold, *The Virtual Community* (Reading, MA: Addison Wesley, 1993); and Pierre Levy, *Collective*

Intelligence: Mankind's Emerging World in Cyberspace (New York: Plenum Press, 1997).

14 Lewin, *Complexity*, p. 191.
15 Ibid., pp. 191, 192.
16 Dillon, 'Governing Terror', p. 14.
17 Richard Doyle, *Wetwares: Experiments in Postvital Living* (Minneapolis: University of Minnesota Press, 2003), p. 19.
18 If Fritz Kahn's images of 'The Man Machine' provide a meaningful representation of the vital industrial subject, the depiction of life in the Wachowski brothers' *Matrix* trilogy encapsulates brilliantly life as a complex system of encoding.
19 Howard Stevenson and Susan Harmeling, 'Entrepreneurial Management's Need for a More "Chaotic" Theory', *Journal of Business Venturing*, vol. 5, no. 1 (1990), p. 3.
20 Holland, *Emergence*, p. 7.
21 See in particular John Urry, *Global Complexity* (Cambridge: Polity Press, 2003).
22 Friedrich von Hayek, *Individualism and Economic Order* (Chicago: University of Chicago Press, 1980).
23 Michael Silberstein and John McGeever, 'The Search for Ontological Emergence', *The Philosophical Quarterly*, vol. 49, no. 195 (1999), p. 186.
24 See *http://www.nytimes.com/2011/09/10/arts/magazine-covers-about-911.html?pagewanted = all* (accessed 15 June 2012).
25 See *http://www.time.com/time/beyond911/* (accessed 15 June 2012).
26 Benedict Anderson, *Imagined Communities: Reflections on the Origin and Spread of Nationalism* (London: Verso, 1983), p. 6.
27 Ibid., p. 7.
28 George Orwell, *Notes on Nationalism* (London: Polemic, 1945). Online at: *http://orwell.ru/library/essays/nationalism/english/e_nat* (accessed 15 June 2012).
29 Dillon, *The Politics of Security*, p. 33.
30 Marcos, 'The Fourth World War Has Begun'.
31 See, for example, Frantz Fanon, *The Wretched of the Earth* (London: Penguin Books, 1990).
32 Stuart Hall, 'Culture, Community, Nation', *Cultural Studies*, vol. 7, no. 3 (1992), p. 361.

33 Frederic Jameson, *Archaeologies of the Future: The Desire Called Utopia and Other Science Fictions* (London: Verso, 2005), p. 15.

34 Miller and Rose, *Governing the Present*, p. 217.

35 Dillon, 'Governing Terror', p. 7.

36 Michael Shermer, *How We Believe: Science, Skepticism and the Search for God*, 2nd edn (New York: Henry Holt, 2007), p. 217.

37 Massumi, 'National Enterprise Emergency', p. 162.

38 Gilles Deleuze, *Difference and Repetition* (New York: Columbia University Press, 1994), p. 208.

39 Gilles Deleuze, *The Logic of Sense* (New York: Columbia University Press, 1990), p. 212.

40 Deleuze and Guattari, *A Thousand Plateaus*, p. 257.

41 Peter Scott, 'Massification, Internationalization and Globalization', in Peter Scott (ed.), *The Globalization of Higher Education* (Buckingham: Open University Press, 2000), pp. 108–29.

42 Jean Baudrillard, *The Transparency of Evil: Essays on Extreme Phenomena* (New York: Verso, 1993), p. 7.

43 Dillon and Reid, *The Liberal Way of War*, p. 44.

44 Sloterdijk, *Terror from the Air*, pp. 69, 70.

45 Robert Pepperell, *The PostHuman Condition: Consciousness beyond the Brain* (Portland: Intellect, 2003), p. 20.

46 Foucault, *The Birth of Biopolitics*, pp. 270–1.

47 Ibid., p. 283.

48 Bruce Mann, 'Protecting the UK's Critical National Infrastructure', Contingency Today, 1 July 2007. Online at: *http://www.contingencytoday.com/online_article/Protecting-the-UK_s-Critical-National-Infrastructure/416* (accessed 15 June 2012).

49 Jacques Derrida, *Points: Interviews 1974–94* (Stanford: Stanford University Press, 1995), p. 387.

50 Michael Dillon, 'Virtual Security: A Life Science of (Dis)Order', *Millennium: Journal of International Studies*, vol. 32, no. 3 (2003), p. 535.

51 Baudrillard, *The Spirit of Terrorism*, p. 3.

52 Wendell Berry, 'Thoughts in the Presence of Fear', *The South Atlantic Quarterly*, vol. 101, no. 2 (2002), p. 279.

53 Brian Michael Jenkins, 'Have We Succumbed to Nuclear Terror?', in Jenkins and Godges (eds), *The Long Shadow of 9/11*, p. 89.

54 US Government, *Joint Inquiry into Intelligence Community Activities before and after the Terrorist Attacks of September 11, 2011*, p. 128. Online at: *http://www.globalsecurity.org/ intell/library/congress/2003_rpt/intell-911-report-072403. pdf* (accessed 15 June 2012).

55 HM Government, *Report of the Official Account of the Bombings in London on 7 July 2005* (Norwich: HMSO, 2006), p. 2 (emphasis added).

56 Ibid., p. 31 (emphasis added).

57 Ibid., p. 1.

58 Jonathan Haidt, 'Why We Celebrate a Killing', *The New York Times*, 7 May 2011. Online at: *http://www.nytimes. com/2011/05/08/opinion/08haidt.html* (accessed 15 June 2012).

59 HM Government, *A Strong Britain in an Age of Uncertainty: The National Security Strategy* (London: The Stationery Office, 2010), p. 3.

60 Ibid., p.19.

61 Ibid., p. 16.

62 Ibid., p. 18.

63 Ibid., pp. 15, 25.

64 Massumi, 'National Enterprise Emergency', p. 159.

65 George Chesterton, 'Britain's Love Affair with Our Military is Dangerous', *The Guardian*, 23 December 2011. Online at: *http://www.guardian.co.uk/commentisfree/2011/dec/23/ military-love-affair-dangerous* (accessed 15 June 2012).

66 Massumi, 'National Enterprise Emergency', p. 163.

Chapter 4   On Divine Power

1 Giorgio Agamben, *The Kingdom and the Glory: For a Theological Genealogy of Economy and Government* (Stanford: Stanford University Press, 2011), pp. 45, 3.

2 Jean Baudrillard, *The Intelligence of Evil or the Lucidity of the Pact* (New York: Berg, 2005), p. 14.

3 George Bush, 'Address One Year After Operation Iraqi Freedom', Washington, DC, 19 March 2004.

4 Charles Mathewes, *Evil and the Augustinian Tradition* (Cambridge: Cambridge University Press, 2001), p. 27.

5 See in particular Alain Badiou, *Saint Paul: The Foundation of Universalism* (Stanford: Stanford University Press, 2003); and Simon Critchley, *The Faith of the Faithless: Experiments in Political Theology* (New York: Verso, 2012).

6 Leo Strauss, *Natural Right and History* (Chicago: University of Chicago Press, 1953), p. 317.

7 Neiman, *Evil in Modern Thought*, pp. 8, 9.

8 Hannah Arendt, *Eichmann in Jerusalem: A Report on the Banality of Evil* (New York: Penguin Books, 2006), p. 23.

9 Theodor Adorno, Else Frenkel-Brunswik, Daniel J. Levinson, and R. Nevitt Sanford, *Authoritarian Personality* (New York: Harper & Row, 1950).

10 Hannah Arendt, *The Human Condition* (Chicago: University of Chicago Press, 1958).

11 Hannah Arendt, *The Origins of Totalitarianism* (Fort Washington, PA: Harvest Books, 1976), p. 438.

12 Richard Bernstein, 'Did Hannah Arendt Change Her Mind? From Radical Evil to the Banality of Evil', in Larry May and Jerome Kohn (eds), *Hannah Arendt: Twenty Years Later* (Cambridge, MA: MIT Press, 1997), p. 127.

13 Neimann, *Evil in Modern Thought*, p. xi.

14 Ibid., p. 282.

15 William Connolly, 'Faith, Territory and Evil', in Alan Schrift (ed.), *Modernity and the Problem of Evil* (Bloomington: Indiana University Press, 2005), p. 133.

16 John Gray, *Black Mass: Apocalyptic Religion and the Death of Utopia* (London: Penguin, 2011), p. 1.

17 Ibid., p. 7.

18 Ibid., p. 105.

19 Online at: *http://www.whitehouse.gov/the-press-office/remarks-president-acceptance-nobel-peace-prize* (accessed 22 June 2012).

20 Tony Blair, 'Prime Minister's Address to the Labour Party Conference October 2001'. Online at: *http://www.guardian.co.uk/politics/2001/oct/02/labourconference.labour6* (accessed 22 June 2012).

21 Tony Blair, 'Speech to US Congress' (18 July 2003) Online at: *http://www.guardian.co.uk/Iraq/Story/0,2763,1000734,00.html* (accessed 22 June 2012).

22 Bauman, *Society under Siege*, p. 86.
23 Carl Schmitt, *Political Theology: Four Chapters on the Concept of Sovereignty* (Chicago: University of Chicago Press, 2006), p. 36.
24 James Martel, *Divine Violence: Walter Benjamin and the Eschatology of Sovereignty* (London: Routledge, 2011), p. 23.
25 Jacques Derrida, *Rogues: Two Essays on Reason* (Stanford: Stanford University Press, 2005), p. 17.
26 Wendy Brown, *Walled States, Waning Sovereignty* (Cambridge, MA: Zone Books, 2010).
27 Arendt, *The Human Condition*, p. 250.
28 Bauman, *Society under Siege*, p. 107.
29 John MacMillan, 'Liberalism and the Democratic Peace', *Review of International Studies*, vol. 30, no. 2 (2004), pp. 179–200.
30 Michael Doyle, 'Liberal Internationalism: Peace, War and Democracy', Nobelprize.org, June 2004. Online at: *http:// www.nobelprize.org/nobel_prizes/peace/articles/doyle/* (accessed 25 June 2012). On Kant's specific work see Immanuel Kant, 'Perpetual Peace', in Hans Reiss (ed.), *Kant: Political Writings* (New York: Cambridge University Press, 1991), pp. 93–130.
31 Mary Midgley, *Wickedness: A Philosophical Essay* (London: Routledge, 1984), p. 208 n. 7.
32 See Gilles Deleuze, *Le Cours de Gilles Deleuze* (1978). Online at: *http://www.webdeleuze.com* (accessed 22 June 2012).
33 Michel Foucault, 'What Is Revolution?', in Sylvère Lotringer (ed.), *Michel Foucault: The Politics of Truth* (Los Angeles: Semiotext(e), 2007), pp. 83, 84.
34 Hardt and Negri, *Empire*, p. 81.
35 Immanuel Kant, *Religion within the Limits of Reason Alone* (New York: Harper & Row, 1960), p. 66.
36 Ibid., p. 28.
37 Ibid., p. 46.
38 Martin Matuštík, 'Violence and Secularization, Evil and Redemption', in Schrift (ed.), *Modernity and the Problem of Evil*, p. 44.
39 Ibid., p. 43.

40 Sharon Anderson-Gold, *Unnecessary Evil: History and Moral Progress in the Philosophy of Immanuel Kant* (New York: State University Press, 2001), pp. xi, 3, 7.
41 Ibid., p. 15.
42 Allen Wood, *Kant's Moral Religion* (Ithaca, NY: Cornell University Press, 1970), p. 219.
43 Kant, *Religion within the Limits of Reason Alone*, p. 49.
44 Ibid., p. 32.
45 Gordon Michalson Jr, *Fallen Freedom: Kant on Radical Evil and Moral Regeneration* (Cambridge: Cambridge University Press, 1990), p. x.
46 Ibid., p. 7.
47 Ibid., pp. 58, 59.
48 Ibid., pp. 88, 89.
49 Adrian W. Moore, 'Aspects of the Infinite in Kant', *Mind Association*, vol. 96, no. 386 (1988), p. 209.
50 Immanuel Kant, *Critique of Pure Reason* (New York: St Martin's Press, 1929), p. Bxxx.
51 Michalson, *Fallen Freedom*, p. 142.
52 Moore, 'Aspects of the Infinite in Kant', p. 218.
53 Michalson, *Fallen Freedom*, p. 28.
54 Ibid., pp. xi, 28
55 John Locke's view on the possibility for salvation and redemption of the savages is well documented. In his 'Letter Concerning Toleration', for instance, he noted: 'That any man should think it fit to cause another man, whose salvation he heartily desires, to expire in torments, and that even in an unconverted estate, would, I confess, seem rather strange to me . . . .' John Locke, *Two Treatises of Government and a Letter Concerning Toleration* (New York: Yale University Press, 2003), p. 217. He would, however, qualify this, notably in his *Essays Concerning Human Understanding*, in which he stresses that the savages, along with children and the unlearned, are incapable of innate ideas – they must be taught the ways of civilization. Eduardo Galeano pointed out that Montesquieu in particular had problems with accepting the 'degraded men of the New World as fellow humans'. Eduardo Galeano, *Open Veins of Latin America: Five Centuries of the Pillage of a Continent* (New York and London: Monthly Review Press,

1973), p. 41. The same can be said about Rousseau, who was never a real egalitarian. As Charles W. Miller observed, for Rousseau the 'only natural savages cited are non-white savages, examples of European savages being restricted to reports of feral children raised by wolves and bears . . . even if some of Rousseau's non-white savages are "noble" . . . they are still savages. . . . So the praise for non-white savages is a limited paternalistic praise, tantamount to admiration for healthy animals, in no way to be taken to imply their equality, let alone their superiority to the civilized Europeans of the ideal polity. The underlying racial dichotomization of civilized and savage remains quite clear.' Charles W. Miller, *The Radical Contract* (Ithaca, NY: Cornell University Press, 1997), pp. 68–9.

56 Immanuel Kant, *Metaphysics of Morals* (Cambridge: Cambridge University Press, 1991), p. 16, emphasis added.

57 Ibid., pp. 110, 111.

58 Immanuel Kant, 'On the Different Races of Man', in Earl Count (ed.), *This Is Race* (New York: Henry Schuman, 1950), p. 16.

59 Immanuel Kant, 'Physical Geography', in Emmanuel C. Eze (ed.), *Race and the Enlightenment* (Oxford: Blackwell, 1997), p. 61.

60 It is perhaps instructive that Smith's use of the term appeared first in his work on astronomy, then in his *Theory of Moral Sentiments*, before the familiar economic usage found in *The Wealth of Nations*. On this see Duncan Foley, *Adam's Fallacy: A Guide to Economic Theology* (Cambridge, MA: Harvard University Press, 2006).

61 Adam Smith, *The Wealth of Nations* (London: Penguin Books, 1986), p. 264.

62 Max Weber, *The Protestant Ethic and the Spirit of Capitalism* (New York: Charles Scribner, 1958), p. 7.

63 Agamben, *The Kingdom and the Glory*, p. xi.

64 Ibid., p. 1.

65 Ibid., p. 44.

66 Giorgio Agamben, *What Is an Apparatus?* (Stanford: Stanford University Press, 2009), pp. 23, 24.

67 Antonio Negri, 'Sovereignty: That Divine Ministry of Earthly Life', *Journal for Cultural and Religious Theory*, vol. 9,

no. 1 (2008), p. 97. Online at: *http://www.jcrt.org/archives/09.1/Negri.pdf*.

68 Ibid., p. 99.

69 See Jean-François Lyotard, *Heidegger and 'the Jews'* (Minneapolis: University of Minnesota Press, 1990), p. 77.

70 Friedrich von Hayek, *The Road to Serfdom* (London: Routledge, 1944).

71 See Alex Shand, *Free Market Morality: The Political Economy of the Austrian School* (London: Routledge, 1992); and Michael Baurmann, *The Market of Virtue: Morality and Commitment in a Liberal Society* (The Hague: Kluwer Law International, 1996).

72 Hayek, *The Road to Serfdom*, p. 69.

73 Ibid., p. 163.

74 Friedrich von Hayek, *Studies in Philosophy, Politics and Economics* (Chicago: University of Chicago Press, 1980), p. 194.

75 Milton Friedman, *Capitalism and Freedom* (Chicago: University of Chicago Press, 2002), p. 12.

76 Ibid., p. 194.

77 Doyle, 'Liberal Internationalism'.

78 Smith, *The Wealth of Nations*, p. 385.

79 Charles Montesquieu, *The Spirit of the Laws* (Cambridge: Cambridge University Press, 1989), p. 338.

80 Patrick McDonald, *The Invisible Hand of Peace: Capitalism, the War Machine, and International Relations Theory* (Cambridge: Cambridge University Press, 2009), pp. 22, 23, 15.

81 Online at: *http://www.totalpolitics.com/speeches/policy/religion/34433/dimbleby-lecture-on-the-struggle-for-the-soul-of-the-21st-century.thtml* (accessed 22 June 2012).

82 Jonathan Goodhand and David Hume, 'From Wars to Complex Political Emergencies: Understanding Conflict and Peace-Building in the New World Disorder', *Third World Quarterly*, vol. 20, no. 1 (1999), p. 14.

83 Bridget Byrne, *Gender, Conflict, and Development: Volume I* (London: Institute of Development Studies, 1995), p. 3.

84 Joanna Macrae and Nicholas Leader, *Shifting Sands: The Search for 'Coherence' between Political and Humanitarian Responses to Complex Emergencies* (London: Overseas Development Institute, 2000), pp. 30–1.

85 Blair, 'Prime Minister's Address to the Labour Party Conference October 2001'.
86 For full details of this organizational initiative, its panel members, along with considered reports, see *http://www. un-globalsecurity.org/* (accessed 22 June 2012).
87 United Nations, *A More Secure World: Our Shared Responsibility* (Report of the High-Level Panel on Threats, Challenges, and Change, 2004), pp. 1, 3.
88 Foucault, *Society Must Be Defended*, p. 53.
89 David Miliband's full NATO speech can be found online at: *http://www.fco.gov.uk/en/news/latest-news/?view=Speech&id =20621074* (accessed 22 June 2012, emphasis added).
90 RAND, *War by Other Means: Building Complete and Balanced Capabilities for Counter Insurgency* (Santa Monica, CA: Rand Corporation, 2008), pp. iii–iv.
91 David Kilcullen, *The Accidental Guerilla: Fighting Small Wars in the Midst of a Big One* (Oxford: Oxford University Press, 2009).
92 Colleen Bell and Brad Evans, 'Terrorism to Insurgency: Mapping the Post-Intervention Security Terrain', *Journal of Intervention & State Building*, vol. 5, no. 1 (2010), pp. 371–90.
93 Christopher Paul, 'Winning Every Battle But Losing the War against Terrorists and Insurgents', in Jenkins and Godges (eds), *The Long Shadow of 9/11*, pp. 106, 109, 111.

Chapter 5 A New Leviathan

1 Norman Myers, 'Population, Environment and Conflict', *Environmental Conservation*, vol. 14, no. 1 (1987), pp. 15–22; Norman Myers, 'Environment and Security', *Foreign Policy*, vol. 74 (Spring 1989), pp. 23–41; Norman Myers, 'Population, Environment and Development', *Environmental Conservation*, vol. 20, no. 3 (1993), pp. 1–12; and Norman Myers, *Ultimate Security: The Environmental Basis of Political Stability* (New York: Norton, 1993).
2 Michael Diederich, '"Law of War" and Ecology – A Proposal for a Workable Approach to Protecting the Environment through the Law of War', *Military Law Review*, no. 136 (1992), pp. 137–60.

3 Myers, *Ultimate Security*, p. 20.

4 World Commission on Environment and Development, *Our Common Future* (Oxford: Oxford University Press, 1987), p. 291.

5 Ibid., p. 310.

6 Robert Kaplan, 'The Coming Anarchy', *The Atlantic*, February 1994.

7 United Nations, *A More Secure World: Our Shared Responsibility* (Report of the High-Level Panel on Threats, Challenges, and Change, 2004), p. 24.

8 UNDP, *Fighting Climate Change: Human Solidarity in a Divided World* (New York: United Nations Development Programme, 2007), p. 3.

9 Online at: *http://www.whitehouse.gov/the-press-office/remarks-president-acceptance-nobel-peace-prize* (accessed 22 June 2012).

10 World Bank, *Development and Climate Change* (New York: World Bank, 2010), p. 37.

11 UNDP, *Fighting Climate Change*, p. 2.

12 Mark Duffield and Brad Evans, 'Biospheric Security: The Development-Security-Environment-Nexus [DESNEX], Containment and Retrenching Fortress Europe', in J. Peter Burgess and Serge Gutwirth (eds), *A Threat against Europe? Security, Migration and Integration* (Brussels: VUB Press, 2011), pp. 93–110.

13 UNDP, *Fighting Climate Change*, p. 1.

14 Jeremy Rifkin, *Biosphere Politics: A New Consciousness for a New Century* (New York: Crown Publishing Group, 1991), p. 4.

15 Beck, *Power in the Global Age*, pp. 253–4.

16 Ibid., p. 253.

17 Ibid., pp. 255, 256.

18 Ulrich Beck and Johannes Willms, *Conversations with Ulrich Beck* (Cambridge: Polity Press, 2003), p. 264.

19 Mikkel Rasmussen, *The Risk Society at War: Terror, Technology and Strategy in the 21st Century* (Cambridge: Cambridge University Press, 2006), p. 308.

20 Beck and Willms, *Conversations with Ulrich Beck*, p. 264.

21 Bauman, *Society under Siege*, p. 10.

22 Ibid., p. 101.

23 Hans J. Morgenthau, 'The Problem of Sovereignty Reconsidered', *Columbia Law Review*, vol. 48, no. 3 (1948), p. 350.

24 Thomas Hobbes, *Leviathan* (Cambridge: Cambridge University Press, 1991), pp. 121, 129.

25 Jens Bartelson, 'On the Indivisibility of Sovereignty', *Republics of Letters: A Journal for the Study of Knowledge, Politics, and the Arts,* vol. 2, no. 2 (2011) Online at: *http://rofl. stanford.edu/node/91* (accessed 26 June 2012).

26 Derrida, *The Beast & the Sovereign*, p. 76.

27 Brown, *Walled States, Waning Sovereignty*, p. 66.

28 Hardt and Negri, *Empire*, pp. xii–xiii.

29 Hardt and Negri, *Multitude*, p. 22.

30 Foucault, *Security, Territory and Population*, p. 70.

31 Dean, *Governmentality*, p. 13.

32 Foucault, *The Birth of Biopolitics*, p. 74.

33 Philip Bobbit, *The Shield of Achilles: War, Peace and the Course of History* (London: Penguin, 2003), p. 21.

34 Bobbit, *Terror and Consent*, p. 458.

35 Nikolas Rose, 'Government and Control', *The British Journal of Criminology*, vol. 40, no. 2 (2000), p. 325.

36 See William Walters, 'Mapping Schengenland: Denaturalizing the Border', *Environment and Planning D: Society and Space*, vol. 20, no. 5 (2002), pp. 561–80.

37 Schmitt, *The Nomos of the Earth*, p. 354.

38 Ibid., p. 351.

39 Agamben, *Homo Sacer*, p. 171.

40 Ibid., p. 179.

41 Ibid., pp. 174–5.

42 Agamben, *State of Exception*, p. 4.

43 Ibid., p. 22.

44 Agamben, *Homo Sacer*, p. 19.

45 Schmitt, *The Nomos of the Earth*, p. 29.

46 Dillon, 'Governing Terror', p. 11.

47 Judith Butler, 'Restaging the Universal', in Judith Butler, Ernesto Laclau, and Slavoj Žižek (eds), *Contingency, Hegemony, Universality* (London: Verso, 2000), p. 35.

48 Didier Bigo and Elspeth Guild, *Controlling Frontiers: Free Movement into and within Europe* (Aldershot: Ashgate, 2005).

49 Jef Huysmans, *The Politics of Insecurity: Fear, Migration and Asylum in the EU* (London: Routledge, 2006).

50 Jef Huysmans, 'The European Union and the Securitization of Migration', *Journal of Common Market Studies*, vol. 38, no. 5 (2000), pp. 751–77.

51 Scott Peterson, *Me against My Brother: At War in Somalia, Sudan and Rwanda* (London: Routledge, 2000).

52 Kevin Grove, 'Insuring Our Common Future? Dangerous Climate Change and the Biopolitics of Environmental Security', *Geopolitics*, vol. 15, no. 3 (2010), pp. 538–9.

53 Nicole Gelinas, 'A Perfect Storm of Lawlessness', *City Journal: Online Edition*, September 2005. Online at: *http://www.city-journal.org/html/eon_09_01_05ng.html* (accessed 26 June 2012).

54 Bauman, *Society under Siege*, p. 113.

55 IDMC, *Internal Displacement: Global Overview of Trends and Developments in 2006* (Geneva: Norwegian Refugee Council, 2007).

Chapter 6 The Event Horizon

1 Edmund Husserl, *Cartesian Meditations: An Introduction to Phenomenology* (The Hague: Martinus Nijhoff, 1960).

2 Jacques Derrida, *Edmund Husserl's Origin of Geometry: An Introduction* (New York: Bison Press, 1989), p. 117.

3 Gilles Deleuze, *Bergsonism* (New York: Zone, 1988), p. 113.

4 Constantine Boundas, 'Deleuze–Bergson: An Ontology of the Virtual', in Paul Patton (ed.), *Deleuze: A Critical Reader* (Oxford: Blackwell Publishers, 1996), p. 91.

5 Ibid., p. 92.

6 William Connolly, 'The Politics of the Event', April 2011. Online at: *http://contemporarycondition.blogspot.com/2011/04/politics-of-event.html* (accessed 27 June 2012).

7 Ibid.

8 Friedrich Nietzsche, *Thus Spoke Zarathustra* (Cambridge: Cambridge University Press, 2006).

9 Frank Stevenson, 'On the Horizon: Nietzsche's Lady Dawn and Deleuze's Sky Chance', *Concentric: Literature & Cultural Studies*, vol. 35, no. 2 (2009), p. 361.

10 Deleuze, *Difference and Repetition*, pp. 198, 202.

11 On this see François Raffoul, 'Heidegger and the Aporia of History', *Poligrafi: Natural History*, vol. 16, nos 61–2 (2011), pp. 91–118. It should be noted here that Heidegger actually uses historical time to designate the time of the event. Historical time is, however, being presented here as that which stands in opposition in a Nietzschean sense.
12 Deleuze, *The Logic of Sense*, p. 63.
13 Cabinet Office, *National Security Strategy of the United Kingdom: Security in an Interdependent World* (Norwich: TSO, 2008), p. 57.
14 Virilio, *The Original Accident*, p. 49.
15 Brian Jenkins, *Redefining the Enemy: The World Has Changed, But Our Mindset Has Not* (Santa Monica, CA: RAND Corporation, 2004).
16 Michael Wermuth, 'Improving Terrorism Warnings – The Homeland Security System', testimony presented to the House Committee on Government Reform, Subcommittee on National Security, Emerging Threats and International Relations, 16 March 2004. Online at: *http://www.rand.org/pubs/testimonies/CT220.html* (accessed 26 June 2012).
17 I am borrowing here from the observations of Bauman, who, pointing to the work of Susan Neiman and Jean-Pierre Dupuy, notes that the quick successions of earthquake, fire, and high tide in Lisbon 1755 marked this precise separation and thus ushered in the modern. See Bauman, *Liquid Fear*, p. 58.
18 Virilio, *The Original Accident*, p. 3.
19 Melinda Cooper, 'Pre-empting Emergence: The Biological Turn in the War on Terror', *Theory, Culture & Society*, vol. 23, no. 4 (2006), p. 119.
20 See Bruce Hoffman, *Inside Terrorism* (New York: Columbia University Press, 2006).
21 Paul Davies, *Analytical Architecture for Capabilities-Based Planning, Mission Systems Analysis and Transformation* (Santa Monica, CA: RAND Corporation, 2008), pp. 1–2.
22 Brian Jackson, *Marrying Prevention and Resiliency: Balancing Approaches to an Uncertain Terrorist Threat* (Santa Monica, CA: RAND Corporation, 2008), p. 2.
23 Ibid., p. 10.

24 Ibid., p. 16.
25 It is important to note that the infinite here does not refer to the potentially limitless, neither does it value the alterior, but it is a totalizing, absolute, and internalizing composite.
26 Quentin Meillassoux, *After Finitude: An Essay on the Necessity of Contingency* (London: Continuum, 2008).
27 Dillon and Reid, *The Liberal Way of War*, p. 108.
28 Brian Massumi, 'Potential Politics and the Primacy of Pre-emption', *Theory & Event*, vol. 10, no. 2 (2007) (online).
29 Ibid.
30 Ibid.
31 Badiou, *Infinite Thought*, p. 109.
32 HM Government, *Report of the Official Account of the Bombings in London on 7 July 2005* (Norwich: HMSO, 2006).
33 NIOS and RAND, *Protecting Emergency Responders, Volume 3: Safety Management in Disaster and Terrorism Response* (US National Institute for Occupational Safety and Health and the RAND Corporation, May 2004). Online at: *http://www.cdc.gov/niosh/docs/2004–144/* (accessed 27 June 2012).
34 'Three-Day Bioterrorism Drill Begins in an Oklahoma Town', *The New York Times*, 13 April 2002, p. A11. Online at: *http://www.nytimes.com/2002/04/13/us/nation-challenged-bioterror-threat-three-day-bioterrorism-drill-begins-oklahoma.html* (accessed 27 June 2012).
35 'UK Terror Attack Exercise Planned', British Broadcasting Corporation, 3 March 2003. Online at: *http://news.bbc.co.uk/1/hi/uk_politics/2814087.stm* (accessed 27 June 2012).
36 RAND, *Using Probabilistic Terrorism Risk Modelling for Regulatory Benefit–Cost Analysis* (Santa Monica CA: RAND Corporation, 2007).
37 Stephen Graham, 'Olympics 2012: Welcome to Lock-Down London', *The Guardian*, 12 March 2012. Online at: *http://www.guardian.co.uk/sport/2012/mar/12/london-olympics-security-lockdown-london* (accessed 27 June 2012).
38 Slavoj Žižek, *The Sublime Object of Ideology* (London: Verso, 1989), pp. 132, 133.
39 Žižek, *Welcome to the Desert of the Real*, p. 32.
40 Jenny Edkins, *Trauma and the Memory of Politics* (Cambridge: Cambridge University Press, 2003), p. 9.

41 Maja Zehfuss, 'Forget September 11', *Third World Quarterly*, vol. 24, no. 3 (2003), pp. 525, 526.

42 George W. Bush, 'President's Remarks to the Nation', 11 September 2002. Online at: *http://news.bbc.co.uk/1/hi/world/americas/2252515.stm* (accessed 27 June 2012).

43 Jacques Derrida, 'Autoimmunity: Real and Symbolic Suicides', in Giovanna Borradori (ed.), *Philosophy in a Time of Terror: Dialogues with Jürgen Habermas and Jacques Derrida* (Chicago: University of Chicago Press, 2003), p. 90.

44 James Der Derian, 'Global Events, National Security, and Virtual Theory', *Millennium: Journal of International Studies*, vol. 30, no. 3 (2001), p. 672.

45 David Campbell, *Politics without Principle: Sovereignty, Ethics, and the Narratives of the Gulf War* (Boulder, CO: Lynne Rienner, 1993), p. 7.

46 Timothy Rayner, 'Time and the Event: Reflections on September 11, 2001', *Theory & Event*, vol. 5, no. 4 (2002) (online).

47 Deleuze, *The Logic of Sense*, p. 172.

48 Foucault, *Security, Territory, Population*, p. 20.

49 Deleuze, *Difference and Repetition*, pp. xv, 167.

50 Gilles Deleuze, *Nietzsche and Philosophy* (New York: Columbia University Press, 2006), p. 10.

51 Brian Massumi, 'Introduction: Like a Thought', in Brian Massumi (ed.), *A Shock to Thought: Expression after Deleuze and Guattari* (London: Routledge, 2002), p. xxvii.

52 Jacques Derrida, *Margins of Philosophy* (Brighton: Harvester Press, 1982), p. 9.

53 Deleuze, *The Logic of Sense*, p. 54.

54 Ibid., p. 73.

55 Ibid., p. 197.

56 Gerald Prince, *A Dictionary of Narratology* (Lincoln: University of Nebraska Press, 1987), p. 28.

57 Alain Badiou, *Being and Event* (London: Continuum, 2007), pp. xii–xiii.

58 Alain Badiou, *The Logic of Worlds: Being and Event Vol. 2* (London: Continuum, 2009).

59 Gilles Deleuze, *Empiricism and Subjectivity: An Essay on Hume's Theory of Nature* (New York: Columbia University Press, 1991), p. 87.

60 Derrida, 'Autoimmunity: Real and Symbolic Suicides', p. 90.
61 Ibid., p. 86.
62 Judith Butler, *Frames of War: When Is Life Grievable?* (London: Verso, 2009), pp. 3–4.
63 Ibid., p. 4.
64 Henry Giroux, 'Counter-Memory and the Politics of Loss', Truthout, 13 September 2011. Online at: *http://www.truth-out.org/counter-memory-and-politics-loss-after-911/1315595429* (accessed 27 June 2012).
65 Ibid.
66 Simon Critchley, 'September 11 and the Cycle of Revenge', The Stone, 8 September 2001. Online at: *http://opinionator.blogs.nytimes.com/2011/09/08/the-cycle-of-revenge/* (accessed 27 June 2012).
67 Jacques Derrida, *On Cosmopolitanism and Forgiveness* (New York: Routledge, 2005), p. 32.
68 Ibid., p. 37.
69 Richard Posner, *Catastrophe: Risk and Response* (Oxford: Oxford University Press, 2004), p. 8.

Select Bibliography

Theodor W. Adorno, Else Frenkel-Brunswik, Daniel J. Levinson, and R. Nevitt Sanford, *Authoritarian Personality* (New York: Harper & Row, 1950)

Giorgio Agamben, *Homo Sacer: Sovereign Power and Bare Life* (Stanford: Stanford University Press, 1995)

Giorgio Agamben, *The Kingdom and the Glory: For a Theological Genealogy of Economy and Government* (Stanford: Stanford University Press, 2011)

Giorgio Agamben, *State of Exception* (Chicago: University of Chicago Press, 2005)

Giorgio Agamben, *What Is an Apparatus?* (Stanford: Stanford University Press, 2009)

Benedict Anderson, *Imagined Communities: Reflections on the Origin and Spread of Nationalism* (London: Verso, 1983)

Sharon Anderson-Gold, *Unnecessary Evil: History and Moral Progress in the Philosophy of Immanuel Kant* (New York: State University Press, 2001)

Hannah Arendt, *Eichmann in Jerusalem: A Report on the Banality of Evil* (New York: Penguin Books, 2006)

Hannah Arendt, *The Human Condition* (Chicago: University of Chicago Press, 1958)

Hannah Arendt, *The Origins of Totalitarianism* (Fort Washington, PA: Harvest Books, 1976)

John Arquilla and David Ronfeldt, *In Athena's Camp: Preparing for Conflict in the Information Age* (Santa Monica, CA: RAND Corporation, 1997)

John Arquilla and David Ronfeldt (eds), *Networks and Netwars: The Future of Terror, Crime and Militancy* (Santa Monica, CA: RAND Corporation, 2001)

Alain Badiou, *Being and Event* (London: Continuum, 2007)

Alain Badiou, *Infinite Thought: Truth and the Return to Philosophy* (London: Continuum, 2005)

Alain Badiou, *The Logic of Worlds: Being and Event Vol. 2* (London: Continuum, 2009)

Alain Badiou, *Saint Paul: The Foundation of Universalism* (Stanford: Stanford University Press, 2003)

Jean Baudrillard, *The Intelligence of Evil or the Lucidity of the Pact* (New York: Berg, 2005)

Jean Baudrillard, *The Spirit of Terrorism and Other Essays* (London: Verso, 2003)

Jean Baudrillard, *The Transparency of Evil: Essays on Extreme Phenomena* (New York: Verso, 1993)

Zygmunt Bauman, *Liquid Fear* (Cambridge: Polity Press, 2006)

Zygmunt Bauman, *Liquid Modernity* (Cambridge: Polity Press, 2000)

Zygmunt Bauman, *Liquid Times: Living in an Age of Uncertainty* (Cambridge: Polity Press, 2007)

Zygmunt Bauman, *Society under Siege* (Cambridge: Polity Press, 2002)

Michael Baurmann, *The Market of Virtue: Morality and Commitment in a Liberal Society* (The Hague: Kluwer Law International, 1996)

Ulrich Beck, *Power in the Global Age* (Cambridge: Polity Press, 2006)

Ulrich Beck and Johannes Willms, *Conversations with Ulrich Beck* (Cambridge: Polity Press, 2003)

Walter Benjamin, *Illuminations: Essays and Reflections* (New York: Schocken Books, 1968)

Didier Bigo and Elspeth Guild, *Controlling Frontiers: Free Movement into and within Europe* (Aldershot: Ashgate, 2005)

Philip Bobbit, *The Shield of Achilles: War, Peace and the Course of History* (London: Penguin, 2003)

Phillip Bobbit, *Terror and Consent: The Wars for the 21st Century* (New York: Penguin, 2008)

Ken Booth (ed.) *Critical Security Studies and World Politics* (Boulder, CO: Lynne Rienner, 2005)

Giovanna Borradori (ed.), *Philosophy in a Time of Terror: Dialogues with Jürgen Habermas and Jacques Derrida* (Chicago: University of Chicago Press, 2003)

Boutros Boutros-Ghali, *Uncommon Opportunities: An Agenda for Peace and Equitable Development* (London: Zed Books, 1994)

Wendy Brown, *Walled States, Waning Sovereignty* (Cambridge, MA: Zone Books, 2010)

Graham Burchell, Colin Gordon, and Peter Miller (eds), *The Foucault Effect: Studies in Governmentality* (Chicago: University of Chicago Press, 1991)

J. Peter Burgess and Serge Gutwirth (eds) *A Threat against Europe? Security, Migration and Integration* (Brussels: VUB Press, 2011)

Judith Butler, *Frames of War: When is Life Grievable?* (London: Verso, 2009)

Judith Butler, Ernesto Laclau, and Slavoj Žižek (eds), *Contingency, Hegemony, Universality* (London: Verso, 2000)

Barry Buzan, *People, States and Fear: An Agenda for International Security Studies in the Post-Cold War Era* (Boulder, CO: Lynne Rienner, 1991)

Barry Buzan, Ole Waever, and Jan de Wilde, *Security: A New Framework for Analysis* (Boulder, CO: Lynne Rienner, 1998)

Bridget Byrne, *Gender, Conflict, and Development: Volume I* (London: Institute of Development Studies, 1995)

Matthew Calarco and Steven DeCaroli (eds) *Giorgio Agamben: Sovereignty and Life* (Stanford: Stanford University Press, 2007)

David Campbell, *Politics without Principle: Sovereignty, Ethics, and the Narratives of the Gulf War* (Boulder, CO: Lynne Rienner, 1993)

David Campbell, *Writing Security: United States Foreign Policy and the Politics of Identity* (Minneapolis: University of Minnesota Press, 1998)

Manuel Castells, *End of Millennium* (Oxford: Blackwell, 1998)

Manuel Castells, *The Informational City: A Framework for Social Change* (Toronto: University of Toronto Press, 1990)

Drucilla Cornell, Michael Rosenfeld, and David Gray Carleson (eds), *Deconstruction and the Possibility of Justice* (New York: Routledge, 1992)

Earl Count (ed.), *This Is Race* (New York: Henry Schuman, 1950)

Simon Critchley, *The Faith of the Faithless: Experiments in Political Theology* (New York: Verso, 2012)

Paul Davies, *Analytical Architecture for Capabilities-Based Planning, Mission Systems Analysis and Transformation* (Santa Monica, CA: RAND Corporation, 2008)

Mitchell Dean, *Governing Societies: Political Perspectives on Domestic and International Rule* (Maidenhead: Open University Press, 2007)

Mitchell Dean, *Governmentality: Power and Rule in Modern Society* (London: Sage, 1999)

Gilles Deleuze, *Bergsonism* (New York: Zone, 1988)

Gilles Deleuze, *Difference and Repetition* (New York: Columbia University Press, 1994)

Gilles Deleuze, *Empiricism and Subjectivity: An Essay on Hume's Theory of Nature* (New York: Columbia University Press, 1991)

Gilles Deleuze, *Foucault* (London: Continuum, 1999)

Gilles Deleuze, *The Logic of Sense* (New York: Columbia University Press, 1990)

Gilles Deleuze, *Negotiations: 1972–1990* (New York: Columbia University Press, 1995)

Gilles Deleuze, *Nietzsche and Philosophy* (New York: Columbia University Press, 2006)

Gilles Deleuze and Félix Guattari, *Anti-Oedipus: Capitalism and Schizophrenia* (London, Continuum: 2003)

Gilles Deleuze and Félix Guattari, *A Thousand Plateaus: Capitalism and Schizophrenia* (London: Continuum, 2002)

Jacques Derrida, *The Beast & the Sovereign: Volume 1* (Chicago: University of Chicago Press, 2009)

Jacques Derrida, *Edmund Husserl's Origin of Geometry: An Introduction* (New York: Bison Press, 1989)

Jacques Derrida, *Margins of Philosophy* (Brighton: Harvester Press, 1982)

Jacques Derrida, *On Cosmopolitanism and Forgiveness* (New York: Routledge, 2005)

Jacques Derrida, *Points: Interviews 1974–94* (Stanford: Stanford University Press, 1995)

Jacques Derrida, *Rogues: Two Essays on Reason* (Stanford: Stanford University Press, 2005)

Michael Dillon, *The Politics of Security: Towards a Political Philosophy of Continental Thought* (London: Routledge, 1997)

Michael Dillon and Andrew Neal (eds), *Foucault on Politics, Security and War* (London: Palgrave, 2008)

Michael Dillon and Julian Reid, *The Liberal Way of War: Killing to Make Life Live* (London: Routledge, 2009)

Richard Doyle, *Wetwares: Experiments in Postvital Living* (Minneapolis: University of Minnesota Press, 2003)

Mark Duffield, *Development, Security and Unending War: Governing the World of Peoples* (Cambridge: Polity Press, 2007)

Jenny Edkins, *Trauma and the Memory of Politics* (Cambridge: Cambridge University Press, 2003)

Emmanuel C. Eze (ed.) *Race and the Enlightenment* (Oxford: Blackwell, 1997)

Richard Falk, *On Humane Governance: Towards a New Global Politics* (Cambridge: Polity Press, 1995)

Frantz Fanon, *The Wretched of the Earth* (London: Penguin Books, 1990)

Duncan Foley, *Adam's Fallacy: A Guide to Economic Theology* (Cambridge, MA: Harvard University Press, 2006)

Michel Foucault, *The Birth of Biopolitics: Lectures at the Collège de France 1978–1979* (New York: Palgrave Macmillan, 2008)

Michel Foucault, *Ethics: Subjectivity and Truth* (New York: The New Press, 1998)

Michel Foucault, *The Order of Things: An Archaeology of Human Sciences* (London: Routledge, 2001)

Michel Foucault, *Power/Knowledge: Selected Interviews and Other Writings, 1972–1977* (New York: Pantheon, 1980)

Michel Foucault, *Security, Territory and Population: Lectures at the Collège de France 1977–1978* (New York: Palgrave Macmillan, 2007)

Michel Foucault, *Society Must Be Defended: Lectures at the Collège de France 1975–1976* (New York: Picador, 2003)

Milton Friedman, *Capitalism and Freedom* (Chicago: University of Chicago Press, 2002)

Francis Fukuyama, *The End of History and the Last Man* (Harmondsworth: Penguin, 1993)

Frank Furedi, *Culture of Fear Revisisted: Risk Taking and the Morality of Lower Expectation* (London: Continuum, 2006)

Eduardo Galeano, *Open Veins of Latin America: Five Centuries of the Pillage of a Continent* (New York and London: Monthly Review Press, 1973)

John Gray, *Black Mass: Apocalyptic Religion and the Death of Utopia* (London: Penguin, 2011)

John Hall, *Apocalypse: From Antiquity to the Empire of Modernity* (Cambridge, Polity Press: 2009)

Beatrice Hanssen, *Critique of Violence: Between Post-structuralism and Critical Theory* (London: Routledge, 2000)

Michael Hardt and Antonio Negri, *Empire* (Cambridge, MA: Harvard University Press, 2000)

Michael Hardt and Antonio Negri, *Multitude: War and Democracy in the Age of Empire* (London: Hamish Hamilton, 2004)

Tom Hayden (ed.), *The Zapatista Reader* (New York: Nation Books, 2002)

Friedrich von Hayek, *Individualism and Economic Order* (Chicago: University of Chicago Press, 1980)

Friedrich von Hayek, *Law, Legislation and Liberty* (London: Routledge, 1973)

Friedrich von Hayek, *The Road to Serfdom* (London: Routledge, 1944)

Friedrich von Hayek, *Studies in Philosophy, Politics and Economics* (Chicago: University of Chicago Press, 1980)

Martin Heidegger, *Pathmarks* (Cambridge: Cambridge University Press, 1998)

Martin Heidegger, *The Question Concerning Technology and Other Essays* (New York: Harper & Row, 1977)

Thomas Hobbes, *Leviathan* (Cambridge: Cambridge University Press, 1991)

Bruce Hoffman, *Inside Terrorism* (New York: Columbia University Press, 2006)

John H. Holland, *Emergence: From Chaos to Order* (Oxford: Oxford University Press, 1998)

Human Genome Project, *Genomics and Its Impact on Society* (US Department of Energy Office of Science, 2006)

Human Security Centre, *The Human Security Report 2005: War and Peace in the 21st Century* (University of British Columbia: Human Security Centre, 2005)

Edmund Husserl, *Cartesian Meditations: An Introduction to Phenomenology* (The Hague: Martinus Nijhoff, 1960)

Jef Huysmans, *The Politics of Insecurity: Fear, Migration and Asylum in the EU* (London: Routledge, 2006)

Michael Ignatieff, *Empire Lite: Nation-Building in Bosnia, Kosovo and Afghanistan* (London: Vintage, 2003)

Brian Jackson, *Marrying Prevention and Resiliency: Balancing Approaches to an Uncertain Terrorist Threat* (Santa Monica, CA: RAND Corporation, 2008)

Frederic Jameson, *Archaeologies of the Future: The Desire Called Utopia and Other Science Fictions* (London: Verso, 2005)

Brian Jenkins, *Redefining the Enemy: The World Has Changed, But Our Mindset Has Not* (Santa Monica, CA: RAND Corporation, 2004)

Brian Michael Jenkins and John Paul Godges (eds), *The Long Shadow of 9/11: America's Response to Terrorism* (Santa Monica, CA: RAND Corporation, 2011)

Steven Johnson, *Emergence: The Connected Lives of Ants, Brains, Cities and Software* (London: Penguin, 2001)

Robert Kagan, *Paradise and Power: America and Europe in the New World* (London: Atlantic Books, 2003)

Mary Kaldor, *Human Security: Reflections on Globalization and Intervention* (Cambridge: Polity Press, 2007)

Mary Kaldor, *New and Old Wars: Organized Violence in a Global Era* (Cambridge: Polity Press, 1999)

Mary Kaldor and S.D. Beebe, *The Ultimate Weapon Is No Weapon: Human Security and the New Rules of War and Peace* (New York: Public Affairs, 2010)

Immanuel Kant, *Critique of Pure Reason* (New York: St Martin's Press, 1929)

Immanuel Kant, *Metaphysics of Morals* (Cambridge: Cambridge University Press, 1991)

Immanuel Kant, *Religion within the Limits of Reason Alone* (New York: Harper & Row, 1960)

Stuart Kaufman, *Investigations* (New York: Oxford University Press, 2000)

Lily Kay, *Who Wrote the Book of Life? A History of the Genetic Code* (Stanford: Stanford University Press, 2000)

David Kilcullen, *The Accidental Guerilla: Fighting Small Wars in the Midst of a Big One* (Oxford: Oxford University Press, 2009)

Pierre Levy, *Collective Intelligence: Mankind's Emerging World in Cyberspace* (New York: Plenum Press, 1997)

Roger Lewin, *Complexity: Life at the Edge of Chaos* (Chicago: University of Chicago Press, 1999)

Sylvère Lotringer (ed.), *Michel Foucault: The Politics of Truth* (Los Angeles: Semiotext(e), 2007)

Jean-François Lyotard, *Heidegger and 'the Jews'* (Minneapolis: University of Minnesota Press, 1990)

Patrick McDonald, *The Invisible Hand of Peace: Capitalism, the War Machine, and International Relations Theory* (Cambridge: Cambridge University Press, 2009)

Joanna Macrae and Nicholas Leader, *Shifting Sands: The Search for 'Coherence' between Political and Humanitarian Responses to Complex Emergencies* (London: Overseas Development Institute, 2000)

James Martel, *Divine Violence: Walter Benjamin and the Eschatology of Sovereignty* (London: Routledge, 2011)

Brian Massumi, *The Politics of Everyday Fear* (Minnesota: University of Minnesota Press, 1993)

Brian Massumi (ed.), *A Shock to Thought: Expression after Deleuze and Guattari* (London: Routledge, 2002)

Charles Mathewes, *Evil and the Augustinian Tradition* (Cambridge: Cambridge University Press, 2001)

Larry May and Jerome Kohn (eds), *Hannah Arendt: Twenty Years Later* (Cambridge, MA: MIT Press, 1997)

Quentin Meillassoux, *After Finitude: An Essay on the Necessity of Contingency* (London: Continuum, 2008)

Maurice Merleau-Ponty, *Humanism and Terror* (Boston: Beacon Press, 1969)

Gordon Michalson Jr, *Fallen Freedom: Kant on Radical Evil and Moral Regeneration* (Cambridge: Cambridge University Press, 1990)

Mary Midgley, *Wickedness: A Philosophical Essay* (London: Routledge, 1984)

Charles W. Miller, *The Radical Contract* (Ithaca, NY: Cornell University Press, 1997)

Peter Miller and Nikolas Rose, *Governing the Present: Administering Economic, Social and Personal Life* (Cambridge: Polity Press, 2008)

Charles Montesquieu, *The Spirit of the Laws* (Cambridge: Cambridge University Press, 1989)

Stephen Morton and Stephen Bygrave (eds), *Foucault in an Age of Terror* (London: Palgrave, 2008)

Chantal Mouffe (ed.), *The Challenge of Carl Schmitt* (London: Verso, 1999)

Norman Myers, *Ultimate Security: The Environmental Basis of Political Stability* (New York: Norton, 1993)

Susan Neiman, *Evil in Modern Thought: An Alternative History of Philosophy* (Princeton: Princeton University Press, 2002)

Friedrich Nietzsche, *Thus Spoke Zarathustra* (Cambridge: Cambridge University Press, 2006)

George Orwell, *Notes on Nationalism* (London: Polemic, 1945).

Paul Patton (ed.), *Deleuze: A Critical Reader* (Oxford: Blackwell Publishers, 1996)

Robert Pepperell, *The PostHuman Condition: Consciousness beyond the Brain* (Portland: Intellect, 2003)

Scott Peterson, *Me against My Brother: At War in Somalia, Sudan and Rwanda* (London: Routledge, 2000)

Richard Posner, *Catastrophe: Risk and Response* (Oxford: Oxford University Press, 2004)

Ilya Prigogine, *The End of Certainty* (New York: Free Press, 1997)

Paul Rabinow (ed.), *The Foucault Reader: An Introduction to Foucault's Thought* (London: Penguin Books, 1991)

William Rasch, *Sovereignty and Its Discontents: On the Primacy of Conflict and the Structure of the Political* (London: Birkbeck Law Press, 2004)

Mikkel Rasmussen, *The Risk Society at War: Terror, Technology and Strategy in the 21st Century* (Cambridge: Cambridge University Press, 2006)

Hans Reiss (ed.), *Kant: Political Writings* (New York: Cambridge University Press, 1991)

Howard Rheingold, *The Virtual Community* (Reading, MA: Addison Wesley, 1993)

Paul Ricoeur, *Time and Narrative* (Chicago: University of Chicago Press, 1984)

Jeremy Rifkin, *Biosphere Politics: A New Consciousness for a New Century* (New York: Crown Publishing Group, 1991)

Daniel Rosenberg and Susan Harding (eds) *Histories of the Future* (Durham, NC: Duke University Press, 2005)

Naoki Sakai and Jon Solomon (eds), *Translation, Biopolitics, Colonial Difference* (Hong Kong: Hong Kong University Press, 2004)

Saskia Sassen, *The Global City: New York, London, Tokyo* (Princeton: Princeton University Press, 2001)

Carl Schmitt, *The Concept of the Political* (Chicago: University of Chicago Press, 1996)

Carl Schmitt, *The Nomos of the Earth: In the International Law of the Jus Publicum Europaeum* (New York: Telos Press, 2003)

Carl Schmitt, *Political Theology: Four Chapters on the Concept of Sovereignty* (Chicago: University of Chicago Press, 2006)

Alan Schrift (ed.), *Modernity and the Problem of Evil* (Bloomington: Indiana University Press, 2005)

Peter Scott (ed.), *The Globalization of Higher Education* (Buckingham: Open University Press, 2000)

Alex Shand, *Free Market Morality: The Political Economy of the Austrian School* (London: Routledge, 1992)

Michael J. Shapiro, *Cinematic Geopolitics* (New York: Routledge, 2009)

William Shawcross, *Deliver Us from Evil: Peacekeepers, Warlords and a World of Endless Conflict* (New York: Touchstone, 2001)

Michael Shermer, *How We Believe: Science, Skepticism and the Search for God*, 2nd edn (New York: Henry Holt, 2007)

Herbert A. Simon, *The Sciences of the Artificial* (Cambridge, MA: MIT Press, 1981)

Peter Sloterdijk, *Terror from the Air* (Los Angeles: Semiotext(e), 2009)

Adam Smith, *The Wealth of Nations* (London: Penguin, 1986)

Rupert Smith, *The Utility of Force: The Art of War in the Modern World* (London: Penguin, 2006)

Leo Strauss, *Natural Right and History* (Chicago: University of Chicago Press, 1953)

John Urry, *Global Complexity* (Cambridge: Polity Press, 2003)

US Department of the Army, *Field Manual 3–24: Counterinsurgency* (Washington, DC: Department of the Army, 2006)

Paul Veyne, *Writing History: Essay on Epistemology* (Middletown, CT: Wesleyan University Press, 1984)

Paul Virilio, *City of Panic* (London: Berg, 2007)

Paul Virilio, *The Original Accident* (Cambridge: Polity Press, 2007)

Paul Virilio, *Speed and Politics* (Los Angeles: Semiotext(e), 1986)

Paul Virilio, *The University of Disaster* (Cambridge: Polity Press, 2009)

Duncan Watts, *Six Degrees: The Sciences of a Connected Age* (New York: Norton, 2002)

Max Weber, *The Protestant Ethic and the Spirit of Capitalism* (New York: Charles Scribner, 1958)

Eyal Weizman, *Hollow Land: Israel's Architecture of Occupation* (London: Verso, 2007)

Nicholas Wheeler, *Saving Strangers: Humanitarian Intervention in International Society* (Oxford: Oxford University Press, 2000)

White House, *The National Security Strategy of the United States of America* (Washington, DC: White House, 2006)

Allen Wood, *Kant's Moral Religion* (Ithaca, NY: Cornell University Press, 1970)

Richard Wyn-Jones, *Security, Strategy, and Critical Theory* (Boulder, CO: Lynne Rienner, 1999)

Slavoj Žižek, *The Sublime Object of Ideology* (London: Verso, 1989)

Slavoj Žižek, *Welcome to the Desert of the Real* (London: Verso, 2002)

Index